THE AFTERMATH
OF THE NAPOLEONIC WARS

TSAR ALEXANDER I,
portrait by Monnier, 1806

THE AFTERMATH
OF THE
NAPOLEONIC WARS

THE CONCERT OF EUROPE—AN EXPERIMENT

by

H. G. SCHENK

New York · HOWARD FERTIG · 1967

First published in 1947
by Kegan Paul, Trench, Trubner & Co., Ltd.

HOWARD FERTIG, INC. EDITION 1967

Library of Congress Catalog Card Number: 66-25859

PRINTED IN THE UNITED STATES OF AMERICA
BY NOBLE OFFSET PRINTERS, INC.

CONTENTS

ERRATA

Page 48, third footnote, line 1: "le Desiré" should read "le Désiré"

Page 51, line 5: "11s.7d. for 1816, 14s.3d. for 1817, and 11s.8d. for 1818" should read "11.7d for 1816, 14.3d for 1817, 11.8d for 1818"

Page 91, first footnote, lines 3 and 4: "Jesetzesdespolie" should read "Gesetzesdespotie"

Page 143, line 5 from bottom: "absolutionist" should read "absolutist"

Page 171, fourth footnote, line 1: "case" should read "cause" fourth footnote, line 4: "au" should read "an"

Page 216, fourth footnote, line 2: "Affairs" should read "Affaires"

Page 220, line 6 from bottom: "unendlischen" should read "unendlichen"

ILLUSTRATIONS

PREFACE

This book could not have been written without stimulation and help from many quarters. I can mention here only a few outstanding examples.

Of my teachers and friends at Prague, Dr. Eugen Lieben taught me to appreciate the humane, Josef Mirovský and Ladislav Knotek the human approach to social and political problems of the past and the present. At the University, Professor Robert Neuner stimulated my interest in the history of ideas ; Professor Hans Kelsen whose assistant I had the privilege to be, introduced me to the intricate problems of international organization.

Among those who early in 1939 generously assisted me in finding a refuge in this country, or afterwards in bridging over very difficult times, I should like to mention with special gratitude Barclay Baron, H. Salter Nichols, Harrison Barrow, the Reverend Rosamund Lee, Dr. Beryl Smalley, the Reverend J. M. Thompson, R. P. Bell, Mrs. M. G. Hazell, and my uncle Karl Schenk.

To Oxford University, and Exeter College in particular, I am indebted for having accepted me in 1940 as a research student, and for granting me the privileges of decrees 3 and 4 of October 31, 1939. While working on this book I enjoyed research grants from the Society for the Protection of Science and Learning, the Post-Graduate Aid Committee, and the Warden of All Souls' Committee (formerly Magdalen College Refugee Scholars Fund).

I have had the privilege of working with Professor G. D. H. Cole since April 1940. He introduced me to English social history, discussed with me each chapter of this book, and helped me in many other ways ; I am extremely grateful to him. To Professor B. H. Sumner, Ernst Eisler, and Dr. Franz von Pollack-Parnau I am indebted for valuable bibliographical advice. My thanks are due also to those of my students at Oxford with whom I was able to discuss several aspects dealt with in this book. In matters of English style, I have been assisted by Mr. A. S. B. Glover, Peter F. Copping, Dr. L. C. Knights and Ronald G. Chapman. To Mrs. Copping and J. Cowan I am grateful for their help with the typescript.

The illustrations from the Curzon and Firth Collections are reproduced by kind permission of Bodley's Librarian.

The debt of gratitude which I owe to my brother and my wife is deeper than I feel able to express.

H. G. S.

Exeter College, Oxford,
April 29, 1945

PART I

THE ORIGINS OF THE HOLY ALLIANCE

Nur die Religion kann Europa wieder auferwecken und die Völker sichern.

Novalis (1799).

CHAPTER I

THE IDEOLOGICAL BACKGROUND

The religious aspirations expressed in the project of the Holy Alliance, if not in its conclusion, are still the subject of much controversy among historians. Recent writers have tended to pour scorn on them. This attitude seems to me misleading, for it implies a serious underestimate of the part which religion, after a long period of retreat, began at this time to exercise upon the minds of men.

When the French Revolution broke out, secular thought, in the Western half of Europe, had come to occupy much of the place formerly reserved for religion. One main cause of this was that religion had given up many of its old pretensions, and had to some extent ceased to interfere in political struggles. Cause and effect, however, were intermingled : while the gradual withdrawal of religion to occupy itself exclusively with transcendental problems paved the way for the gradual progress of secular political philosophy, that progress was itself to some extent a cause of the withdrawal.

But a tendency in the opposite direction had already begun while French, and for that matter Western, Enlightenment, was still in full swing. As early as 1755 Rousseau, in a draft of his *Contrat Social*, had attacked the rationalism of Diderot. Rousseau had already come to realize that reason by itself would never bring men together, if they were concerned with their individual happiness alone, as the current theory of the Encyclopædists supposed. A stronger bond was required. About half a century later, during the long period of Wars which ensued upon the Revolution, when the churchyard assumed the rôle of preacher,[1] the need for a reintegration of society was felt with growing intensity. An increasing number of people in all classes of society came to look upon Christianity as its only safe foundation. The social

[1] Jean Paul, *Politische Fastenpredigten* (written between 1809 and 1816).

building to be constructed upon it was naturally visualized in very different ways, for the function of religion as a social ideology may be either to justify or to undermine the old social order.

It is due to the comparative neglect of the religious background of the Holy Alliance that its original intention has been thought by some historians to have been in line with the religion of restoration as represented, for example, by Joseph de Maistre. In fact two different trends can be quite distinctly traced : a conservative trend of which the religion of restoration was one aspect, and a radical trend which can be shown to have led direct to Tsar Alexander's draft Treaty for the Holy Alliance.

The herald of conservative religion was Edmund Burke in the latter years of his life, mainly, though not exclusively, by reason of his *Reflections on the Revolution in France*. The influence which this aspect of Burke's thought exercised upon political speculation in England and even more on the Continent cannot be overestimated. It is with this aspect, and this aspect alone, that these pages will be concerned.

The *Reflections* mark the culmination of the attitude which Mr. Basil Willey in *The Eighteenth Century Background* (1940) has called optimism of acceptance.[1] In a letter to the Comte de Mercy, in August 1793, Burke wrote :

> It is not the cause of nation against nation, but, as you will observe, the cause of mankind against those who have projected the subversion of that order of things, under which our part of the world has so long flourished, and, indeed, been in a progressive state of improvement. The limits of which, if it had not been thus rudely stopped, it would not have been easy for the imagination to stop.[2]

Such an attitude, of course, implied a denial that the old social system had any serious shortcomings. Burke himself had formerly attacked the notorious black-and-white method when he said : " We cannot look upon men as delinquents in the mass." He still objected to this method, but only when it was used by his antagonists. In a letter to William Weddell, on January 31st, 1792, he pointed out :

> That these [the best born, the best bred, and those possessed of rank and hereditary settlement] should be all scoundrels, and that the virtue, honour, and public spirit of a nation should be only found

---

[1] P. 55.   Cf. Lord Morley : " He had all his life surrounded himself with a mental paradise of order and equilibrium " (*Burke*, London, 1923, p. 215.)

[2] *Correspondence of the Rt. Hon. Edmund Burke between the Year 1744 and the period of his decease in 1797*, IV, London, 1844, p. 138.

in its attorneys, pettifoggers, stewards of manors, discarded officers of police, shop boys, clerks of counting-houses and rustics from the plough, is a paradox, not of false ingenuity, but of envy and malignity.[1]

He himself, however, used the same demagogic method to excess in this very letter. He referred to the vast body of French nobility and gentry as " the very first for disinterested services to their country ".[2] All the evidence at our disposal, on the other hand, confirms the judgment of Coleridge who, though highly critical of the Revolution, spoke of the " extravagantly false and flattering picture which Burke gave of the French nobility and hierarchy ".[3] In order to be able to attack the mass of the French people, Burke invented the paradox that France was " out of itself ", the moral France being separated from the geographical.[4]

What, in Burke's view, lay at the root of all the trouble ? In the letter to the Comte de Mercy quoted above, the answer is : " It is the contempt of property, and the setting up against its principle certain pretended advantages of the state (which, by the way, exists only for its conservation) that has led to all the other evils which have ruined France, and brought all Europe into the most imminent danger." [5] It is at this point that God comes into the argument. For example, in a letter to the Duke of Portland, Burke spoke of " this struggle, perhaps the last struggle, in favour of religion, morality, and property ".[6] This juxtaposition was by no means accidental. A similar passage occurs in the *Reflections*. There we are told : " Our manners, our civilization and all the good things which are connected with manners and with civilization, have, in this European world of ours, depended for ages upon two principles, . . . the spirit of a gentleman and the spirit of religion." [7] So far as France was concerned, this statement was corroborated two years later by the Archbishop of Narbonne, who said that the resistance of the French higher clergy in 1791 was due, not to their faith, but to their honour as gentlemen.[8] The degree of their attach-

---

[1] Ibid., III, p. 407.   [2] Ibid., pp. 392–3.
[3] *The Friend : A Series of Essays*, London, 1866, Section I, Essay 5, p. 135, n. 1. Cf. also Lord Acton's unpublished MS. on Burke : " His attachment to whatsoever things are of good repute." And again : " Burke had no conception of the evil of class government, being a defender of antiquity." (Cf. page 6, note 4 of this book.)
[4] " Remarks on the Policy of the Allies," *Works*, IV, London, 1802, p. 110.
[5] *Correspondence*, IV, pp. 142–3.
[6] Ibid., IV, p. 221.
[7] *Reflections*, London, 1790, p. 117.
[8] Frederick B. Artz, *France under the Bourbon Reaction*, Cambridge (Mass.), 1931, p. 102.

ment to the old feudal order seems indeed to have been remarkably high.[1]

As to property, Burke was not only opposed to equal, but in favour of the most unequal division :

It [i.e. property] can never be safe from the invasions of ability, unless it be out of all proportion predominant in the representation. It must be represented too in great masses of accumulation or it is not rightly protected. . . . The perpetuation of property in our families is the most valuable and most interesting circumstance attending it . . . and that which tends the most to the perpetuation of society itself.[2]

And here again the responsibility is put upon God. In *Thoughts and Details on Scarcity* (1795), Burke wrote that one ought

manfully to resist the very first idea, speculative or practical, that it is within the competence of government, or even of the rich, as rich, to supply to the poor those necessaries which it has pleased the Divine Providence for a while to withhold from them. We, the people, ought to be made more sensible that it is not in breaking the laws of commerce, which are the laws of nature, and consequently the laws of God, that we are to place our hope of softening the Divine displeasure to remove any calamity under which we suffer, or which hangs over us.[3]

The link between property and religion was thus twofold. In the first place, God had sanctioned economic inequality. Secondly, God had provided the poor with a suitable consolation : the hope of a better life in another world. This is clear from the following passage :

They [the body of the people] must respect that property of which they cannot partake. They must labour to obtain what by labour can be obtained ; and when they find, as they commonly do, the success disproportioned to the endeavour, they must be taught their consolation in the final proportions of eternal justice. Of this consolation, whoever deprives them, deadens their industry, and strikes at the root of all acquisition as of all conservation.[4]

A society which seeks to preserve inequality of property, especially if this is to be " out of all proportion ", cannot dispense

---

[1] Cf. Katharina Heinrichs, *Die politische Ideologie des französischen Klerus bei Beginn der grossen Revolution*, Berlin, 1934, pp. 97, 138, 147, 153.

[2] *Reflections*, p. 75.

[3] *Works*, new ed., VII, London, 1826, p. 404.

[4] *Reflections*, p. 351. Cf. also : " Where trade and manufacture are wanting to a people, and the spirit of nobility and religion remains, sentiment supplies, and not always ill supplies their place." But if, Burke continues, the same event takes place with a people who have lost this spirit, the consequences may be frightful, for then these barbarians are " possessing nothing at present, and hoping for nothing hereafter ". (*Reflections*, p. 118.)

with a certain amount of transcendental religion.[1] This idea had a certain tradition behind it. Voltaire had already spoken of religion as good enough for his tailor. Shaftesbury and Bolingbroke regarded enlightened ideas as the privilege of the upper classes, and Thomson had referred to the " Godlike enlightn'd few ". In 1757, Soame Jenyns in *A Free Enquiry into the Nature and Origin of Evil* had written :

Ignorance or the want of literature, the appointed lot of all born to poverty, and the drudgeries of life, is the only opiate capable of infusing that insensibility which can enable them to endure the miseries of the one, and the fatigues of the other. It is a cordial administered by the gracious hand of Providence : of which they ought never to be deprived by an ill-judged and improper Education. It is the basis of all subordination, the support of society, and the privilege of individuals.[2]

Then came Burke, and, perhaps under his influence, Paley, in 1793, published his *Reasons for Contentment, addressed to the Labouring Part of the British Public.* Here the social function of transcendentalism is stated quite bluntly : " Religion ", the reverend writer maintains, " smooths all inequalities, because it unfolds a prospect which makes all earthly distinctions nothing." [3] Paley was in agreement with Burke also on the point that the poor have in reality many compensations even in this world. He represented frugality, for example, as a pleasure in the guise of a hardship,[4] and even went so far as to assert that the law defended the weak against the strong.[5] Similarly, Mrs. Crewe, recording Burke's Table Talk, noted : " Mr. Burke ever disliked a sort of cant which was kept up and made a fashion of concerning

---

[1] " The necessity of artificial religion " (Burke, *A Vindication of Natural Society, 1756*), or, to use Max Weber's terminology, the case for transcendental religion as a means of domestication has never been put forward more bluntly than by Napoleon Bonaparte. In August 1800, the First Consul said in conversation with Roederer : " La société ne peut exister sans l'inégalité des fortunes, et l'inégalité des fortunes ne peut subsister sans la religion. Quand un homme meurt de faim à côté d'un autre qui regorge, il lui est impossible d'accéder à cette différence, s'il n'y a pas là une autorité qui lui dise : ' Dieu le veut ainsi ; il faut qu'il y ait des pauvres et des riches dans le monde ; mais, ensuite et pendant l'éternité, le partage se fera autrement.' " (Comte P. L. Roederer, *Œuvres*, III, Paris, 1854, p. 335.) In March 1806, the Emperor's statement with regard to religion was more concise : " Quant à moi, je n'y vois pas le mystère de l'incarnation, mais le mystère de l'ordre social ; la religion rattache au ciel une idée d'égalité qui empêche le riche d'être massacré par le pauvre." (H. Taine, *Le Régime Moderne*, II, Paris, 1894, p. 8.)

[2] P. 34. On the other hand, Jenyns, unlike Burke, perceived the vicious circle : " Trade and wealth . . . must certainly produce luxury which no less certainly must produce their destruction " (p. 141).

[3] Paley, p. 21.   [4] Ibid., p. 11.

[5] Ibid, p. 6. Coleridge later referred to him as a mere time-serving casuist. (Hazlitt, *My First Acquaintance with Poets*, Complete Works, xvii, London, 1933, p. 114.)

the Poor. . . . The poor are not poor, said he, but men as we are, all born to be, and perhaps happiest for being, without more resource than their own hands, and common powers from Nature." [1] Mrs. Crewe asked Burke whether he had read Paley's last book. He replied : " No, but I would recommend it, because I have good reason to believe it to be one of our best performances." [2] Accordingly, in *Thoughts and Details on Scarcity* he recommended to the poor : " Patience, labour, sobriety, frugality, and religion." [3]

Faced with this evidence, it seems difficult not to agree with Lord Acton's judgment on Burke contained in one of his numerous unpublished manuscripts. Acton speaks of Burke's appeal to insincerity, and says expressly that he was : " Not even thoroughly sincere in his religious belief." [4] Even Mr. Cobban, who in his *Edmund Burke and the Revolt against the Eighteenth Century* (1929) undertakes to defend Burke against Acton, has to admit that " the political benefits conferred by religious organizations, in particular by the Church of England, tended in his mind, as in the minds of most of his contemporaries, to outweigh spiritual values ".[5] The truth of this was never more obvious than on the occasion when a few of the clergy petitioned to be relieved from some of the severities of subscription. Burke resisted them on the sophistic ground that the truth of a proposition deserves less attention than the effect which adherence to it would have upon the established order of things.[6]

Political benefits might be expected also from religious organizations other than the Church of England. Owing to the French War, a close and friendly communication existed, for the first time since the Glorious Revolution, between the English Government and the Vatican.[7] It was at that time, on October 10th, 1793, to be exact, that Burke wrote to Sir John Hippisley : " I confess I would, if the matter rested with me, enter into much more distinct and avowed political connections with the court of Rome than hitherto we have held. If we decline them, the bigotry will be on our part, and not on that

[1] " Extracts from Mr. Burke's Table Talk, at Crewe Hall." *Miscellanies of the Philobiblon Society*, VII, London, 1862–3, p. 29.
[2] Ibid., p. 58. Cf. Harold Laski : " The road from Burke to Paley was more direct than it is comfortable to admit." (*The Rise of European Liberalism*, 1936, p. 205.)
[3] *Works*, ed. 1826, VII, p. 377.
[4] Acton MSS. Add. 4967, Cambridge University Library. Hazlitt arrived at the same conclusion : " There was always a dash of insincerity ; a sinister bias in his disposition." (" Arguing in a Circle ", *The Liberal*, July 1823.)
[5] P. 240.   [6] Morley, op. cit., p. 247.
[7] Lecky, *A History of England in the Eighteenth Century*, VII, London, 1890, p. 461.

of his Holiness." [1] Lord Acton, in the manuscript mentioned above, emphasizes Burke's influence on Catholic political writers, and without going into details of analogies, indicates the progression : Burke—de Maistre—Bonald—Chateaubriand—Gentz [2] —Müller. So far as the French aristocrat *émigrés* are concerned, this analogy will now be examined.

The French aristocrat *émigrés* who on the Continent became the heralds of the religion of restoration had a great deal in common with Edmund Burke. They too were alive to the imperative necessity for a counter-ideology which religion alone could offer. In 1802, Bonald prophesied : " Il faut se pénétrer de cette vérité philosophique de toutes les vérités, que la Révolution a commencé par la Déclaration des Droits de l'homme, et qu'elle ne finira que par la déclaration des droits de Dieu." [3] They too realized that the youthful impetus of the new revolutionary ideas had to be checked by emphasizing the high value of tradition. In order to reject the ideas of the present, they glorified those of the past often simply on account of their antiquity.[4] This tendency went so far that whenever Bonald quoted Bossuet, he treated him as if he were a contemporary.

However, there were limits to the analogy ; limits which arose from the fact that Burke was still able to rely on the solid background of England's social institutions, whereas the feudal society so much beloved of the French aristocrat *émigrés* had broken down. But there still existed the Roman Catholic Church ; infinitely weaker, it is true, than it had been for instance in the eleventh and twelfth centuries, but, broadly speaking, never as yet defeated. That is why Catholic tradition could assume the function which otherwise might have been performed by feudal tradition. If this had not been interrupted in so drastic a manner, Bonald and de Maistre might not have undertaken to justify their entire political views on Catholic grounds. Karl Ludwig von Haller's [5] example seems to bear out the truth of this assumption. Haller, a patrician of Berne,[6] the social structure of which

---

[1] Sir John Hippisley, *The Substance of Additional Observations intended to have been delivered in the House of Commons*, London, 1806, p. 93.

[2] Gentz, however, always remained a Protestant. It has truly been said of him that he felt more strongly about the value of religion than about religion itself.

[3] *Législation primitive*, Paris, 1802, p. 93.

[4] Cf. R. Mauduit, *Les Conceptions Politiques et Sociales de Bonald*, Thèse, Paris, 1913, p. 156.

[5] His *chef-d'œuvre*, *Restauration der Staatswissenschaften*, 6 vols., was not published until 1816 ; but all its essential points were anticipated in his *Handbuch der allgemeinen Staatenkunde* (1808).

[6] Cf. a delightful entry in Lord Broughton's *Recollections of a Long Life* : " Arrived

had been comparatively little affected by the French Revolution, made feudal tradition the pivot of his system of political thought, so much so that he created the notion of the *Patrimonialstaat*. This is all the more significant since he openly confessed that he had never read a single book on mediæval history.[1] The social relations of everyday life were his only material of observation.[2] These he knew pretty well, for his statement was corroborated, though with a different bias, by Laharpe in 1818, who referred to " aristocratisme " as a malady endemic in the city-cantons.[3] The glorification of feudal tradition retained its eminent place in Haller's system even after his conversion to the Catholic faith, at a time, that is, when he had come to appreciate the Church as a powerful ally in the great common struggle against social innovation.

Political Catholicism appealed to the French aristocrat *émigrés* for another reason also. Not only was the Church's tradition unbroken and its sympathies unmistakably on their side, but its very structure and organization were to a large extent similar to that of the monarchical state. In October 1797, Louis XVIII, in his instructions to the bishops who had remained faithful to the dynasty, strongly emphasized " the intimate connexion which existed between altar and throne ".[4] A year earlier, Bonald had written : " Dans chaque société le gouvernement doit faire un secret effort pour établir la religion qui a le plus d'analogie avec ses principes." In this respect Bonald followed Montesquieu, whose doctrine he rejected in practically all other matters of importance : " Montesquieu a bien senti cette conformité secrète des religions et des gouvernements. La religion catholique convient, nous dit-il, à une monarchie, et la protestante s'accommode mieux d'une république."[5] But this similarity between Catholicism and monarchism could bind to the Church only those members of the privileged aristocracy whose intellectualism demanded some sort

at Lausanne on August 24th, 1816 . . . Met young Blomfield who took us to Gibbon's house. Blomfield told us scarcely any one here thinks of Gibbon. They think nothing but of nobility. Voltaire is not remembered, Rousseau partially ; Haller they commemorate as a patrician of the place." (Vol. II, pp. 5–6.)

[1] *Restauration der Staatswissenschaften*, 2nd ed., VI, Winterthur, 1825, p. 572.

[2] " Nicht am Alten und Unbekannten, sondern an dem, was vor unseren Augen liegt, haben wir jene Gesetze wahrgenommen, die sowohl in älteren als in mittleren und neueren Zeiten stets die nämlichen gewesen sind, und in alle Zukunft die nämlichen bleiben werden." (Ibid.)

[3] *Quellen zur Schweizer Geschichte*, XII, 1891, p. 229.

[4] F. Baldensperger, *Le mouvement des idées dans l'émigration française*, II, Paris, 1924, p. 225.

[5] *Théorie du pouvoir politique et religieux*, 1796, livre VI, ch. II.

of systematization ; for the rest of the populace the social function of religion had to be different. For them the transcendental element, common to so many different interpretations of Christianity besides Catholicism, must be stressed : " La religion agît comme consolatrice en nous faisant espérer que toutes les iniquités seront réparées dans la vie future." [1]

In fervently advocating " absolute monarchy ", what Bonald and de Maistre really had in mind was such a state of affairs as had existed in their country before 1789. The monarch was then, of course, far from absolute in relation to the aristocracy. Bonald, it is true, praised the great advantages of an hereditary monarchy, but at the same time he did not forget the hereditary aristocracy and feudal institutions. [2] Despite all this, there is a sincere note about Bonald's religiosity. His bias did not blind him to the fact that eighteenth-century France had suffered from certain abuses. [3] Moreover, he was consistent in rejecting wealth and technical progress at the same time as political reforms. He certainly idealized feudal society, but at least he saw that the worship of Mammon is incompatible with the worship of Christ.

De Maistre's sincerity, on the other hand, is open to some doubt. In a letter to Comte Potocki, written in 1810, he analyses the causes of the breakdown of feudal societies thus :

Il y a dans tous les pays un certain nombre de familles conservatrices sur lesquelles repose l'État : c'est ce qu'on appelle l'aristocratie ou la noblesse. Tant qu'elles demeurent pures et pénetrées de l'esprit national l'État est inébranlable, en dépit des vices des souverains ; dès qu'elles sont corrompues, surtout sous le rapport religieux, il faut que l'État croule, quand il serait gouverné de Charlemagne en Charlemagne. Le patricien est un prêtre laïque : la religion est sa première propriété et la plus sacrée, puisqu'elle conserve son privilège, qui tombe avec elle. [4]

He thus arrives at the conclusion : " Il n'y a pas de plus grand crime pour un noble que celui d'attaquer les dogmes." This letter, an almost unique testimony of class-consciousness, shows with unsurpassable clarity that de Maistre's system of thought centred round his fervent desire to preserve feudal aristocracy. The social function of religion, as he interpreted it, was to preserve the privileges of his own class, and moreover it was bound

---

[1] *Essai analytique sur les lois naturelles de l'ordre social*, 1800, p. 22.
[2] Cf. A. Viatte's verdict : ". . . dévot de monarchie plus que de religion ". (*Le Catholicisme chez les Romantiques*, Paris, 1922, p. 65.)
[3] *Pensées sur divers sujets, et discours politiques*, I, Paris, 1817, p. 67.
[4] *Lettres et opuscules inédits*, II, Paris, 1851, pp. 262–3.

to act in this way in order that it might itself survive.   In view of all this evidence it might be well to revise the opinion that de Maistre developed Legitimist views which were based on his religious convictions.   Is it not equally possible to assume that he developed religious views which were based on his Legitimist convictions ? [1]   At any rate, the two were inextricably bound up with each other.

Religiosity which could not be regarded as wholly disinterested was to be observed in Germany also.   Lichtenberg in 1796 described the situation thus :

I know on good authority that since the Revolution religious scepticism is said no longer to be found among people of rank and family where it previously dominated.   People have learnt to pray ; many ladies who formerly wished to hear nothing about it, are now altogether " pour la religion des nos pères ".   (Some people never pray until it thunders.)   It is believed, however, that they have something more in mind, and that they mean also " Le Gouvernement des nos pères." [2]

Schleiermacher, who was hoping for a genuine revival of Christianity, noticed the same tendency :

The men of the world [he wrote in 1804] have some recollection that formerly when more outward religiosity dominated the people, many other things too were different and more pleasing.   The people lived in a more secluded and decorous manner, they worked more cheaply and more untiringly, they showed themselves more submissive ; nor did they allow themselves all kinds of opinions or even aspirations for a better life.   These excellent qualities have disappeared together with religiosity and would perhaps come back with it. [3]

To the increasing number of his upper-class contemporaries who were thinking in this way, Schleiermacher aptly referred as " religion's political protectors ". [4]   With equal indignation Jean

---

[1] Baader, one of the representatives of radical Christianity, blamed de Maistre for his purely political conception of the Church.

[2] " Aphorismen ", ed. A. Leitzmann, 5. Heft, *Deutsche Literaturdenkmale*, No. 141, Berlin, 1908, p. 109.   Lichtenberg's " good authority " was Miss Williams' *Tour in Switzerland*, I, London, 1798, pp. 73–4, but it is obvious that that country was only a starting-point for Lichtenberg's more general observations on the subject.   (Cf., e.g., Eichendorff, Deutsches Adelsleben am Schlusse des achtzehnten Jahrhunderts, 1857.) Cf. also J. W. Ward's remark to the Bishop of Llandaff in 1815 : " The French Revolution had frightened people, and they began to perceive that atheism was not quite so good a joke." (*Letters of the Earl of Dudley to the Bishop of Llandaff*, London, 1840, p. 116.)

[3] " Über die Mittel, dem Verfall der Religion vorzubeugen ", *Sämmtliche Werke*, I. Abt., V, Berlin, 1846, pp. 96–7.

[4] Ibid., p. 100.   Cf. also Saint-Martin : " Woe, woe, to you speculators who give no foundation to religion but politics." (*Le Ministère de l'Homme-Esprit*, 1802.) I quote from the English translation *Man : His True Nature and Ministry*, by E. Burton Penny, London, 1864, p. 343.

Paul wrote in 1809 : " Religion is not a church parade of the State, . . . heaven cannot become the lackey of earth, nor can a sacristy and sanctuary be transformed into the State's cook-shop." [1]

The heralds of a radical Christian revival were Saint-Martin, " le Philosophe Inconnu ", Novalis and Baader, Novikov and Madame de Krüdener. The only analogy of any importance between this trend and that described above, save for the general idea of the social importance of religion, is the concept which Burke expressed as follows : " All persons possessing any portion of power ought to be strongly and awfully impressed with an idea that they act in trust and that they are to account for their conduct to the one great Master, Author and Founder of Society." [2] However, by virtue of the very different function which religion served for Burke on the one hand, and for Saint-Martin on the other, there was, so far as that idea was concerned, an enormous difference of emphasis. In Burke's system of thought, that idea had no prominent place ; in Saint-Martin's it was the leitmotif. According to the latter, the divine right of the monarch was only a presumption which in each case had to be lived up to by the monarch himself. Every government constitutes in reality a secret combination of elements of democracy, aristocracy, and monarchy.[3] Therefore the form of a government is less important than its spirit ; to bring rulers nearer to perfection is at least as urgent as to improve modes of government.[4] The only suitable form of government is the theocratical.[5]

There are many other ways of demonstrating how different was Saint-Martin's conception of religion from that adopted by the prophets of conservatism. While Burke's optimism of acceptance made him write : " I would not exclude alteration . . . but even when I changed, it should be to preserve ",[6] Saint-Martin, on the other hand, envisaged a society in which the associative principle of " amour " should be paramount, as opposed to the domination of law and of power. Whereas Burke was, as we have seen, highly pleased with the trend of Western civilization up to 1789, Saint-Martin saw in our very trades and " industries "

---

[1] " Über die jetzige Sonnenwende in der Religion ", *Sämmtliche Werke*, XIV, Weimar, 1939, p. 144.   [2] *Reflections*, 1790, p. 81.
[3] *Lettre à un ami*, Paris, an III, 1795, p. 56.   [4] Ibid., p. 59.
[5] *Éclair sur l'association humaine*, Paris, an V, 1797, p. 33.
[6] *Reflections*, p. 199.

a proof of the injury it had done to the world.[1]   While de Maistre
denounced Rousseau as a dangerous madman who had perhaps
made more mistakes than anyone else in the world, Saint-Martin
wrote, in 1795, in his *Lettre à un ami, ou considérations politiques
philosophiques et religieuses sur la révolution française* this encomium
of Rousseau :

> Jean-Jacques lui-même, dont le cœur et la plume étoient si propres
> à faire descendre la vérité sur la terre, ce Jean-Jacques que je regarde
> comme un envoyé, comme un prophète de l'ordre sensible, comme
> celui de tous les publicistes qui a le mieux rempli sa mission, qui a
> le mieux entrevu, quoique par éclair et par intervalle, ces principes
> supérieurs que je t'expose, enfin qui a le plus respecté la nature de
> l'homme. . . . [2]

While Bonald and de Maistre saw salvation only in Catholicism,
Saint-Martin in *Le Ministère de l'Homme-Esprit* uttered the warning
that Christianity should not be confounded with Catholicism ;
for " Christianity belongs to eternity ; Catholicism to time ".[3]

Finally, Burke and the French aristocrat *émigrés* were compet-
ing with each other in the strongest expressions of sorrow, disgust
and rage over the French Revolution. Saint-Martin, in his
Lettre à un ami, above-mentioned, placed the burden of responsibility clearly on the ruling class. As to the clergy, on whose
account Burke during his visit to pre-1789 France perceived little
or no private uneasiness,[4] Saint-Martin accused them of lust of
power and glory as well as of covetousness,[5] which in their turn
were due to the secularization of the Church. In these tragic
circumstances, the Revolution was to be regarded as a baptism
of blood and tears. Out of this ordeal Christianity might arise
purified, strengthened, and set free.

The contrast is equally obvious if the dogmas of conservative
religion are compared with the politico-religious system of the
German Romanticist, Friedrich von Hardenberg (Novalis). We
have seen that the main characteristic of conservative religion
was complacency. Those who were satisfied with the existing
order of things, or with the situation as it had been up to the
Revolution respectively, were pleased with the kind of religion
which glorified that state of affairs ; an intensification of that

---

[1] *Man : His True Nature and Ministry*, p. 65.
[2] *Lettre à un ami*, p. 33. For the antithesis Saint-Martin—de Maistre, cf. M.
Matter, *Saint-Martin le Philosophe Inconnu. Sa vie et ses écrits*, Paris, 1862, pp. 249–50 ;
also A. Franck, *La philosophie mystique en France à la fin du XVIIIe siècle*, Paris, 1866,
p. 134.
[3] P. 399 in the English translation.
[4] *Reflections*, p. 214.   [5] *Lettre à un ami*, pp. 13 sqq.

religiousness was all they were after. Novalis, on the other hand, though he agreed in holding that " Christendom had again to become living and active ",[1] was yet of the opinion that : " As yet there is no Religion. We must first found a training-school of genuine Religion. Think ye that there is Religion ? Religion must be made and produced through the union of a number of men. The fullest germs of the new Religion lie in Christianity, but they also lie comparatively neglected." [2] And in another passage : " Who says that the Bible is finished ? May it not be that the Bible is still in process of growing ? " [3] We find a similar idea among the aphorisms of the young Friedrich Schlegel who, Novalis hoped, would become the Paul of the new religion.[4] He wrote in 1797 : " Oh these blind people who are talking about atheism ! Does a theist as yet exist ? Is any human intellect already master of the idea of divinity ? " [5]

Though he agreed with Burke's view that religion was the basis of civil society, or as Novalis himself put it, that it was the unifying social principle *par excellence*,[6] his conception of a unified civil society was, nevertheless, totally different from Burke's.[7] So far as the State itself was concerned, Novalis, as opposed to Burke, saw in the Christian religion the germ of democracy.[8] This made him stress the importance of equality : everyone should become eligible for the throne. The union between liberty and equality could alone, in his view, establish a genuine harmony.[9] Therefore he shed no tears over the *ancien régime*. He saw quite clearly that " its administration must have been extremely defective for so many parts to become imperfect and such an obstinate weakness to take root ".[10] He also wrote :

[1] *Hymns and Thoughts on Religion*, transl. by W. Hastie, Edinburgh, 1888, p. 134.
[2] Ibid., p. 112. Cf. Madame de Krüdener's letter, in 1814, to a theological student at Strasbourg : " Every Christian ought to be a missionary, but you need not go to the North Pole for that ; you will find plenty of Samoyedes in your own country ; and hearts colder than those of the Lapps." (Clarence Ford, *The Life and Letters of Madame de Krüdener*, London, 1893, p. 149.)
[3] *Fragmente*, ed. E. Kamnitzer, Dresden, 1929, p. 546.
[4] Novalis' marginal note to Schlegel's aphorism in which he addresses his friend. (Paul Kluckhohn, " Novalis und Friedrich Schlegel ", *Deutsche Rundschau*, CXCI, 1922, p. 167.)
[5] Ed. J. M. J. Minor, *Friedrich Schlegel. Seine prosaischen Jugendschriften*, II, Wien, 1882, p. 302.
[6] " Durch Religion werden die Menschen erst recht eins."
[7] The accepted opinion is that Burke's *Reflections* inspired the politico-religious system of Novalis. Cf., for example, Carl Schmitt-Dorotic, " Politische Theorie und Romantik ", *Historische Zeitschrift*, CXXIII, 1921, p. 380. Cf. also Paul Kluckhohn, *Persönlichkeit und Gemeinschaft*, Halle a. d. Saale, 1925, p. 36. Meinecke (*Weltbürgertum und Nationalstaat*, 3. Aufl., München, 1915) establishes an antithesis, albeit not very sharply. [8] *Hymns and Thoughts on Religion*, pp. 99–100.
[9] *Fragmente*, p. 495. [10] Ibid., p. 516.

" The old and new world are engaged in warfare and the imperfections and weakness of state-governments are made public
in frightful phenomena." [1]   As to the more subtle causes of the
Revolution, every contemporary can find them in himself.[2]

Novalis' concern for equality went so far that some of the
thoughts which he collected for his proposed encyclopædia or
" scientific Bible ", as he called it, clearly point in the direction
of what later came to be called Socialism.   So, for example,
when he wrote :   " Whatever a private person possesses, he has
received from the State." [3]   And :   " Every citizen is a civil
servant.   Only as such does he possess his income." [4]   And the
far-sighted remark :   " The whole economy in the State could
be run on a large scale (im grossen)." [5]   That these remarks were
by no means accidental is proved by Novalis' deep insight into
the hollowness of the philosophical foundation of economic
liberalism.   " The principle of the old notorious system is ", he
said, " to bind everyone to the State by means of self-interest . . .
great efforts have been made to effect this political squaring of
the circle :   but crude self-interest seems to be absolutely im-
measurable and anti-systematic." [6]   It is also, I think, highly
significant that Novalis even anticipated the Utopian and Marxian
Socialist expectation that there will be no need for a legal order
in the society of the future, or at any rate that the number of
laws will decrease, for :   " Laws are the complement of imperfect
characters." [7]

The borders of the State were too narrow for the comprehensive concept of salvation which Novalis had in mind.   Moreover,
he realized that States could achieve all their constructive purposes only by taking their measures in common.   He was concerned, therefore, above all else, to find a solution for Europe.
The pamphlet Die Christenheit oder Europa in which he outlined
this solution was not published until 1825, but the manuscript
was completed as early as 1799, and soon became known to a
large number of sympathizers.   We find in it the same emphasis
on the paramount importance of religion :   " It is impossible for
secular powers to find their balance ;   a third element, secular
and transcendental at the same time, can alone fulfil this task.
. . .   Religion alone can again awaken all Europe, it alone can

---

[1] *Christianity or Europe*, transl. by the Rev. John Dalton, London, 1844, p. 26.
[2] Novalis' marginal note to Schlegel's aphorism on the Revolution.   (Kluckhohn,
op. cit., p. 165.)   [3] *Fragmente*, p. 489.
   [4] Ibid., p. 502.   [5] Ibid., p. 489.
   [6] Ibid., p. 510.   [7] Ibid., p. 493.

safeguard the nations." [1]   For it was real security and real peace, not an uneasy Balance of Power, for which he was longing : " Between the conflicting powers no peace can be established : the name of peace is but an illusion—a mere truce." [2]   Utterly dissatisfied with the solution attempted in the years immediately preceding, Novalis, like so many Utopians, turned his eyes to the far distant past : " Princes referred their dispute to the father of Christianity, and willingly cast down their crowns and dignities at his feet." Here we have a typical example of a Utopia attributed to a past period ; it goes almost without saying that such a state of affairs as Novalis described, never existed. But that is not the point at issue ; all we have to note in this connection is that Novalis advocated a revolutionary change in the outlook on international as well as national politics, and, secondly, that he proclaimed with romantic fervour that such a new order was already visible : " . . . a new golden Period, with heavenly features, a prophetic wonder-working, wound-healing one, comforting us and enkindling hopes of eternal life ". And in another passage : " The old and new world are engaged in warfare . . . Perchance, in these events, as in the sciences, a more intimate and varied connection between the European States is at hand." And Novalis' ultimate aim was that : " Europe may again awaken and the states form but one."

In this connection it is, I believe, for a variety of reasons, indispensable to subject Franz von Baader's system of thought to a careful examination. It is more or less generally admitted that Baader, by reason of the famous memoranda which he is said to have addressed to the rulers of Russia, Austria and Prussia in the spring of 1815, represents an important link between political romanticism, as expressed in the politico-religious writings of that time, on the one hand, and Tsar Alexander I, author of the original draft of the Holy Alliance Treaty, on the other. Far more controversial is the question of the character of Baader's own system. This may be due to the fact that Baader, unlike Novalis, attempted on more than one occasion to exercise a direct influence on European politics. Novalis, as we have seen, proclaimed that a completely new, genuinely Christian age was just about to begin ; by his proclamation he desired only to accelerate this fortunate course of events. Baader, on the other

---

[1] *Schriften*, ed. Minor, II, Jena, 1907, pp. 42-3.
[2] This and the following passages are quoted from the English translation by the Rev. J. Dalton.

hand, though on the whole pursuing the same ideal, sought a different path for its achievement. In one case, in the spring of 1815, he probably chose the method of direct approach by letter to the most powerful monarchs of the Continent, or at any rate to Tsar Alexander, and kept in touch for a considerable time afterwards with very influential Russian orthodox circles. This may account to some extent for the striking ambiguity of some of his ideas. In order to influence the political struggle, and thus, as he hoped, to eradicate that fatal conflict once and for all, he had to play the game whose first rule demanded compromise. This need by no means have been the result of conscious deliberation.

Baader shared with both Saint-Martin, whose works he had read in his youth, and Novalis, the fervent desire that the spirit of Christianity should permeate public as well as private life. As to the international sphere, he was aware that without a League of Souls there could be no League of States. He was of the opinion that no Christian State had ever as yet existed,[1] and that the time had at last come to receive again and with renewed intensity the principles of religion, love and liberty into the realm of politics.[2] Replying to those who failed to see any element in Christianity besides the transcendental, he wrote : " It cannot well be denied that a religion which announced the message of the approach of the Kingdom of God among men has a cosmopolitan tendency, and although that Kingdom is not of this World, it is coming for it and into it." [3] These ideas he expressed in his pamphlet, *Über das durch die Französische Revolution herbeigeführte Bedürfnis einer neueren und innigeren Verbindung der Religion mit der Politik* (1815), which seems to have been identical or almost identical with the above-mentioned memoranda to the three monarchs. But this pamphlet contained an even bolder assertion : " In fact no secular and no ecclesiastical despot has as yet been sincere in his Christianity, and each of them has sought in his own way to suppress it. The worst method of suppression has always been that of hypocrisy." [4] As opposed to Novalis and Saint-Martin, he deplored the event of the French Revolution ; yet he tried to divide his accusation fairly between the ruling class and the people by blaming them both for having renounced Christianity :

[1] *Sämmtliche Werke*, VI, Leipzig, 1834, p. 25.
[2] Ibid., p. 26.   [3] Ibid., p. 25.
[4] Ibid., p. 21.

L.C. DE SAINT MARTIN

dit le Philosophe inconnu

Tiré du Cabinet de Mr. Matter.

SAINT MARTIN,
le Philosophe Inconnu

[*face p.* 16

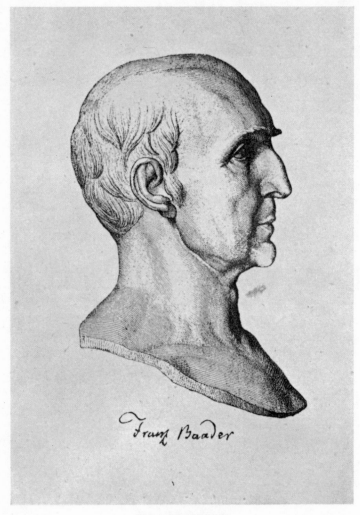

FRANZ BAADER

[face p. 17

In proportion as love, the real spirit of community between the elements of a State, vanishes, and thus *hubris* and baseness become predominant, that State approaches its decline. It makes no difference how these two attitudes are divided among the various ranks of society, or whether the haughtiness reaches its climax first in the higher and only afterwards in the lower ranks, or whether the baseness in the higher ranks produces the haughtiness in the lower, whether, that is, the despotism assumes a monarchical, aristocratic or democratic form.[1]

Another aspect of Baader's doctrine is equally important for our purpose : The deep respect which he, a Roman Catholic, felt for the other branches of Christianity. De Maistre and Bonald also stressed the necessity for religious unity in Europe ; but all that they meant was that the heretics should return in penitence to the bosom of the Roman Catholic Church. Baader, who likewise regarded religious unity as one of the main preliminary conditions for a genuine peace in Europe, did not, however, expect it to come about unless Roman Catholicism, Protestantism and Russian Orthodoxy were prepared to learn from each other's merits and faults. Here, indeed, we have one of the main characteristics of that radical interpretation of Christianity which, it can be shown, came to assume actual political importance in connection with Tsar Alexander's scheme of the Holy Alliance. What did the differences between the actual branches of Christianity matter, in view of this interpretation, one of the cardinal points of which was precisely their unification ?

The roots of supra-denominationalism can be traced back to the end of the Middle Ages. A new emphasis was given to the movement at the beginning of the seventeenth century. By then the momentous theological battle between Protestantism and Catholicism had, in many places,[2] degenerated into sophistic and sophisticated squabbles. Ecclesiastics on both sides eagerly professed Christian love for their fellow-creatures, but only too often this feeling was superseded by hatred for each other. From about that time there was, among the common people, a definite trend towards a more broad-minded conception of religion. The following lines, written by an Augsburg craftsman in 1602, express a fairly widespread feeling in Southern Germany :

---

[1] Ibid., pp. 19–20.
[2] Not at that time in England. It might perhaps be said that in this country the Reformation in the full religious sense of the word came considerably later than on the Continent.

Ablasbriff tu ich nit kauffen,
Zu keiner Walfarth mag ich nit lauffen,
Ich ehr aber Gottes Mutter,
Und glaub nicht an Doctor Luther.
Dennoch bin ich kein Papist,
Desgleichen auch kein Calvinist,
Ich glaub an Herrn Jesum Christ,
Der vor mich und mein Sündt gestorben ist.[1]

In the course of the Thirty Years' War people in some regions were forced to change their denomination three or four times. Such treatment could not fail to produce still greater indifference towards the distinctions between the contending creeds.[2]   There exist from that period innumerable satires and cartoons in which zealots of both Catholic and Protestant affiliation are alike savagely ridiculed.

In the eighteenth century the main impulse in this direction came from the Moravian Brethren. This very important remnant of the old Hussite movement, reorganized in Saxony from 1722 onwards by Count Zinzendorf, never felt the need to erect dogmatic barriers between itself and the other Protestant churches or sects, since, as has been pointed out, it did not originate from any other Evangelical Church.[3]   Since, on the one hand, the Brethren themselves claimed to represent the genuine Catholic Church, and on the other, as a result of the terrible persecutions suffered in the period of the Counter-reformation the number of their followers was very small, their tendency was naturally in the direction of a new unity of believers.[4]   To leave the door wide open was certainly a promising plan for pursuing that goal. Zinzendorf, too, was very favourable to the idea that the *Unitas Fratrum* should stand above the various Christian denominations.

Supra-denominationalism in itself is, however, by no means an auspicious basis for a radical or newly reorganized religious movement ; for it implies a certain amount of scepticism.   Friedrich Carl von Moser, the Würtemberg Pietist and politician, who demanded of a truly religious statesman that he should feel neither hatred nor bitterness against the followers of another

[1] Quoted by Gustav Freytag, *Bilder aus der deutschen Vergangenheit*, IV, Leipzig, 1867, p. 11.

[2] Sometimes, however, the result was religious indifference rather than supra-denominationalism. Fanaticism, as Arnold Toynbee put it, was sterilized " at the cost of extinguishing Faith ". (*Study of History*, V, p. 671.)

[3] Cf. article " Moravians " in Hastings' *Encyclopedia of Religion and Ethics*.

[4] The sixth of the eight main points of doctrine as set forth in the Church book of the *Unitas Fratrum* is the Fellowship of Believers.

Church,[1] was yet aware of the affinity between tolerance and indifference in religious matters.[2] However, there is always the chance of diverting that scepticism to issues of minor importance. The easiest way to do this is to declare all matters to which scepticism inclines to extend, to be such minor issues. But this can succeed only if a new or a resuscitated creed exists to which all the currents of fervent belief which used formerly to flow to the old creed are being diverted.

Among the main features which characterized the deepening of the religious feeling was humility, which afforded a marked contrast to the proud Calvinist feeling of predestination.[3] The new Reformation which, as Zinzendorf had already pointed out, set in after the Thirty Years' War, made men once more alive to man's sinfulness, and in particular to the dangers to which their own salvation was continuously exposed. Zinzendorf's followers retained this humility. Unlike the Methodists, the Herrenhutians did not venture to contemplate the possibility of their becoming faultless and perfect Christians.[4]

Bound up with humility was the feeling which might be described as suspicion of the world. That love of the world is dangerous for the salvation of the soul, because the Word is choked thereby (Matt. xiii. 22) was an idea with a long and venerable tradition behind it. Mediæval monks, later sects like the Joachimites, the Fraticelli, the Lollards and the Hussites, and later still, the Anabaptists, the Mennonites, some of the Baptists, the Diggers, and the early Quakers were perhaps the most notable links in this chain of radical Christians. German Pietism forms a bridge in this respect, between the above-mentioned movements on the one hand, and the radical Christian revival at the turn of the eighteenth century on the other. Pietist suspicion of the world was at its strongest after the Thirty Years' War, and again shortly before the French Revolution and during the period of wars that ensued. Seventeenth-century Pietist preachers warned true Christians to beware of the " respectable world ".[5] Again in late eighteenth- and early nineteenth-century Würtemberg, Pietists such as Bengel considered it to be an honour for true Christians to be at loggerheads with the world.

---

[1] *Reliquien*, Frankfurt am Mayn, 1766, p. 220.
[2] Ibid., p. 345.
[3] Max Weber, " Die protestantische Ethik und der Geist des Kapitalismus ", in : *Gesammelte Aufsätze zur Religionssoziologie*, 2. Aufl., Tübingen, 1922, p. 143.
[4] Max Weber, op. cit., p. 148, n. 4.
[5] Albrecht Ritschl, *Geschichte des Pietismus*, III, 2. Abt., p. 96.

Quite unlike the Puritans, Bengel thought highly of those who were hard pressed and miserable in the outward affairs of life. The belief was very widespread among the Pietists of Würtemberg that all the present rulers of the world are in possession of their power unlawfully, and that they owe it only to the patience of God.[1]

A growing suspicion of the world on the part of genuinely religious persons was all the more justified since worldly powers did much, during the seventeenth century, to annul an essential tradition of the Church : the tradition of community. The nobility succeeded in gaining all kinds of privileges, for example the right to receive Holy Communion in private, to have reserved pews in Church, to approach the altar separately from the lower orders, and even to have their funerals celebrated without a funeral sermon. Church patrons who were members of the nobility interfered to an increasing degree in purely ecclesiastical matters, especially after the Thirty Years' War.[2]

The Pietist movement was, in some of its aspects, a reaction against this far-reaching profanation of the Church. The Herrenhutians in particular may be said to have revived the community ideal.[3] Zinzendorf himself, however, pointed out that radical Pietism was confined to the lower classes. Very broadly speaking, his statement was undoubtedly true. In Central and Northern Germany, where Pietism hardly penetrated the middle and lower strata of society, the movement remained, on the whole, very respectable. On the other hand, the radical character of the movement in Würtemberg was due to the fact that the middle and peasant classes with their remarkably democratic tradition had been its supporters from the beginning. As applied to whole strata of society, the generalization thus seems to hold. It is all the more remarkable that some of the apostles of radical Christianity, Novalis and Madame de Krüdener for example, definitely belonged to the higher classes.

Although the Pietist movement, as we have seen, manifested a certain suspicion of the world, and although it reacted against the profanation of the Church, it did not remain altogether uninfluenced by the trend towards rationalization. Zinzendorf's postulate was typical : " A reasonable man should not be without

[1] H. Ph. C. Henke, *Religionsannalen*, Achtes Stück, Braunschweig, 1805, p. 161.
[2] Cf. Paul Drews, " Der Einfluss der gesellschaftlichen Zustände auf das kirchliche Leben ", *Zeitschrift für Theologie und Kirche*, XVI, 1906, pp. 45 seqq.
[3] Cf. Hans Walter Erbe, *Zinzendorf und der hohe Adel seiner Zeit*, Diss., Leipzig, 1928, pp. 122 seqq.

faith, and a man with faith should not be unreasonable." Similarly, F. C. von Moser declared : " Any religion which seeks to make reason suspect and its gifts open to objection, is itself suspect and open to objection." The Swiss thinker Lavater, also, concentrated on the elements common to both Enlightenment and radical Christianity, when he wrote : " He who loves Christ and calls Him his master from his inmost heart, and allows himself to be guided by Christ's teaching, is a Christian and a saint, whether he be called a Jesuit or a non-Catholic, a hero of reason (*Vernunftheld*) or an enthusiast." [1]

Nor should it be overlooked that radical Christianity owed its social impetus to some extent to the humanitarian tendencies of the eighteenth century, manifested, for example, in the poor-relief [2] of the *Aufklärung* and expressed in the social utopias of the *philosophes*. In Germany, Jung-Stilling may be said to have personified the union between reinterpreted Christianity and reinterpreted humanitarianism.

It is equally imperative to determine what was the essential difference between these two trends. For on frequent occasions they denounced each other with such bitterness that the fact that they were fighting against the common enemy, Conservatism, was almost forgotten. While pursuing, on the whole, the same social ideals as the *philosophes*, the representatives of radical Christianity differed widely as to the methods of achieving their goal. Their appeal was, after all, directed essentially to the emotions. That is why Madame de Krüdener, the great prophetess of the resuscitated creed, spoke of " the barren comfort of philosophic reasoning " [3] and compared the whole race of philosophers to extinct volcanoes. [4] Similarly, Saint-Martin complained of the " cold metaphysicians ".[5] And why are they so cold ? " Leur paroles sont vides et froides," says Madame de Krüdener, " car ce qui ne vient pas du cœur, ne retourne pas au cœur." [6]

The appeal to the emotional side of man's mind implied, at the same time, a sharp contrast to Christianity as interpreted by the organized churches and respectable sects of the day. In opposition to each of them and as a challenge to all, perfect

[1] Quoted from Ritschl, op. cit., I, p. 508.
[2] Cf. G. Uhlhorn, *Die christliche Liebesthätigkeit seit der Reformation*, Stuttgart, 1890, pp. 283 seqq.   [3] Ford, op. cit., p. 151.
[4] Ernest J. Knapton, *The Lady of the Holy Alliance. The Life of Julie de Krüdener*, New York, 1939, p. 197.
[5] *Man : His True Nature and Ministry*, p. 343.
[6] Ch. Eynard, *Vie de Madame de Krüdener*, II, Paris, 1849, pp. 299–302.
A.N.W.

agreement of opinion on dogmatic and ritual questions was declared an issue of secondary importance. What mattered above all else was Christian life and Christian character. Emotion by itself, of course, was insufficient. Purely emotional Pietism, in fact, as put into practice by the leisured classes, was only playing with religion. For serious Pietists, however, the exact interpretation of Christ's words became of less importance in view of the new emphasis on the love of Christ for mankind.[1] Charity—that was to be the main if not the only dogma, for Christianity and charity were in fact more or less identical : " Though I have all faith, so that I could remove mountains, and have not charity, I am nothing." The most outstanding point among the doctrines of the Moravian Brethren was, in- dubitably, the fifth, which demanded good works as evidence of faith. Thus Madame de Krüdener's bitterest accusation against her contemporaries was that they were " indolent in regard to everything which is good ".[2] E. J. Knapton, her latest biographer, who cannot be suspected of too much sympathy for her faith, which he summarizes as " bizarre and ill-founded ",[3] yet scrupulously testifies to the fact that, even in face of constant persecution from the authorities, she distributed charity with a lavish hand,[4] thus living up to her belief.

One more aspect of radical Christianity remains to be men- tioned, and one which was to assume special importance in connection with the origins of the Holy Alliance : its strong chiliastic expectation. Several types of chiliastic ideas can be distinguished at that time ; they varied from the dark colours of apocalyptic to the bright hues of messianism. As an example of the latter—which was on the whole predominant—the following passage from Lavater's letter to Jung-Stilling, written in 1800, is significant :

I understand by this Kingdom of the Lord not merely an indefinite, general and heavenly felicity, like many thousand pious Christians,

---

[1] J. F. Fontaines, pastor of the Alsatian town of Sainte-Marie-aux-Mines, seemed, according to Knapton, op. cit., p. 108, " to care little for the rites and dogmas of his church, but chose instead to speak in impassioned language of Christ's love for man, and of the power of prayer, and of the impending approach of the millennium ". Pastor Fontaines was for a considerable time closely associated with Madame de Krüdener's endeavours for a religious awakening of Europe.

[2] " Die heutige Welt, besonders die aufgeklärte und gebildete, ist schlimmer als lasterhaft ; sie ist träge zu allem Guten, schlaff und matt, weder kalt noch warm. Sie hat keinen Glauben und keine Liebe." (W. T. Krug, " Gespräch unter vier Augen mit Frau von Krüdener in bezug auf den Ursprung des Heiligen Bundes ", Politische und Juridische Schriften, I, Braunschweig, 1834, p. 270.)

[3] Op. cit., p. 226.   [4] Ibid., pp. 169–70.

but a regularly organized state whose visible King is the God-man, Jesus Christ. I believe that He will reign on the earth, in his most peculiar, visible, tangible human form and in a perfect corporality.[1]

Apocalyptic features were prominent in Bengel's vision. According to a prophecy of his made some time before the Revolution, the Antichrist was to open his struggle against the Church in the year 1790.

Messianism was likewise one of the main features of radical Christianity as manifested in the religious awakening in Russia. In 1784, Nikolas Ivanovich Novikov, the prominent Freemason, who like Saint-Simon endeavoured to bring about a reconciliation of religion and science, wrote : " Et tous les souverains croyants de tout l'univers uniront leurs forces pour préparer et établir sur la terre le Royaume de Jésus-Christ et de son Amour divin et spirituel. Ils auront en vue avant tout la Volonté, la Gloire, et le Règne de Dieu et le Bonheur éternel de tous les hommes." [2] In these lines all the essential tenets of radical Christianity are, as it were, summarized : first, the emphasis upon charity ; second, the concern for a wide international organization ; [3] and last the chiliastic expectation that the Paradise thus defined will actually be established on this planet.

[1] Sequel to *Heinrich Stilling*, trans. by Samuel Jackson, London, 1836, p. 109.
[2] Quoted from J. Vernadskij, " Le Césarévich Paul et les Francs-Maçons de Moscou ", *Revue des Études Slaves*, III, 1923, pp. 283-4.
[3] In this respect, the Quakers were the first to work out detailed proposals. In 1692, William Penn wrote his *Essay towards the Present and Future Peace of Europe*. In 1710 his example was followed by John Bellers in his pamphlet *Some Reasons for an European State, proposed to the Powers of Europe*.

CHAPTER II

DIPLOMATIC OVERTURE

During the first few years of his reign, Tsar Alexander I was interested chiefly in domestic policy. With the help of his collaborators Novosiltsev, Stroganov, Czartoryski, and Kochubey, he tackled first the problem of administrative reform. It was not long before his interest began to centre on social questions : on many occasions when he met his young collaborators [1] at the Informal Committee, he made quite clear his strong dislike of class privilege. [2] Nor was this merely a matter of phrases for the Tsar, for after he had made his vow to grant no more crown peasants into serfdom, he really kept it. In matters of agrarian reform, however, neither the Tsar, autocrat though he was believed to be, nor his enthusiastic Committee were, as a rule, in a position to impose their will upon the obstinate and unruffled body of landowners. In vain had Radishchev hoped to stir their consciences by his realistic *Journey from St. Petersburg to Moscow* (1790). Catherine II had not greatly exaggerated when she wrote on the margin of a copy of that book : " He tries to persuade the squires to liberate their serfs, but nobody will listen to him." A case in point was the way in which S. P. Rumyantsev's proposal, which had Alexander's full support, was received by the Council of State. Rumyantsev's memorandum was based on the idea of a gradual extinction of serfdom. The Council of State, while admitting that the scheme might be very useful, expressed their conviction that to proclaim it would lead the peasants to believe that general emancipation was approaching, and that they were to obtain unrestricted freedom. The same reluctance to accept the proposal was shown by Derzhavin, the Minister of Justice. He agreed with Rumyantsev only in holding that under the old laws proprietors had no rights over their serfs, but added that " political views having bound the peasants to the land, serfdom became a custom, which, being rooted by time, became so far divine, that great discretion is required to touch

---

[1] The oldest, Novosiltsev, was 39, the youngest, Stroganov, only 29 years of age. Kochubey and Czartoryski were just over 30, when Alexander ascended the throne at the age of 24.
[2] Detailed reports of the Committee's proceedings are to be found in Nicolas Mikhaïlovich, *Le Comte Paul Stroganov*, II, Paris, 1905, annexes IX and X.

it without harmful consequences ".[1] Derzhavin also wrote an " Ode to God " in which he exhorted his fellow-countrymen to stand for God in poetry, and for serfdom in politics.

In spite of such formidable opposition a few tangible improvements were achieved in agrarian matters ; for example, the right of squires to punish their peasants was restricted. But on the whole the results were very small indeed in relation to the amount of discussion and the number of ukases on agrarian affairs, many of which proved almost entirely inoperative. An outstanding example was the ukase drafted by Rumyantsev. The Council of State, in spite of grave doubts which they did not conceal, eventually approved it. The idea of the new law of February 20th, 1803, was to encourage landowners to liberate their peasants as well as to provide a certain amount of governmental supervision of the process and to establish a new class of freemen. During the twenty-two years between the issue of the ukase and the death of Alexander I, less than 1 per cent. of the peasants were liberated. The main cause of this extraordinary failure was the fact that many of the proprietors made exorbitant demands on their peasants as the price of their liberty. Peasants of good proprietors, the historian Karamzin explained, did not want freedom, and those of bad ones were too poor to buy it. When all was said and done, there remained but one sphere, namely public education, in which the reforms of the new régime were entirely successful. Soon after his accession to the throne, the Tsar founded, besides many other schools, three new universities. But this was not enough for his ambitions nor for those of his collaborators.

Having been brought up by his tutor Laharpe on ideals— albeit not on Christian ideals—Alexander I soon became disgusted with domestic politics and recognized them to be an unclean business. Of foreign politics he did not as yet know a great deal. While engaged on reforms in his own country, he had instructed his diplomats to keep Russia out of war as long as possible. The alternative to social reform was evidently reform in the international sphere. This change of interest,[2] while necessitated by the aversion of the Russian gentry to his reforming schemes, was in a paradoxical way facilitated by the expansionist aspirations of that class. When he was Crown Prince, Alexander had

[1] Quoted from James Mavor, *An Economic History of Russia*, 2nd ed., London, 1925, pp. 317–18.
[2] Cf. Nicolas Mikhaïlovich, op. cit., I, p. 76.

written to Kochubey in 1796 : " Incredible disorder prevails in
the administration ; robbery goes on everywhere ; all depart-
ments are ill-managed ; order seems to have been banished, but
the empire recks nothing, and strives only after expansion." The
land-owning yet land-hungry Russian aristocracy was able to think
of Russian interference in the politics of Europe only in terms
of an increase of Russia's power leading to the expansion of her
territory. When the Tsar first began to show an interest in
European politics, therefore, he met with their genuine approval.
Later on, when on ideological grounds Alexander turned more
and more against Napoleon, the Russian squires also turned anti-
French, but for more material reasons : the Continental blockade
had reduced Russian wheat exports from 174,558 tons between
1801 and 1805 to 29,000 tons between 1806 and 1810. The
export trade in oats, rye, and timber also suffered heavily. It
was not until 1810–11 that the entry of colonial goods into
Russia was first permitted, and that Russia gradually abandoned
the system by which the entry of British goods was forbidden ;
she soon went so far as to prohibit the importation of certain
luxury articles until then imported from France. Yet the mis-
understanding on which the Russian aristocracy—apart from a
few who shared the Tsar's views—based their approval of Alexander's foreign policy soon became apparent. This happened,
probably for the first time, in the spring of 1804 on the occasion
of the kidnapping of the Duc d'Enghien from German territory
by French agents, and his subsequent execution. A Council was
held, over which the Tsar presided. The foreign minister
Czartoryski pointed out that France had violated international
law, and that Russia was therefore entitled to demand satisfaction.
If it was refused, she should break off diplomatic relations with
France. In the debate that followed, Czartoryski was opposed
by N. P. Rumyantsev, a diplomat of the old style, who stressed
the importance of " Russia's interest " as opposed to Czartoryski's
" policy of principle and sentiment ".

The older members of the Russian diplomatic staff did not
show much understanding of the new line which Alexander
intended to take in foreign policy. This became obvious on
another occasion in the spring of the same year. In May 1804,
a new British Cabinet was constituted, Pitt again becoming Prime
Minister. It was then that a memorandum was sent to St.
Petersburg by S. Vorontsev, the Russian Ambassador in London,
urging the necessity of a perpetual alliance with England for the

mutual advantage of the two countries and the pacification of Europe. In the following month, the scheme was amplified by Vorontsev to provide that Russian land-power and British sea-power should supplement each other, and the two countries become each other's markets. The possibility of conflict was ruled out, for the countries were not neighbours, and Russia possessed no colonies. The gist of the scheme was thus an appeal to the self-interest of both Russia and Britain, sentiments which were supposed to be compatible and even to tend in the same direction. There was no essential difference between Vorontsev's conception of 1804 and the programme of the Second Coalition of 1798. The rise of Napoleon seemed, in a way, to justify the maintenance of the traditional outlook. The revolutionary changes which Napoleon made in the map of Europe were from the beginnings of his conquests on so large a scale that the alliances formed to oppose him naturally emphasized above all else their desire to bring to a halt the expansion of France.

All the more striking is the contrast between this old-fashioned policy of alliances and the scheme for a new international law outlined for the first time in an official document in Novosiltsev's Instructions in the autumn of 1804. Novosiltsev was sent to London in order to suggest a new alliance on what really deserved to be called new principles. The despatch of a special envoy from the Tsar's circle of personal and political friends was decided upon, because the ordinary ambassador could hardly be expected to perform this delicate task in a manner which would satisfy Alexander and Czartoryski. This was the first occasion on which the Tsar's distrust of officials in general and diplomats in particular became apparent.

For two reasons Novosiltsev's Instructions meant a revolution in diplomatic history. A complete change in the outlook on international affairs was envisaged among Napoleon's actual and potential enemies, especially, of course, in Great Britain and Russia. But internal politics, too, were to be viewed from a new angle. The foundation upon which the Instructions were based was the conviction that the main ideas of the French Revolution were sound. Indeed we have Czartoryski's testimony to the fact that Alexander, in 1796, wished the French Republic success even though he condemned the terrible excesses of the Revolution.[1] The sincerity of his tutor Laharpe, who in his turn had been a pupil of Rousseau, certainly made a strong impression on Alex-

[1] *Alexandre Ier et le prince Czartoryski*, Paris, 1865, p. xviii.

ander's susceptible mind.   But there were other influences besides
Laharpe.   In fact, many of the ideas expressed in Novosiltsev's
Instructions can be traced back to a memorandum which
Czartoryski's teacher, the Italian Scipione Piattoli, wrote for the
Russian Foreign Office in 1803.   The independence of small
nations, constitutionalism, and the federation of Europe—these
are the main features of the memorandum.   They are also the
main features of the Instructions.[1]   Arbitrariness was regarded
as the cause of all evil, in the life of the State as well as in European
relations.   Therefore certain legal barriers would have to be
erected against arbitrariness showing itself in either way.[2]   The
barriers proposed were, as said above, constitutionalism à la
Montesquieu and European federalism à la Rousseau.   It is
true that the Instructions speak also of " l'intérêt véritable des
autorités légales ", which seems to foreshadow the principle of
legitimacy.   Though the possibility of inconsistency is not to be
excluded, the meaning of " autorités légales ", viewed in the
whole context of the Instructions, seems to have been different :
not every kind of legitimate power was to be preserved, but only
that which was based on constitutional grounds.   France was to
be deprived of her monopoly of *liberté* in the internal and of inter-
nationalism in the European sphere.   Moreover, these weapons
might quite well be used against the country of their origin,
which, the Instructions suggested, used them but in a hypocritical
way.   This was why France would have to be liberated from
Napoleon's yoke, just as the subjected countries of Europe were
to be liberated from the yoke of France in accordance with the
principle of national self-determination—an anticipation of
Wilsonianism : " Il serait nécessaire . . . de composer chaque
État de peuples homogènes qui puissent se convenir entre eux,
et s'harmoniser avec le gouvernement qui les régit." [3]   The
system which should bind together the various member-States
of the European League was to be a new, clearly defined and
codified international law, to which the municipal law of the
member-States was to be subjected.   In this way the League was
to interfere in constitutional questions affecting its Members ;
for it is highly probable that the " tranquillity and safety " it

---

[1] Hildegard Schaeder has shown and carefully proved the importance of Piattoli
in this respect.   (" Die dritte Koalition und die heilige Allianz ", *Osteuropäische
Forschungen*, ed. O. Hoetzsch, XVI, Königsberg, 1934, pp. 12–21.)
[2] *Mémoires du prince Adam Czartoryski et correspondance avec l'Empereur Alexandre Ier*,
tome second, Paris, 1887, pp. 33–4.
[3] Ibid., p. 36.

was to guarantee did not mean external peace alone. All this obviously implied a restriction of State sovereignty. According to Saint-Pierre's suggestion, wars were to be reduced by neutral mediation. Violations of the rules of the new international law were to be punished by the federation itself.

The Instructions indeed owed everything to Western Enlightenment. As early as 1712, at the end of the War of the Spanish Succession, the Abbé de Saint-Pierre had realized that the system of " *Équilibre* " was unsatisfactory. Towards the end of the century, Kant came to the same conclusion.[1] Kant had likewise developed Saint-Pierre's and Rousseau's idea of federalism by pointing to the meetings of the States-General at The Hague as the nucleus of a federal Europe.[2] But the influence of the Enlightenment was obvious above all from the fact that the unifying bond of Christianity was nowhere mentioned in the Instructions. In this respect, too, Saint-Pierre had started a tradition. Whereas the religious tolerance had been of a supra-denominational character, the Abbé's tolerance was based on religious indifference.[3] Therefore, unlike Bellers, he laid no stress on the Christian character of a European federation. Similarly, Kant held that the abolition of war was a requirement of the moral and practical Reason. Kant and Holbach, like so many thinkers of the Enlightenment, thought that no higher legislator was needed.

How did it come about that this enlightened scheme for the establishment of an international organization in Europe arose in Russia, Europe's most backward social milieu? To answer this question, it is certainly not sufficient to point to the Tsar's susceptible character, or to the influence of his tutor, or that of Stroganov who in Paris during the Revolution had become a member of one of the Jacobin sections, and later became a close friend of the Tsar. We have also to take into account the mentality of a considerable part of the Russian diplomatic corps, namely of those foreigners who had only recently entered the Russian diplomatic service, or whose ancestors had emigrated to Russia from Germany, the Baltic, or Western Europe. Unwilling to submerge themselves in the Russian culture which could not fail to compare unfavourably with that of their ancestors, they kept aloof—many of them spoke Russian very badly—and

---

[1] " Über den Gemeinspruch : Das mag in der Theorie richtig sein, taugt aber nicht für die Praxis ", (1793), *Werke*, V, Leipzig, 1838, p. 410.
[2] " Metaphysische Anfangsgründe der Rechtslehre ", ibid., p. 189.
[3] Cf. Joseph Drouet, *L'Abbé de Saint-Pierre. L'homme et l'œuvre*, Paris, 1912, p. 296.

became markedly cosmopolitan,[1] which at that time was tant-
amount to being good Europeans.   Because of Russia's backwardness,[2] these intellectuals had not yet been absorbed into Russian
society.   They were therefore to some extent *déracinés*, and as
such ready to regard Europe as their country.   The Tsar, on the
other hand, was always keen to receive distinguished foreigners
into his service, as much now as later when he came to look
upon Europe as one big family, as he put it in Vienna.[3]

The far-reaching extent of the change in the political outlook
which Alexander and Czartoryski suggested to Pitt through
Novosiltsev can be judged, apart from an analysis of the Instructions, from the way in which these suggestions were received.
It was more than a matter of phraseology when Pitt, summarizing
his conversations with Novosiltsev and with the ordinary ambassador Vorontsev in the memorandum of January 19th, 1805,
used the expression " re-establishing a general system of public
law in Europe " [4] instead of " un nouveau code du droit des
gens " which had been suggested to him.   The English ruling
class, though willing to go some way to meet Alexander's proposals,
was by no means prepared to give up its claim for British sovereignty by subordinating it to European control.   The second
main point, namely the idea of basing the new State system, at
least in part, on the principle of national self-determination, was
also omitted in Pitt's memorandum.   In this a concern for the
ruling classes of Austria and Prussia may have played a certain
part.   For these two Powers, which Pitt hoped to draw into the
Alliance against Napoleon, had to be bribed by the prospect of
territorial expansion in Italy and the Rhineland respectively.
Nevertheless a certain readjustment in British foreign policy did
take place.   Pitt agreed that it would be advisable to keep the
alliance in being, even after victory had been won.   By 1804
the fear of France had become so great that this concession was
regarded as inevitable, just as in 1904 the fear of Germany was
to lead Britain to make a " rapprochement " with France, thus
breaking with her tradition of " splendid isolation ".

[1] Cf. Michailowski-Danilewski, " Die Vertreter Russlands auf dem Wiener
Kongress ", in Th. Schiemann, *Geschichte Russlands unter Nikolaus I*, Vol. I, Berlin,
1904, pp. 547–53.
[2] A symptom of this backwardness is that in 1812 only 4.4 per cent. of Russia's
total population lived in towns.
[3] Note in Stein's diary on May 8th, 1813.   (*Briefwechsel, Denkschriften und
Aufzeichnungen*, ed. E. Botzenhart, V, Berlin 1933, p. 237.)
[4] C. K. Webster, *British Diplomacy 1813–1815.   Select Documents dealing with the
Reconstruction of Europe*, London, 1921, p. 390.

The practical result of these negotiations, which at the beginning of 1805 were continued in St. Petersburg, was the treaty between Russia and Britain of April 11th, 1805.[1] Eventually the British negotiator, Lord Gower, had to make some further concessions to the " Russian speculative tendency ", as he called it, proud as he apparently was of Britain's more practical approach ; as a proof of which he succeeded in postponing the revision of maritime international law which Alexander had desired to be tackled at once. The concession was a statement that in setting up new governments in the countries which were to be liberated, the will of the people was to be decisive. The Treaty between Russia and Prussia of November 1805 to which Austria acceded on the day of its conclusion, went further. It defined the task of the future federal system in the following terms : " Un objet essentiel des travaux du Congrès sera de donner à l'Europe entière le système qui lui a manqué, en mettant, non plus comme autrefois, tel objet particulier sous la garantie de telle Puissance, mais tous les objets sous la garantie de toutes." [2] This article obviously envisaged the restriction of State sovereignty.

Just as the Tsar, in Novosiltsev's Instructions of 1804, had been the first to suggest in a diplomatic document the restriction of State sovereignty, he was also the first to introduce, eight years later, some of the principles of radical Christianity into diplomatic correspondence. We are thus entering the period characterized by the diplomatic documents which, as will be shown, led up to the Pact of the Holy Alliance. Before analysing these documents, however, it is necessary to illustrate the contact which existed between Alexander I and the European movement of religious awakening.

Koshelev, who as president of the Committee for Petitions enjoyed an independent position subordinate to the Tsar alone, was an enthusiastic disciple of Saint-Martin, Ekhartshausen, and Lavater, and his correspondence with the Tsar extended at least from 1812 to 1814.[3] Indeed, Alexander, in a letter to Koshelev of December 13th, 1815, acknowledged that his friend had been

[1] For the text of the treaty with its secret articles, cf. John Holland Rose, *Select Despatches from the British Foreign Office Archives relating to the Formation of the Third Coalition against France*, London, 1904, pp. 265–76.

[2] Article VI of the Treaty, cf. F. de Martens, *Recueil des Traités et Conventions conclus par la Russie avec les Puissances Étrangères*, II, St. Petersburg, 1875, p. 486.

[3] Cf. the Tsar's letter to Golitsyn from Laybach in February 1821. (Nicolas Mikhaïlowitch, *L'Empereur Alexandre Ier. Essai d'étude historique*, I, St. Petersburg, 1912, p. 222.)

mainly responsible for showing him the path which he was now following. Labsin's influence worked in the same direction ; he too, like Koshelev, was in contact with Jung-Stilling. Labsin played an important part in the development of Russian masonic lodges which exhibited a peculiar blend of liberalism and mysticism.[1]

There exists an essay written by Alexander himself for his sister Catherine, in which he gives a *résumé* of mystical literature. He distinguishes three kinds of mystical writings. In the first place, there are those whose object is mainly theoretical. Their foundation is abstract. Before reading them, people should be introduced to the rather complicated terminology of mysticism, but Alexander does not attach much importance to these differences in words. The second group is made up of those which contain less theory and more practical moral teaching. The third is occupied exclusively with " moral culture " demonstrating some practical method which has been approved by experience. And the Tsar adds : " This is the most trustworthy and the safest kind. Happy is he who, having devoted some time to intellectual enquiry, finds himself bored by those of the first order, passes on to the second, and proceeds even to the third. Perfection and truth are here fundamental, for in everything perfection is simplicity." [2]

As to the influence of contemporary mysticism upon Alexander, we have seen that Baader's outspoken memoranda probably reached the Tsar in 1814 or early 1815. On April 2nd of the latter year, Alexander Stourdza, himself in close touch with the Tsar, wrote to Stein from Munich : " Une autre connaissance qui fera époque dans ma vie est celle de Franz Baader. Il est difficile de rencontrer un homme plus intéressant." [3] In July 1814 the Tsar met Jung-Stilling and told him that he considered the doctrines of the Moravian Brethren, whom he had visited in the previous year, as the ideal form of Christianity.[4] It is also

---

[1] Cf. Pypin, *Die geistigen Bewegungen in Russland in der ersten Hälfte des XIX. Jahrhunderts*, I, Berlin, 1894, p. 447. It may be noteworthy in this connection that Saint-Martin lodges were founded in Russia. (Cf. G. van Rijnberk, *Un thaumaturge au XVIIIᵉ siècle. Martines de Pasqually*, Lyon, 1935-8.)

[2] P. Pierling, *Problème d'histoire : L'Empereur Alexandre Iᵉʳ est-il mort catholique ?* 2. ed., Paris, 1913, gives a French translation of the Tsar's essay which he seems to have found in the original Russian version in the Russian edition of Nicolas Mikhaïlowitch's *Correspondance de l'Empereur Alexandre Iᵉʳ avec sa sœur Catherine Pavlovna.* (In the French edition—the only one which I have been able to see—this essay is not reprinted.)

[3] Stein, *Briefwechsel* etc., V, p. 164.

[4] Jung, *Lebensgeschichte*, Stuttgart, 1887, p. 331.

KOCHUBEI

NOVOSILTSEV

CZARTORYSKI

STROGANOV

Tsar Alexander's Informal Committee

[*face p.* 32

INCENDIE DE MOSCOU, 1812

From the Curzon Collection in the Bodleian Library

[face p. 33

quite certain that Alexander met Madame de Krüdener on frequent occasions during the summer of 1815, and that the Livonian baroness had sufficient courage to rouse profoundly the Tsar's conscience.

It is more than likely that Alexander's " conversion " was no sudden one. The greater part of his reign, including its earlier years, was a period of far-reaching religious tolerance which, in the supra-denominationalism it implied, was typical of the new religious movement. The foundation of the Russian Bible Society in 1812, was but the most conspicuous proof of the tolerant attitude towards problems of Biblical interpretation. Yet the most important ukase, as regards tolerance, was that dated December 9th, 1806, from which the following passage is taken :

Convient-il à un gouvernement chrétien et civilisé de convaincre les hérétiques par les tortures, l'exil ou d'autres moyens cruels ? L'Église orthodoxe elle-même peut-elle approuver les mesures de persécution si contraires à l'esprit de son chef Jésus-Christ ? On atteindra plus facilement le but dans cette circonstance, en se laissant diriger par l'esprit du véritable christianisme. [1]

The War of 1812, as well as the events which led up to Napoleon's final defeat, contributed a great deal to Alexander's full conversion. In the first instance there was the deep and lasting impression of the fire of Moscow which, in Alexander's own words, lit up his soul. It was then that he found in the Bible " words so suitable to and descriptive of the state of his mind ".[2] As to Vienna, we have his own testimony that on that occasion he was inspired to call the Holy Alliance into being. Then, last but not least, there was the elevating experience of having achieved victory over a gigantic enemy. There is enough evidence in the Tsar's correspondence to show that he saw the cause of that victory in a sanction in that etymological sense of which R. R. Marett reminds us in his article on " The Nature of the Sanction in Primitive Law ",[3] namely an inherent power bringing blessings on the just and curses on the unjust. Not even victory could shatter his aversion to—or, if we are to believe Laharpe,[4] his horror of—war. On the contrary, he came to realize more and more what he eventually put into words in his

[1] Gehring, *Die Sekten der russischen Kirche*, Leipzig, 1890, pp. 190–1.
[2] This is what he told the Quaker Stephen Grellet in 1819.
[3] *Zeitschrift für vergleichende Rechtswissenschaft*, L, 1935, p. 65.
[4] Letter to the *Globe*, July 25th, 1829.

conversation with the Quaker Thomas Clarkson at Paris three days before the Pact of the Holy Alliance was signed : " If men were vital Christians, there could be no Wars . . . I am sure that the Spirit of Christianity is decisive against War." [1]

In addition to all these factors, Russia's appalling backwardness at the period with which we are concerned has to be remembered. The standard of everyday life was so low, the rational prospects of attaining a higher standard to-morrow were so poor, that irrational expectations of a new Messiah came to exert an influence upon large parts of the population, to an extent which a foreigner could hardly imagine. This messianism took various forms. Some believed that Christ Himself would reappear in this world ; another small minority thought that Napoleon was the new Messiah ; [2] but in most cases the Messianic belief was somehow bound up with Alexander I who happened to be Tsar during a more troubled period of Russian history than the country had known for a long time. It is almost certain that Alexander I felt a strong urge to live up to these widespread chiliastic expectations.

In a letter written on July 2nd, 1812, from Drissa to the Prince Regent, the Tsar went a long way towards that goal which, three years later, he was to seek to attain by means of the Holy Alliance. The passage, to which Hildegard Schaeder was the first to draw the attention of historians in this connection, runs thus :

> Qu'il me soit permis d'énoncer toute mon opinion. Il me semble qu'il faudrait moins de transactions, de formes et plus de ces sentiments généreux, ardents qui porteraient à envisager tous les peuples unis pour le salut de leur liberté, comme des frères empressés à se porter mutuellement tous les secours dont ils pourraient avoir besoin et n'envisageant qu'un seul but, celui de leur salut commun. Telle est ma manière d'envisager les choses. L'egoisme soit des individus, soit des états, a amené l'ordre actuel des choses. C'est l'opposé qui seul parviendra à le changer. [3]

This profession of faith is significant mainly for the condemnation of egoism it contains ; it was the first time that a typically liberal conception—the compatibility of differing egoisms—was

---

[1] *Thomas Clarkson's Interviews with the Emperor Alexander I of Russia at Paris and Aix-la-Chapelle in 1815 and 1818 as told by himself*, London, 1930, pp. 29–30. Cf. also *Memoirs of the Life and Gospel Labours of Stephen Grellet*, I, London, 1860, p. 417.

[2] Cf. Gehring, op. cit., p. 187.

[3] N. K. Shilder, *Imperator Aleksandr Pervyi*, III, annex, St. Petersburg, 1897, p. 500.

expressly defined by the Tsar. There is also another striking parallel between this document and the Act of the Holy Alliance as drafted by Alexander I three years later, namely the suggestion that the *nations* (*peuples*) should unite as brothers.

In the following year the Tsar went even further. The treaties between the Allies concluded at Reichenbach in June 1813, and at Teplitz in September of that year, did little, it is true, but repeat the liberal ideas of 1805.[1] But the preceding Treaty of Kalisch between Russia and Prussia, dated February 28th, 1813, contained the famous passage : " Le temps arrivera où les traités ne seront plus de trèves, où ils pourront de nouveau être observés avec cette foi religieuse, cette inviolabilité sacrée auxquelles tiennent la considération, la force et la conservation des empires." [2]

At the Congress of Vienna, on New Year's Eve 1814–15, shortly before the Polish and Saxon questions led to the Secret Treaty of Alliance between Great Britain, France and Austria, Alexander I—in all probability in person [3]—drew up a diplomatic note addressed to Austria, Great Britain and Prussia. It seems worth while to quote from this document, especially since it has so far been rather underestimated by historians. The main passage reads thus :

S. M. Impériale est pénétré de la conviction que l'Europe ne pourra recueillir le fruit de ces sacrifices, de ceux en particulier qui furent faits par leurs Majestés l'empereur d'Autriche et le Roi de Prusse, secondés avec tant d'énergie par la Grande-Bretagne, que lorsque l'édifice de la pacification générale reposera sur les mêmes bases qui ont assuré le succès de leurs armes, savoir sur l'identité de leurs vues et maximes politiques, ainsi que sur l'association franche et loyale de leurs intérêts les plus chers. Pénétrés également des principes immuables de la religion chrétienne commune à tous, c'est sur cette base unique de l'ordre politique comme de l'ordre social que les souverains fraternisant entr'eux *épureront leurs maximes d'état* et garantiront les rapports entre les peuples que la providence leur a confiés.[4]

Once more, as in Novosiltsev's Instructions of 1804, and in the letter to the Regent, mentioned above, the emphasis of this

---

[1] Cf. F. de Martens, *Recueil des Traités et Conventions conclus par la Russie avec les Puissances Étrangères*, III, pp. 105 f., 117 f.

[2] Quoted from A. Sorel, *L'Europe et la Révolution Française*, VIII, 2. ed., Paris, 1904, p. 64.

[3] " It contains unmistakably the true germ of the Holy Alliance, presumably by the same hand." (Gagern, *Mein Antheil an der Politik*, II, Stuttgart, 1826, p. 93.)

[4] D. J. L. Klüber, *Acten des Wiener Congresses in den Jahren 1814 und 1815*, VII, Erlangen, 1817, p. 70.

document lies in the clear realization that a completely new system of international co-operation in Europe would have to be built up. The idea that religion must be the new bond had been anticipated, as we have seen, in the Treaty of Kalisch. Here, in the New Year's Eve document of 1814–15, the vague word " religion " was replaced for the first time by the more precise phrase " Christian religion ". It is obvious that this did not mean Christianity in any such narrow sense of the word as was given to it by most of the mutually exclusive churches and sects. It was precisely its supra-denominational aspect which entitled Christianity to provide the new all-embracing bond. It should also be noted that in contradistinction to the Tsar's letter to the Regent, the New Year's Eve document speaks of " souverains fraternisant ". It is a moot point whether this not unimportant difference was perhaps meant to reconcile the Tsar's fellow-sovereigns, who may have been shocked by his unusual suggestion that they should live up to the standards of a religion to which all of them professed allegiance.

On February 12th, 1815, the Tsar told Lord Castlereagh that he desired to renew the Quadruple Alliance ; Castlereagh's despatch to his Prime Minister, of the following day, testifies to this fact.[1] But what the Tsar actually had in mind was probably that very Federation of Christian Europe whose principles he had outlined a few weeks previously.[2] Varnhagen von Ense, who had been present at the Congress of Vienna, reports in his *Mémoires* that the above-mentioned Secret Treaty had been an open secret from the beginning.[3] In these circumstances it seems strange that Alexander I should have expected that Britain and Austria would not only cancel the Secret Treaty, but also conclude an open Alliance against their secret ally. Whatever the Tsar's suggestion was, the response he received is on record. Firstly, there is Lord Castlereagh's own testimony :

. . . I submitted to the Emperor [he writes to Liverpool on February 13th, 1815] that the best Alliance that could be formed in the present state of Europe was, that the Powers who had made the peace should by a public declaration at the close of the Congress announce to Europe, whatever difference of opinion may have existed in the details, their determination to uphold and support the arrangement agreed upon ; and further, their determination to unite their

---

[1] For the text of the despatch, cf. C. K. Webster, *British Diplomacy 1813–1815*, pp. 303–5.
[2] Cf. Schaeder, op. cit., p. 73.
[3] *Denkwürdigkeiten des eigenen Lebens*, 2. ed., III, Leipzig 1843, p. 320.

influence, and, if necessary, their arms, against the Power that should attempt to disturb it.

But more evidence exists. In a postscript to the same letter, Castlereagh writes : " I enclose the Project of Declaration. . . . It has been prepared by M. Gentz on my suggestion." F. von Gentz's diary contains this " Projet de Déclaration " which, indeed, consists of nothing except Lord Castlereagh's counter-proposal wrapped up in a bombastic framework of complacent platitudes.[1] How striking was the difference of outlook between this document and the Tsar's New Year's Eve message ! Whereas the Tsar envisaged a new era of international organization, and emphasized the need for a purification of the principles of international conduct, the obedient ideologist Gentz, on the other hand, was not infected in the least with this reforming zeal. The twenty-five years since the beginning of the French Revolution, in Alexander's eyes a grave portent exhorting to contrition, were for Gentz only an unpleasant interruption of the *ancien régime.* This is how he described the main task of the Congress of Vienna : " Il s'agissait de refaire ce que vingt années de désordres avaient détruit, de reconstruire l'édifice politique avec les vastes décombres, dont un bouleversement affreux avait couvert le sol de l'Europe . . ." [2]

During the Hundred Days, on May 13th (25th), 1815, Alexander I drew up the " Projet d'instruction générale pour les missions de Sa Majesté Impériale ". On the whole, this document may be regarded as a proof of the assumption that during the " religious period " the Tsar's liberalism had by no means vanished. Special emphasis is laid upon the importance of public opinion ; the necessity is stressed for constitutional régimes all over Europe : the Congress of Vienna is blamed for not having shown sufficient understanding of the true interests of the nations.[3]

The following most interesting fact concerning the Tsar's draft of the Holy Alliance was brought to light so late as 1928 by the Swiss scholar W. Näf, who became interested in the question of Switzerland's accession to that Act, and incidentally came upon a document in the Vienna Haus-, Hof- und Staatsarchiv which contained the Tsar's original draft.[4] This had

---

[1] *Tagebücher von Friedrich von Gentz*, I, Leipzig, 1873, pp. 445–6.
[2] Ibid., p. 443.
[3] Shilder, op. cit., pp. 541 seqq.
[4] W. Näf's pamphlet *Zur Geschichte der Heiligen Allianz*, Bern 1928, is not at present available in this country, though the Interlibrary Service has made every effort to

already been mentioned in some contemporary sources, for example in Capodistria's *Aperçu de ma carrière publique depuis* 1798 *jusqu'à* 1822.[1] It is highly significant that the draft differs from the final wording in some very important respects. Since it can fairly be maintained that W. Näf's discovery has so far not received from historians all the attention it deserves,[2] it seems essential to compare the two documents as accurately as possible.

The first paragraph of the Act of the Holy Alliance, concluded in Paris on September 26th, 1815, runs thus :

In the name of the Most Holy and Indivisible Trinity. Their Majesties the Emperor of Austria, the King of Prussia, and the Emperor of Russia, having, in consequence of the great events which have marked the course of the three last years in Europe, and especially of the blessings which it has pleased Divine Providence to shower upon those States which place their confidence and their hope in it alone, acquired the intimate conviction of the necessity of basing the steps to be observed by the Powers, in their reciprocal relations, upon the sublime truths which the holy religion of our Saviour teaches ;

The Tsar's draft, on the other hand, while precisely equivalent as far as the words " acquired the intimate conviction ", had continued thus : " *that the course which the Powers had previously taken in their reciprocal relations must be fundamentally changed, and that it is urgent to replace it* by an order of things exclusively based upon the sublime truths which the holy religion of our Saviour teaches ". The fact that this passage had to be sacrificed in order to win over Prince Metternich, once more shows the reluctance of the then ruling class to admit that their traditional methods of diplomacy had become out of date. Metternich's " amendments " in the second paragraph of the preamble were very much of the same kind. The wording of the original draft had been as follows :

They solemnly declare that the present Act has no other object than to proclaim, in the face of the whole world, their fixed resolution, both in the administration of their respective States, and in their political relations with every other Government, to take *in future* for their sole guide the precepts of that Holy Religion, namely the precepts of Justice, Christian Charity and Peace, which, far from

get it for me. I have used long extracts from Näf's pamphlet quoted in W. Schwarz, *Die heilige Allianz*, Stuttgart, 1935.

[1] *Sbornik russkogo isstoricheskogo obchestva*, III, 1868, p. 201.

[2] The main part of the present chapter was written in the last months of 1940, before E. J. Knapton published his article on the same subject. (" The Origins of the Treaty of the Holy Alliance." Historical Revision No. XCVIII, *History*, New Series XXVI, September, 1941.)

being applicable only to private concerns, *as was hitherto believed*, must have an immediate influence upon the counsels of Princes, and guide all their steps, as being the only means of consolidating human institutions and remedying their imperfections. In consequence, their Majesties have agreed on the following articles . . .

The words which I have put in italics are missing in the final wording.

The most incisive change, however, took place in Article I. Let us look at the draft :

Conformably to the words of the Holy Scriptures which command all men to consider each other as brethren, *the subjects of the three contracting parties* will remain united by the bonds of a true and indissoluble fraternity, and considering each other as fellow-countrymen, they will, on all occasions, and in all places, lend each other aid and assistance. *The same will apply to the respective armies which will equally consider themselves as belonging only to the same army which is called upon to protect Religion, Peace and Justice.*

In the final wording the " subjects of the three contracting parties " are replaced by the " Three contracting Monarchs " ; moreover the second part of Art. I, which referred to the armies, is completely revised and reads thus :

. . . and regarding themselves towards their subjects and armies as fathers of families, they will lead them, in the same spirit of fraternity with which they are animated, to protect Religion, Peace and Justice.

It is obvious that the object of Metternich's amendments, which were far from being only " verbal alterations ", as he pretended to Castlereagh, was to imbue the whole scheme with the spirit of patriarchism. That also is why he substituted, in Art. II, for the Tsar's metaphor of the *three princes ruling over three provinces of the united Christian nation* the metaphor of the three princes ruling over three branches of a family. In Art. III, too, Metternich's touch is recognizable. Whereas according to the original draft " all the *States* which shall choose solemnly to avow the sacred principles, etc." were invited, the final Act speaks of Powers, thus leaving open the question whether smaller States could accede to the Holy Alliance.

Metternich in his *Mémoires* outlined Austria's and Prussia's motives for the conclusion of the Holy Alliance as follows. Their main desire, he asserted, was to please the Tsar, and they could afford to do this in view of the insignificance of the entire scheme.[1] After all, " the Holy Alliance was only the outcome of a Pietist mood of Tsar Alexander, and the application of the principles of Christianity to politics ". Nothing could have been more revealing than this phrase in which Metternich, " der theoretisierende Realpolitiker " as he has been called,[2] minimized this attempt to reconcile the two spheres of religion and politics. Small wonder that the Pact was described by Metternich as " high-sounding Nothing ", by Talleyrand as a " ludicrous contract ", and by Castlereagh as a " piece of sublime mysticism and nonsense ". Since that time Western historiography has tended to regard Alexander I as an unpractical dreamer, or to use Napoleon's favourite catchword, as an " idéologue ".[3]

What Metternich meant when he wrote that Austria wished " to please the Tsar " by acceding to the Pact, is obvious from this passage of Castlereagh's letter to Liverpool, dated Paris, September 28th, 1815 :

Prince Metternich . . . came to me with the project of the treaty since signed. He communicated to me in great confidence the difficulty in which the Emperor of Austria felt himself placed : that he felt great repugnance to be a party to such an act, and yet was more apprehensive of refusing himself to the Emperor's application ; that it was quite clear his mind was affected ; that peace and goodwill was at present the idea which engrossed his thoughts ; that he had found him of late friendly and reasonable on all points ; and that he was unwilling to thwart him in a conception which, however wild, might save him and the rest of the world much trouble so long as it should last.

The Pact was thus to serve as a safety-valve against Russian expansionist aspirations.

Castlereagh's sympathetic attitude at the time of the conclusion of the Holy Alliance, manifested in his suggestion to the

[1] Cf. the remark of Roxandra de Stourdza, the lady-in-waiting who had helped Madame de Krüdener to get in touch with the Tsar : " The incorporation or cession of the most miserable market town would have meant endless negotiations ; but this was just . . . an idea."

[2] E. Kittel, " Metternichs politische Grundanschauungen ", Historische Vierteljahrsschrift, XXIV, 1929.

[3] To quote only three examples : firstly, Pierre Rain, Un Tsar Idéologue. Alexandre Ier, Paris, 1913. Secondly, W. P. Cresson, Diplomatic Portraits, London, 1924, p. 120 : " In theory, at least, Castlereagh was in sympathy with many of the Tsar's ideals. It was his rôle to recall the realities of the situation to the idéologues at home and abroad." Lastly, W. A. Phillips, The Confederation of Europe. A study of the European Alliance, 1813–1823, as an experiment in the international organization of peace, 2nd ed., London, 1920, p. 147 : " This [Castlereagh's project to hold international conferences at fixed intervals] represented a triumph of British Realpolitik over Alexander's dangerous idealism."

Regent that he should express his sympathy with the scheme,[1]
is similarly to be explained by Castlereagh's fear of Russian
encroachment on Britain's interests. In the above-mentioned
letter to the Prime Minister, he goes on to say :

> Upon the whole this is what may be called a scrape ; and yet in
> the long run it may be attended with more beneficial results than
> many of the acts which are in progress, and which are of a character
> better to suit the eye of Parliament. The fact is, that the Emperor's
> mind is not completely sound. Last year there was but too much
> reason to fear that its impulse would be to conquest and dominion.
> The general belief now is, that he is disposed to found his own glory
> upon a principle of peace and benevolence. Since the point of
> Poland was disposed of, there has been nothing in his political conduct
> in the progress of arrangements which indicates another purpose, and
> he really appears to be in earnest. It is, at all events, wise to profit
> by his disposition as far as it will carry us : and this is peculiarly the
> feeling of Austria and Prussia, who hope to keep down, " now that
> they are compatriots ", much of the spirit of frontier jealousy which
> has hitherto embarrassed them.

Viewed from such a standpoint, the Tsar had fallen into a
trap which he had unwittingly laid for himself. The sane motives
behind the Tsar's initiative seemed beyond comprehension. The
situation was analogous to that which had made Rousseau write
of Saint-Pierre's *Projet* in the following words : " C'est une sorte
de folie d'être sage au milieu des fous." [2]

All the European States, with the exception of Turkey, were
asked to join the Holy Alliance. The invitation was accepted
by Würtemberg, Saxony, Sardinia, France, the Netherlands, the
Hanse towns, Spain and Switzerland. Turkey, which had not
been mentioned in Novosiltsev's Instructions, was once more left
out, but this time the Christian character of the Pact offered a
justification for this course. In view of the uneasy relations
between Russia and Turkey, however, the Ottoman Government
felt disposed to look for ulterior motives behind this exclusion.
After all, it could not easily be forgotten that so recently as in
1808 Russia had laid claim to Constantinople. The apprehension of the Porte was all the more understandable since similar
schemes in the past had often implied a hostile attitude towards
Turkey. The Abbé de Saint-Pierre, it is true, had gone no
further than to suggest, in the third edition of his *Projet* (1716),
the exclusion of Turkey from his European Federal Union. But

---

[1] C. K. Webster, op. cit., p. 383.
[2] *Œuvres*, I, 1844, p. 619. Indeed, ruling circles had ridiculed Saint-Pierre in
his time just as they ridiculed the Tsar a century later.

his disciple, the Marquis d'Argenson, who as Foreign Minister
of Louis XV was far more influential than his teacher, had
already given the idea an aggressive twist. In his *Pensées sur la
Réformation de l'État*, written between 1733 and 1752, he envisaged
the entire globe as " well and sufficiently policed and chris-
tianized ". Cardinal Alberoni's less enterprising *Progetto per
ridurre l'impero turchesco all' obbedienza dei principi cristiani, e per
dividere tra di essi la conquista del medesimo*,[1] which was circulated
in the 1730's, looked grim enough from the Turkish point of view.
And even quite recently, in 1813, the German professor Fichte,
in his lectures in Berlin, had spoken of a permanent union between
the Christian nations, and had added the sinister remark that a
natural state of war existed between these nations on the one
side, and the uncultured non-Christians on the other.[2] Yet
Turkey could derive some reassurance from the fact that the
Tsar, in February 1815, had been prepared to include her
dominions in a general guarantee, subject only to the settlement
of points in dispute between Russia and Turkey by arbitration
—an offer which had been declined.[3] Now, in May 1816, the
Russian Ambassador at Constantinople handed in a note which
emphasized the peaceful character of the Holy Alliance.

The Pope was invited to accede to the Pact, but refused.
The Catholic Church felt strongly irritated by Alexander's supra-
denominationalism which was, of course, the quintessence of the
Holy Alliance. Early in 1816, talking to de Maistre who was
just writing his ultramontane book *Du Pape*, the Tsar remarked
of the different kinds of Christian belief : " Il y a dans le
christianisme quelque chose de plus grand que tout cela. Voilà
l'essentiel. Commençons par attaquer l'incrédulité ; c'est un
assez grand point. Je crois bien que toutes les communions se
réuniront un jour, je le tiens pour sûr ; mais le moment n'est
pas venu." [4] A year later, on March 14th, 1817, an article
under the title " Considérations " appeared in the periodical
Le Conservateur impartial. The author was in all probability the
Tsar himself. Its main purpose was to refute the various objections raised to the Holy Alliance. Among other things it was

---

[1] Cf. Jacob ter Meulen, *Der Gedanke der Internationalen Organisation in seiner
Entwicklung 1300–1800*, Haag, 1917, pp. 223–5.
[2] " Die Staatslehre oder über das Verhältnis des Urstaates zum Vernunftreiche ",
Sämmtliche Werke, IV, Berlin, 1845, p. 600.
[3] C. K. Webster, " Some Aspects of Castlereagh's Foreign Policy ", *Transactions
of the Royal Historical Society*, 3rd series, VI, 1912, pp. 72–3.
[4] De Maistre's letter to Comte de Vallaise. (*Œuvres complètes*, XIII, Lyon, 1886,
pp. 282–3).

said that the intention of those who had signed it had been to establish " un point de rapport également éloigné de tous les extrèmes, également contraire au fanatisme et à l'impiété ". It was opposed only to " la soif du pouvoir en religion comme en politique ". It was quite obvious to whom these lines alluded, especially since the Tsar, immediately upon his return from Paris in 1815, had ordered the expulsion of the Jesuits from the principal cities. Finally the Pope was disquieted by Alexander's continued interest in the Bible Society.[1]

It was de Maistre once more who, in 1819, expressed the horror which the Roman Church felt at this competitor who like herself aimed at τὸ καθόλον. This is what he wrote :

L'empereur de Russie avec le christianisme universel, les dogmes fondamentaux et la Société biblique, peut donc être certain qu'il est dans le grand chemin de la destruction du christianisme, et qu'il y travaille réellement avec toute la puissance et toutes les saintes intentions qui suffiraient pour faire triompher la sainte loi.[2]

The negative attitude towards the idea of the Holy Alliance, which we have found among the great temporal powers, was thus shared by the most widely recognized spiritual power of the Western world. In this way was once more manifested the essentially radical character of Alexander's scheme.

---

[1] Cf. the despatch of the French Ambassador Comte de Noailles from St. Petersburg on May 30th, 1817. (*Sbornik*, CXIX, 1904, p. 207.)
[2] " Lettre à M. le Marquis . . ., sur l'État du Christianisme en Europe ", *Œuvres complètes*, VIII, Lyon, 1893, p. 515.

PART II

THE CONCERT OF EUROPE—AN EXPERIMENT

Ligue entre tous les Gouvernements contre les factions dans tous les États.

Metternich (1820).

CHAPTER III

GREAT BRITAIN

The most striking feature of the post-Napoleonic peace settlement was, beyond doubt, the leniency shown towards the vanquished Power. The wars that preceded it had lasted for almost a quarter of a century; yet three years after their conclusion the conquered party was invited to resume its function as a Great Power in the Concert of Europe. It is an established fact that the two men who, apart from the Tsar, were most responsible for this conciliatory policy, were acting in the name of Great Britain. At the same time it is known that Lord Castlereagh and the Duke of Wellington had to overcome considerable obstacles arising from the opposition within their own class, and, moreover, within their own party. The Prime Minister, for example, advocated a quite different policy. In a despatch to Castlereagh, dated July 15th, 1815, he wrote :

It is argued with much force that France will never forgive the humiliation which she has already received, that she will take the first convenient opportunity of endeavouring to redeem her military glory, and that it is our duty, therefore, to take advantage of the present moment to prevent the evil consequences which may even flow from the greatness of our own success.[1]

Lord Liverpool claimed that he described " the prevailing idea in this country " ; [2] even if we discount this hardly verifiable assertion we are safe in assuming that he expressed the idea of the Prince Regent,[3] the Cabinet and, to a large extent, of his class. Since France would not under any circumstances forgive the humiliation of her defeat, it was apparently argued in these circles that she should be humiliated with a vengeance.

[1] *Correspondence, Despatches, and other Papers of Viscount Castlereagh*, Third Series, Vol. X, London, 1852, p. 432.
[2] Ibid., p. 431.
[3] Cf. F. de Martens, *Recueil des Traités et Conventions conclus par la Russie avec les Puissances Étrangères*, tome XI, St. Petersburg, 1895, p. 242.

In various quarters it has been pointed out that the motives which animated Castlereagh and Wellington were not entirely or even mainly altruistic.[1] One theory tries to explain their attitude mainly in Balance of Power terms. France, it is said, was not crushed, because she was expected to function as a counterweight to the growing power of Russia.[2] There is evidence enough to show that such a conception must have played a considerable part in forming the decision of the British peace-makers. But the decisive consideration seems to have been a different one. It is best summarized in E. L. Woodward's general remark : "The governments after 1815 . . . feared that a renewal of revolutionary fervour would again rouse the fury of a nation in arms."[3] Castlereagh's own words in his despatches to Liverpool may be quoted in this connection, since there is no imaginable reason why he should have misled the Prime Minister on this occasion. This is what he wrote from Paris on July 24th, 1815, referring to the harsh terms which Lord Liverpool had in mind : "I doubt . . . the possibility of the King's holding his ground in France, if, after holding himself out to the nation as a means of appeasing the Allies, they disavow him so far."[4] And again on August 17th, 1815 :

If . . . we push things now to an extremity, we leave the King no resource in the eyes of his own people but to disavow us. . . . The whole of this view on the question turns upon a conviction that the King's cause in France is far from hopeless, if well conducted, and that the European alliance can be made powerfully instrumental to his support, if our securities are framed in such a manner as not to be ultimately hostile to France, after she shall have given protracted proof of having ceased to be a revolutionary State.[5]

To repeat, it is not suggested that the British Foreign Minister was insensible to considerations of strategy. " Our insular situation ", he told Mr. Rose in his despatch of December 28th, 1815, " places us sufficiently out of the reach of danger to admit of our pursuing a more generous and confiding policy."[6]

The war-weariness of the French nation[7] helped to make

---

[1] C. K. Webster, *The Foreign Policy of Castlereagh 1815–1832. Britain and the European Alliance*, London, 1925, pp. 74–5.

[2] C. K. Webster, ibid., p. 75 ; cf. also H. Schaeder, *Die dritte Koalition und die heilige Allianz*, Königsberg–Berlin, 1934, p. 41.

[3] *War and Peace in Europe 1815–1870*, London, 1931, p. 8.

[4] *Correspondence etc., of Viscount Castlereagh*, Vol. X, p. 435.

[5] Ibid., pp. 488–9.   [6] Ibid., Vol. XI, p. 105.

[7] Cf. the following passage from A. de Musset, *La Confession d'un Enfant du Siècle*, ch. II : " Les uns disaient : Ce qui a causé la chute de l'Empereur, c'est que le peuple n'en voulait plus ; les autres : Le peuple voulait le roi ; non, la liberté ;

the King's cause in France appear more hopeful. The great majority of Frenchmen seem, for a time, to have felt somewhat tired of warfare of any kind, whether international or civil. But this passive attitude of mind had its limits. As early as July 15th, 1815, William Cobbett, the great antagonist of the ruling class, in an open letter to Castlereagh had exposed the illusion of those who spoke of France as a conquered country in the old sense of the word :

These are old-fashioned ideas, my Lord. They belong to half a century ago, when men were led to have their brains knocked out for the glory of a grand monarque. The French are not conquered. . . . They have been fighting for freedom. Their struggle has been, and is, against feudal, ecclesiastical, and monarchical tyranny ; against seigneurial courts, convents, tythes, frauds and persecutions of priests, corvées, game laws, privileges of Noblesse and Clergy ; [1] and, until they be compelled to submit to these again, they are not defeated, much less are they conquered. . . . You cannot kill all the French. You cannot knock their foreteeth out. You cannot keep the sun from shining in France. No, nor can you impose even tythes upon the cultivators. You must leave them nearly as they are ; or, if you prevail upon the Bourbons to do any outrageous acts against the people, you must keep up all your subsidized armies in France, in order to prevent another revolution, which might burst forth, against " regular government " with increased means. [2]

It is true that Cobbett's task, as he certainly conceived it, consisted at least as much in influencing events as in analysing them. He therefore over-emphasized the helplessness of the conquerors, and his assertion : " You must leave them nearly as they are ", was, of course, to a certain extent political rhetoric. Yet it contained a good deal of truth, and Castlereagh, whether influenced by Cobbett or not, was well aware of this fact. " The great object ", he wrote to the Prime Minister from Paris on October 1st, 1815, " is to keep the King on his Throne. A moderate system, I believe, is the best chance for doing so." [3]

According to the reports of Comte Pozzo di Borgo, the Russian ambassador in Paris, the same spirit animated Wellington. Being in the very responsible position of Commander-in-

non, la raison ; non, la religion ; non, la constitution anglaise ; non, l'absolutisme ; un dernier ajouta : Non ! rien de tout cela, mais le repos."

[1] Cf. in this connection also the following witty passage from Paul-Louis Courier's *Lettre première au Redacteur du Censeur*, dated July 10th, 1819 : " Nous étions la gent corvéable, taillable et tuable à volonté ; nous ne sommes plus qu'incarcérables." (*Pamphlets Politiques et Lettres d'Italie.*)

[2] *Cobbett's Weekly Political Register*, Vol. XXXVIII, No. 2, pp. 40-1.

[3] *Correspondence, etc., of Viscount Castlereagh*, Vol. XI, p. 39.

Chief of the Allied forces of occupation, the Duke deplored what he called the imprudent conduct of the Ultra-Royalists which tended seriously to compromise the whole enterprise of Restoration.[1] On the other hand, it is known that Wellington, when informed by Louis XVIII in 1816 of his decision to dissolve the *Chambre Introuvable*, expressed his apprehension lest the new Chamber should have a democratic majority.[2] This shows that at times both Castlereagh and Wellington must have felt like men walking on a tight-rope. Beneath them, on both sides, they saw the abyss of Terror. If there was little temptation for them to take the fateful step to the left, the White Terror lurking to their right, if more immediate, was no less calamitous. They had helped very actively to reinstate the banner of the White Lily ; they had thereby raised the hopes of Louis XVIII's fellow-*émigrés* that they would be reinstated in full possession, if not in full glory. This proved absolutely impossible ; for the seizure and redistribution of their former lands would have upset too many *rentiers*. Even so, the returning nobles managed to buy back a large portion of their old estates, and it is estimated that by 1820 they had regained about a half of them. Some of the remainder of the noble and church lands came into the hands of the new Napoleonic aristocracy, who leased them to tenant-farmers. In spite of this, the proportion of land belonging to the peasants was greater than in any other country on the Continent.[3] With the rise in market prices and the slow improvement in agriculture, those peasants who had not materially increased their holdings gained a relative economic improvement which later enabled them to buy up land as it came on the market. The comparative well-being of the peasant population was all the more important since agriculture still held first place among the sources of national wealth in France. As late as 1826, the land represented 66 per cent. of the national wealth, and about two-thirds of the French people lived in rural areas.

A full restoration of the *ancien régime* proved impossible, and

[1] Comte Pozzo di Borgo in a despatch to Comte Nesselrode, Paris, December 18(30), 1815. *Correspondance Diplomatique du Comte Pozzo di Borgo et du Comte de Nesselrode depuis la Restauration des Bourbons jusq'au congrès d'Aix-la-Chapelle 1814–1818*, tome I, Paris, 1890, p. 265.

[2] Cf. Alfred Stern, *Geschichte Europas seit den Verträgen von 1815 bis zum Frankfurter Frieden von 1871*, I, Berlin, 1894, p. 103.

[3] A decade after Louis " le Desiré " had been, in Thomas Moore's words, crammed down the throats of the French, Pestel, the revolutionary Russian thinker, proved from a study of the Bourbon restoration that the French Revolution had been beneficial as well as necessary, for the restored monarchy had left intact the fundamental institutions created by the Revolution.

that for more than one reason. If, however, history could be simplified into short formulæ, the remark made by the French writer, M. Gallais, in a secret report addressed on April 13th, 1816, to Sir Charles Stuart, the British Ambassador in Paris, and eventually to Lord Castlereagh, might be used as a basis for one such formula :

Le bouleversement général causé par la révolution, subsiste encore dans les esprits, parceque l'autorité, longtems deposée en des mains viles, a perdu cette majesté qui lui attiroit la confiance et le respect ;
. . . parceque la religion a perdu tout son empire sur cette classe d'hommes qui, faute d'une éducation convenable, ne connoit point les loix de la morale, et ne peut être conduite que par la crainte des peines de l'enfer ou de l'échafaud.[1]

Translated into non-evaluative language, the report of M. Gallais implied that a full-blooded restoration of the *ancien régime* was impossible, since the old ruling class no longer enjoyed the authority on which its former rule had, to a large extent, been based ; that transcendental religion had lost its sway over the people, and that, purgatory having ceased to be a deterrent factor, the aristocracy of the Restoration would have to rely on the sanctions of this world more than did their predecessors. It is easy to understand that a legal order established on such foundations was causing a great deal of anxiety to its foreign protectors.

Yet it is impossible to appreciate this anxiety fully unless we take into account the situation which existed in the protectors' own countries. If this is true of Austria, Prussia, and at a later date of Russia, it certainly applies to Great Britain as well. Her Foreign Minister was acting simultaneously as leader of the House of Commons. As such he had to spend a great deal of his time in presenting to the House the domestic policy of the Cabinet and rendering it as palatable as possible. This job, by the way, he fulfilled with great circumspection and considerable success ; witness even men like Greville [2] or Creevey,[3] who could not be counted among his admirers. Small wonder that Castlereagh was held responsible not only for the leniency shown towards

---

[1] *Correspondence, etc., of Viscount Castlereagh*, Vol. XI, p. 250.

[2] " I believe he was considered one of the best managers of the House of Commons who ever sat in it . . ." (Charles F. Greville, *A Journal of the Reign of King George IV and King William IV*, Vol. I, London, 1874, p. 53.)

[3] Mr. Creevey wrote to Miss Ord on August 14th, 1822 : " By experience, good manners and great courage, he manages a corrupt House of Commons pretty well with some address." (*The Creevey Papers*, ed. by Sir Robert Maxwell, London, 1903, p. 42.)

France, but to almost the same extent for what many regarded as the severity towards the people of Great Britain.

The conclusion of the Napoleonic Wars, though successful from a military point of view, increased at first rather than decreased the economic trouble in Great Britain. The end of the Continental blockade was, it is true, a blessing for some industries, which were now able to dispose of the stocks they had been accumulating during the previous years. The suspension of the blockade, however, worked both ways, so that industries which had enjoyed a virtual monopoly of trade for many years were now suddenly faced with normal competition from the Continent. Another category of industries had been adjusted to an inflated war demand ; they were now compelled to return to the normal peace-time level. Again friction was caused not by the impracticability of the task of reorganization, but rather by the time it required. The national industrial effort, viewed as a whole, was certain to overcome all these difficulties. Yet this consideration did not go far to console those industrialists who were completely or almost completely ruined, or the workmen who in the former case lost their jobs,[1] and in the second experienced a sharp reduction in wages. Unemployment reached its greatest dimensions among the weavers, particularly, but by no means solely, because a considerable number of discharged soldiers and sailors joined their ranks.[2] The crisis was moreover aggravated by the heavy war debt. Of this, too, it could justly be claimed that a nation of the size and capacity of post-Napoleonic Britain was able to afford a war debt even of £900,000,000. But the growth of indirect taxation, devised by the ruling class, meant that the poor were bearing most of the burden.[3] In addition, the price of wheat, artificially raised by the Corn Bill of 1815, solely for the sake of the " uncountry gentlemen " as Lord Byron satirically dubbed them,[4] was kept high in the following

---

[1] A detailed report of the distress caused in 1817 by unemployment is to be found in M. C. Buer's article : " The Trade Depression following the Napoleonic Wars ", *Economica*, I, 1921, pp. 162–4.

[2] Cf. J. L. Hammond and Barbara Hammond, *The Skilled Labourer 1760–1832*, London, 1919, p. 88. With regard to the discharge of soldiers and sailors, and its effects, cf. *Tyne Mercury* of July 23rd, 1816. (*Place Collection*, vol. 29, Colindale Newspaper Library.)

[3] Cf. G. D. H. Cole, and Raymond Postgate, *The Common People 1746–1938*, London, 1938, p. 194.

[4] *The Age of Bronze : or Carmen Seculare et Annus Haud Mirabilis*, 3rd ed., London, 1823, p. 28. The whole passage runs thus :

Alas the country ! How shall tongue or pen
Bewail her now uncountry gentlemen ?

three years, the first of which, owing to extraordinarily bad weather conditions, brought a very poor harvest ; the result was that the price of household bread in London averaged over 1*s.* per 4 lb. loaf in these critical years ; the exact figures being 11*s.* 7*d.* for 1816, 14*s.* 3*d.* for 1817, and 11*s.* 8*d.* for 1818.[1] Thus it was by no means an exaggeration when Mr. Brougham said in the House of Commons on February 25th, 1817, that certain parts of the population of Britain were exposed to the pressure of hunger ; nor was he far from the mark in asserting that these people's sufferings were wholly without example in the country.[2]

The reaction to the crisis of those who were most affected by it was frequently disorderly and at times very violent. Thus the outward symptoms of a revolutionary attitude were undoubtedly present. In his satirical poem *Peter Bell the Third* Shelley wrote in October 1819 : " There is a great talk of revolution ", adding, however : " and a great chance of despotism." And research undertaken during the last decade or two seems to have convincingly proved that the situation in post-Napoleonic Britain lacked one element which must be regarded as essential for a successful revolution, or even for a serious attempt at one. What was wanted to complete the picture of an attempted revolution was, above all, the co-ordination of the various elements of disaffection. Towards the end of the previous disturbances of 1811–12 General Maitland, whose task it had been to restore order and quiet in the districts concerned, had come to the conclusion that " no concert existed nor no plan was laid further than was manifested in the open acts of violence which were daily committed ".[3] Generals Fane and Byng, charged with the same task in 1817, reached the same conclusion ; the local authorities

> The last to bid the cry of warfare cease,
> The first to make a malady of peace.
> For what were all these country patriots born ?
> To hunt and vote and raise the price of corn ?
> But corn, like every mortal thing, must fall,
> Kings, conquerors and markets most of all.
> And must ye fall with every ear of grain ?
> Why would you trouble Buonaparte's reign
> He was your great Triptolemus ; his vices
> Destroyed but realms, but still maintained your prices ;
> He amplified to every lord's content.
> The grand Agrarian Alchymy high Rent.

[1] *Commerce and Industry, Tables of Statistics for the British Empire from 1815*, ed. by William Page, London, 1919, p. 216.
[2] Hansard, *The Parliamentary Debates from the year 1803 to the present time*, Vol. XXXV, pp. 653–4.
[3] General Maitland, May 4th, 1812, in H.O., 40, i ; quoted in Frank Ongley Darvall, *Popular Disturbances and Public Order in Regency England*, London, 1934, p. 175.

reporting to the Home Secretary, and the local members of Parliament, with but a few exceptions, confirmed this.[1] An earlier report of General Fane, addressed on October 24th, 1816, to the Home Office, dealt with one particular type of disturbance, machine-breaking. As a result of the investigation the General concluded that the riots were " not a war against any particular description of Loom, but against all Looms, let for work below certain fixed rates of wages ".[2] The force of Luddism was hardly ever directed against employers who did not in some particular though not always in the same way provoke this reaction. The same applies to other types of industrial disturbances which, with the gradual disappearance of machine-breaking, became more numerous, and to agricultural disturbances. There too, various grievances were felt, and each was to be cured by a special method. The idea : " Ye are many—they are few ",[3] that is, the idea of ridding society of all these grievances by uniting the forces of disaffection, seems at that time to have entered only very few minds. Those few, with the exception of Shelley and Byron, belonged to the intellectual type of the lower middle and artisan classes. The cheap periodical publications brought out by them contained, indeed, at times challenges to civil war, some of them open, as for example the *Democratic Recorder and Reformer's Guide* of October 2nd, 1819,[4] others, such as the *Black Dwarf*, scarcely concealed. The latter paper said on September 3rd, 1817 :

When the community of interests between those who govern and those who are governed is lost, it is the duty of every party to secure its own interest. Of this political aphorism, all governors are perfectly aware ; and they practise their parts with considerable felicity : their success, however, depends upon the indolence and apathy of the people, who will bear patiently their fetters until they become too heavy to be supported . . .[5]

Without belittling the influence which the cheap periodicals were at that time exerting in an ever-increasing degree, we may, I think, safely assume that this particular challenge was hardly echoed by the working-class. Even those who took an active part

---

[1] Darvall, *Popular Disturbances and Public Order in Regency England*, London, 1934, p. 175.

[2] H.O., 42, 154 ; quoted in Darvall, op. cit., p. 187.

[3] The last line of Shelley's *The Mask of Anarchy*, written shortly after *Peterloo*.

[4] This is the wording : " If ever it was the duty of Britons to resort to the use of arms to recover their freedom and hurl vengeance upon the heads of their tyrants, it is now."

[5] The passage is to be found on p. 507.

in major riots were far from pursuing such plans. Instead, they thought that in response to their own action a general rising would take place over the whole country at an early date, and hoped for the best. One of these disturbances was in fact nothing but a march of Derbyshire peasants upon Nottingham ; [1] it is highly significant for the character of the whole period that such an occurrence has come down to history under the terrifying title of the " Pentridge Revolution " ; that the pathetic March of the Blanketeers was regarded by the authorities as part of a traitorous conspiracy ; that, finally, the St. Peter's Fields meeting, the legal object of which was " to consider the propriety of adopting the most legal and effectual means of adopting Reform in the Commons House of Parliament ", led to the inglorious massacre of Peterloo.

The governing English aristocracy as well as the rising bourgeoisie at that time certainly over-estimated the degree of unity among the " lower orders ", as they were currently called. This misjudgment of the situation was perhaps caused by the very high degree of unity existing inside the higher groups and by their far-reaching solidarity of outlook in regard to the lower orders. Growing more and more class-conscious—becoming, that is, more and more conscious of being all members of the one possessing class,[2]—they imagined by a natural process of analogy that the same development was taking place among the other sections of the population. The terminology which they grew accustomed to use in referring to the poor was proof in itself not only of their growing antipathy, but also of their growing apprehension ; for history seems to show that groups are inclined to call each other names only when they begin to be afraid of each other. So far as our case is concerned, we have Cobbett's testimony to the fact that in his lifetime the tone and language of society about the poor had changed very greatly for the worse, that the old name of " the commons of England " had given way to such

---

[1] Cf. Darvall, op. cit., p. 162.
[2] For example, this is the first part of Lord Redesdale's letter to Lord Sidmouth, dated December 11th, 1816 : " I hope that the ebullition of discontent, manifested in so direct and outrageous an attack on property will have the effect of putting all persons possessing property, whatever may be their opinions on political subjects, on their guard against the ruffians who are now disposed to disturb the public peace. The distresses of the time are unquestionably great, and are felt from the highest to the lowest. I fear that, in many cases, rentals will be reduced one-half. The distress which this will occasion must be of long continuance. Men who have been living on an income of 1000£ a year will find it very difficult to live on 500£." (Cf. George Pellew, *The Life and Correspondence of the First Viscount Sidmouth*, Vol. III, London, 1847, p. 161.)

A.N.W.

names as " the lower orders ", " the peasantry " and " the population ", and that when the poor met together to demand their rights they were invariably spoken of by such contumelious epithets as " the populace " or " the mob ".[1] But the widening of the gulf between the poor on the one side, and the aristocracy and rising bourgeoisie on the other, is testified to from other quarters also. For example, an article published in the *Edinburgh Review* in 1819 contained the following statement : " We take the most alarming sign of the times to be, that separation of the upper and middle classes of the community from the lower, which is now daily and visibly increasing." [2] It was on the same lines that the article described the " manifest indisposition towards universal suffrage prevailing in all those classes of the community which had any property, however inconsiderable ".[3] Canning's Liverpool speech of March 18th, 1820, constitutes a further example. It culminated in these revealing words :

May every man who has a stake in the country, whether from situation, from character, from wealth, from his family, and from the hopes of his children—may every man who has a sense of the blessings for which he is indebted to the form of Government under which he lives, see that the time is come, at which his decision must be taken, and when once taken steadfastly acted upon—for or against the institutions of the British Monarchy ! The time is come, at which there is but that line of demarcation.[4]

The solidarity within the aristocracy itself [5] was, indeed, almost complete so far as the treatment of the poor was concerned. There can, for instance, be no doubt that the great majority of the Whigs were hardly less anxious than the Tories to devise the most efficient method of limiting the influence of the Press ; nor that the bulk of them did not object to prosecutions for what was conveniently stigmatized as seditious and blasphemous libel.[6]

---

[1] *Political Register*, LXXVIII, p. 709. Cf. also Byron in the House of Lords on February 27th, 1812 : " You may call the people a mob, but do not forget, that a mob too often speaks the sentiments of the people." (Hansard, *Parliamentary Debates*, XXI, p. 970.)

[2] Vol. XXXII, p. 294.   [3] Ibid., p. 295.

[4] *The Pamphleteer*, XVI, 1820, p. 231.

[5] Byron saw this as clearly as anyone. In *Don Juan*, Canto XVI, stanza LXX, he speaks of " the other interest " meaning the same self-interest, with a different leaning. Cf. also Princess Lieven's remark in a letter to her brother in 1827 : " There are only men who wish to keep their places, and others who wish to occupy them. These two parties only have a real existence." (*Letters of Dorothea, Princess Lieven, during her Residence in London 1812–1834*, p. 98.)

[6] Cf. W. H. Wickwar, *The Struggle for the Freedom of the Press 1819–1832*, London, 1928, pp. 152–3.

James Mill's general analysis of the Whig party and their
organ, the *Edinburgh Review*, explains this attitude very well :

They must [he wrote] be very careful not to excite any suspicion
that they are in reality less favourable to the aristocratical side of the
account than those whom they wish to supplant. And, therefore,
whatever the zeal of which they make show in favour of the people,
it must still appear to the aristocracy, that it bears upon no points of
which they have any occasion to be afraid ; that it leads to the
diminution of none of the advantages which the monopoly of the
powers of government bestows upon them.[1]

Indeed, only on a single issue of great importance, that of
spies, did the Whigs as a group take a decidedly different line
from that of their class-fellows on the other side of the House.

Viewed as a whole, the bourgeoisie could be said to have
thrown in their lot with the aristocracy against the rest of their
fellow-countrymen. In this connection the numerous cases should
be remembered in which manufacturers understood that it would
serve their particular interests to employ their workers at so low
a wage that they would have to be fed in part out of the Poor
Rate which, as a contemporary shrewdly remarked, served as a
bonus to the capital employed in manufacturing ;[2] except in the
North, this system (the Speenhamland system) was widespread
over a great number of counties. Nor should we forget the
tremendous opposition of most manufacturers to factory legislation even in its mildest form ; an opposition which in certain
cases seems to have extended to attempts at influencing those
who had to give medical evidence as to the potential or actual
harm done to the workers' health under the existing working
conditions.[3] The extraordinary results arrived at by some of
these medical experts point in the same direction, as, for example,
the case of a doctor who, examined by the Committee before
the Lords in 1818, did not have the courage to declare that a
child could not work for 23 hours without suffering.[4] Those
middle-class intellectuals did not hesitate to sacrifice their conscience as intellectuals to the cause which promised to guarantee
their own material well-being.

However, just as among the Whigs, so also among the rich

---

[1] *Westminster Review*, Vol. I, 1824, p. 218. The article is not signed, but we have
John Stuart Mill's testimony to the fact that his father was its author. (*Autobiography*,
World's Classics ed., p. 77.)

[2] Cf. J. L. and Barbara Hammond, op. cit., p. 92, n. 4.

[3] Cf. Alfred (= Samuel Kydd), *The History of the Factory Movement from the Year
1802 to the Enactment of the Ten Hours Bill in 1847*, Vol. I, London, 1857, p. 78.

[4] Ibid., pp. 77–8.

merchants, there existed some notable exceptions ; especially in Manchester, and among the middle-class intellectuals, doctors for example. On the other hand, the story of the middle-class radicals constitutes, in a paradoxical way, additional evidence for the assumption of the solidarity that existed throughout the possessing class. True, those renegades proved by their very existence that the solidarity was not complete ; yet the comparatively mild way in which the government dealt with middle-class Radicals [1] suggests that it was in fact very strong.

A great majority of the members of the ruling class (in the widest sense of the word) were, as we have seen, possessed by the idea that the plans of all the disaffected were converging on the point of the total destruction of society. In a memorandum submitted to Lord Liverpool, Robert Southey, then Poet Laureate, describing his conception of the imminent danger, warningly spoke of the horrors of a " bellum servile ".[2] But it was in the closing passage of Canning's speech in the House on January 29th, 1817, that this mentality found its most poetical expression :

. . . we have not leisure to despond [Canning exclaimed], we cannot indulge, without danger, a gloomy and reckless repose. The festal blazes of the War are at an end, the sun of Peace is scarcely yet above the horizon ; we must take care that during this cold and cheerless twilight, the spoiler and the assassin don't break in and destroy.[3]

It was also more than a stratagem, more than the trick of a constitutional lawyer when Eldon, the Lord Chancellor, used to terrify lay hearers by an account of the legal confusion to which any particular change would inevitably lead ; [4] though perhaps consciously exaggerating to some extent, Eldon in all probability himself believed in his gloomy picture. It was the general opinion throughout government circles that it was inadvisable and, moreover, dangerous to make the slightest concessions to popular demands. The Prince Regent, therefore, in his speech on opening the Session, in January 1817, stated bluntly that the existing system of law and government was the most perfect that had ever fallen to the lot of any people.[5] Canning, of course,

---

[1] Cf. Cole and Postgate, op. cit., p. 219.
[2] Quoted in Charles Duke Yonge, The Life and Administration of Robert Banks, Second Earl of Liverpool, London, 1868, p. 299.
[3] Hansard, XXXV, pp. 134–5.
[4] As to the fact, cf. P. Anthony Brown, The French Revolution in English History, London, 1918, p. 165.
[5] Hansard, XXXV, p. 4.

used more general terms ; a pure democracy, he said in 1820, appeared to him unsusceptible of any limitation.[1] Probably to avoid such excesses, Sidmouth, the Home Secretary, even refused to do anything to help those who because of unemployment and hunger wished to emigrate to the colonies.[2] The impracticability of a full restoration of the *ancien régime* on the other side of the Channel obviously strengthened this unyielding attitude. Moreover, the fact that victory had been achieved under the leadership of men like Eldon helped, in Frederick B. Artz's words,[3] to invest the whole existing social and political system with a halo of sanctity.

A letter of Lord Redesdale to Lord Sidmouth, dated 11th December 1816, may be quoted as an example of this complacent mentality :

Many of the old country gentlemen's families are gone ; and I have not a doubt that the destruction of their hereditary influence has greatly contributed to the present insubordination, which, if not checked, will finally produce great disorder. . . . If landed property has not predominant influence, the British constitution, which is founded on the predominance of landed property, cannot stand.[4]

This much at least is certain : in 1816 the unreformed House of Commons was to a very large extent dominated by the direct or indirect influence of the big landowners.[5] It is not surprising that such a body took little interest in industrial conditions. A perusal of the *Parliamentary Debates* of the time proves that industrial disputes were brought to the attention of the Houses of Parliament only when the Cabinet thought it needed emergency powers or considered it desirable to strengthen the penalties of the law. Byron, in his first speech in the House of Lords, on February 27th, 1812, had remarked :

. . . had proper meetings been held in the earlier stages of these riots, had the grievances of these men and their masters (for they also had their grievances) been fairly weighed and justly examined, I do

---

[1] Speech delivered at the Liverpool dinner, given in celebration of his re-election, March 18th, 1820 ; cf. *Pamphleteer*, XVI, p. 225.
[2] Cf. J. L. and Barbara Hammond, op. cit., pp. 189–90.
[3] *Reaction and Revolution 1814–1832*, New York, 1934, p. 119.
[4] George Pellew, *Life of Sidmouth*, Vol. III, p. 162.
[5] Cf. Edward Porritt, *The Unreformed House of Commons*, Vol. I, Cambridge, 1903, p. 311. Cf. also John Stuart Mill's speech on the British Constitution before the Debating Society in 1825 : " We are told by one that our Constitution is a balance ; by another that it is a representation of classes ; by others that it is an aristocratical republic efficiently checked by public opinion. To this I will add my theory that it is an aristocratical republic insufficiently checked by public opinion." (*Autobiography*, Appendix, World's Classics ed., p. 280.)

think that means might have been devised to restore these workmen to their avocations, and tranquillity to the country. . . . In what state of apathy have we been plunged so long, that now for the first time the House has been officially apprised of these disturbances ? [1]

It is also significant that in 1817 the debates on popular distress and on popular disturbances were quite distinct, no attempt being made to connect the two.[2] Thus severed from their context, the riots appeared to the members of Parliament far more mischievous and dangerous. In these circumstances, the Cabinet found no great difficulty in persuading a large majority in both Houses that the situation required drastic measures.

It was widely argued—and with plausibility—that the Cabinet as compared with Parliament or anyone else, was in possession of many more data which gave them a deeper insight into the threatening situation. But the same argument is, as everyone knows, always applied by Cabinets which want to have their own way. It may be granted that the men who were directing the post-Napoleonic State machine did have all the means which were at that time available of finding out what they required to know. But the causation of social facts is a highly complicated matter ; the prejudices and preconceived ideas of the investigators necessarily influence their choice of the methods of investigation.[3] In the present case, the investigators were strongly inclined to credit the exaggerated reports of official and unofficial spies, and therefore they availed themselves of this questionable source of information more than any British government before or after them.[4] It is, I think, incorrect to say that the spies were merely a substitute for a regular police, which, we must admit, hardly existed at the time.[5] There is enough evidence to show that Lord Sidmouth in his deep-rooted antipathy towards the Spencean Society greatly overestimated the influence which it was able to wield,[6] and that for this reason he sent informers to that Society who, for motives

---

[1] Hansard, *Parliamentary Debates*, XXI, p. 969.
[2] Cf. Darvall, op. cit., p. 222.
[3] Cf. Max Weber, " Die ' Objektivität ' sozialwissenschaftlicher und sozialpolitischer Erkenntnis ", (*Gesammelte Aufsätze zur Wissenschaftslehre*, Tübingen, 1922) ; and " Der Sinn der ' Wertfreiheit ' der soziologischen und ökonomischen Wissenschaften " (Ibidem), *passim*.
[4] In his delightful satirical poem, " The Fudge Family in Paris " (London, 1818), Thomas Moore, hiding behind the pseudonym Thomas Brown the Younger, refers to the informers as the Regent's ears ; he compares them to the fabulous golden ears of King Midas, " meaning informers, kept at high rent " (p. 44).
[5] The latter point has, I think, been over-emphasized, for example by Carl Brinkmann. Cf. *England seit 1815*, 2nd ed., Berlin, 1938, p. 24.
[6] Cf. Cole and Postgate, op. cit., p. 214.

only too obvious, obliged his Lordship with alarming reports. As to those motives, this is what the *Edinburgh Review* said in 1817 : " . . . these emissaries, being secure of impunity, and installed in an office, the continuance of which is to depend on the continuance of disaffection, they cannot be expected to be very hostile to the growth of it ".[1] Besides, it is known that the spies in 1816, though more efficient than four years previously, were far from competent ; in their ignorance some of them, in their turn, were inclined to believe rumours, however unfounded. The Cabinet must have realized this to some extent. They seem to have known nothing of Oliver's character when they took him into their employ ; soon afterwards, however, their own correspondents sent them information which was anything but recommendatory.[2] But the Cabinet apparently continued to credit Oliver's fantastic reports, or, at any rate, to use them as one of the most important means of proving that they were right in their judgment of the situation. It may be doubted whether the Cabinet really believed what Oliver told them. There are grounds enough for a strong suspicion that they did not care whether the information on which their preconceived verdict was to be based, was at all reliable. J. L. and Barbara Hammond deserve the credit for having collected the evidence.[3] The main point is that on June 17th, 1817, Lord Fitzwilliam sent an important letter to the Government in which among other things he stated : " There certainly is very generally in the Country a strong and decided opinion that most of the events that have recently occurred in the Country are to be attributed to the presence and active agitation of Mr. Oliver. He is considered as the main spring, from which every movement has taken its rise." The Government withheld this letter from the Secret Committee, unquestionably a strange procedure in view of its extreme importance.

Once the Cabinet had decided to rely in such measure on the reports of spies, it was quite consistent that the democratic principle of publicity was not applied in Parliament as far as these matters were concerned. Nor did the Lord Chancellor conceal the reason. If inquiries of this kind were conducted publicly, he told Parliament on February 27th, 1818, those who gave information to the Government would be made known and

---

[1] Vol. XXVIII, p. 538.
[2] J. L. and Barbara Hammond, op. cit., p. 374.
[3] Ibid., pp. 363-73.

exposed to their enemies.[1] It was too much to expect that the highly anti-democratic measures which were in preparation could be arrived at by democratic methods. The Secret Committees of the House of Commons, chosen by ballot, had of course to base their judgment on the evidence which the Government and in particular the Home Office had prepared for them. Thus it was that they affirmed the existence of a plot not only for " the overthrow of all the political institutions of the kingdom " but, with special reference to the small and rather uninfluential Spencean Society, for " a division of the landed and extinction of the funded property of the country ".[2]

Everything clearly depended on the opinion of the Cabinet Ministers and of Wellington who, both through Castlereagh and directly, was able to exert a considerable influence on the Cabinet. We have seen that the Home Secretary's mind was full of gloomy apprehension. As to the Duke's attitude, this is perhaps best summarized in his assertion that the disturbances were principally caused by the idleness, dissipation and improvidence of all the middling and lower classes in England, produced by a long course of prosperity and of flattery of their vices by the higher orders and the Government.[3] If the keynote of this utterance is con- tempt, Lord Castlereagh, to judge from his several speeches in Parliament, seems to have entirely shared the Home Secretary's outlook. It has to be remembered that Castlereagh in his func- tion as Leader of the House of Commons probably consciously overstated the case which the Cabinet was presenting to the House. But his deep apprehension sounded quite sincere when in the debate on the Seditious Meetings Bill on February 24th, 1817, he warned the House that the threatening " conspiracy was of a desperate character, on the point of exploding, and that it had in fact exploded ".[4] He was greatly assisted by Canning who, in the same debate, went so far as to declare that

the danger to be apprehended was not to be defined in one word. It was rebellion ; but not rebellion only ; it was treason ; but not treason merely ; it was confiscation ; but not confiscation within such bonds as have been usually applied to it in the changes of Dynasties, or the Revolution of States :—it was an aggregate of all

[1] Horace Twiss, *The Public and Private Life of Chancellor Eldon*, London, 1844, p. 310.
[2] Hansard, *Parliamentary Debates*, XXXV, p. 438.
[3] Wellington to Major-Gen. Sir H. Torrens, dated Cambrai, 3rd December 1816. (*Supplementary Despatches, Correspondence and Memoranda of Field-Marshal Arthur, Duke of Wellington*, Vol. XI, London, 1864, p. 561.)
[4] Hansard, XXXV, p. 593.

these evils ; it was all that dreadful variety of sorrow and of suffering which must follow the extinction of loyalty, morality and religion ; which must follow upon the accomplishment of designs tending not only to subvert the Constitution of England, but to overthrow the whole frame of society.[1]

Although deeply anxious about this menacing state of affairs, the Cabinet was far from despair. Parliament was reassured by Castlereagh of the fair chance of overcoming all these dangers. It must be allowed, he told the House, that the treasonable disposition prevailed chiefly in the inferior orders of society. Looking to the history of the revolutionary spirit in England, it appeared to him to have been gradually descending from those higher and better informed ranks in which it formerly showed itself to the lower orders. And indeed we may add that 75 per cent. of the children belonging to that class were illiterate. Castlereagh continued that " the poison now operated only on those classes to which an antidote could perhaps be more easily discovered, and more effectively applied ".[2] In this connection it is well to remember how John Stuart Mill described Castlereagh's attitude towards the people in general : " Was there ever a more unpopular minister than Lord Castlereagh ? Was there ever a minister who cared so little about it ? " Mill asked in a speech on the British Constitution before the Debating Society in 1825. He went on to explain : " The reason was that although he had the people against him, the predominant portion of the aristocracy was for him, and all his concern about public dissatisfaction was to keep it below the point of a general insurrection." [3] A line similar to Castlereagh's was taken, in December 1819, by the Bishop of Llandaff, who felt that, unlike the reasoned arguments on infidelity which were addressed to the educated classes during the eighteenth century, the anti-Christian writings of the nineteenth were too unreasonable to be suppressed by anything less than the terrors of the law.[4]

The antidote, duly produced according to the Cabinet's prescription, consisted indeed of nothing less than the law of terror. In 1817, the notorious " Gagging Bills " were passed, by which all public meetings were forbidden except under licence from the magistrate, and the Habeas Corpus Act was suspended ; thus Lord Sidmouth was enabled to send out his Circular in-

---

[1] Ibid., p. 633. [2] Ibid., p. 591.
[3] *Autobiography*, World's Classics ed., p. 286.
[4] Hansard, XLI, pp. 987-8. The occasion was the third reading of the Blasphemous Libel Bill.

forming magistrates of their power to imprison anyone whom they suspected of libel. In 1819, at a time when depression was again as great as two years previously, the even severer Six Acts followed, introducing among other things a heavy newspaper tax. Viewed as a whole, the Six Acts, as Mackintosh rightly pointed out in the House, amounted to an almost complete suspension of the constitution. All these highly repressive measures were presented as a remedy in order to save, among other things, liberty.[1] For example, this is how Canning, the eloquent mouthpiece of the ruling class, wound up his speech mentioned above :

It is for the House to say, whether or not the Constitution shall be guarded by those new outworks which the perils of the time have rendered necessary, against the assaults of furious and desperate men :— whether that system of law and liberty, under which England has so long flourished in happiness and glory—in internal tranquillity, and external grandeur—shall be sacrificed or saved.[2]

And the Lord Chancellor, who on other occasions, as we have seen, used to make a special point of the sacredness of the constitution, said in the House of Lords on March 21st, 1817, that what he advocated was " to suspend their liberties for a short time, in order to have the full enjoyment of them ever after ".[3]   In the same style Eldon by a surprising twist went on to justify this measure by saying that for his part he thought it wiser to look for prevention rather than punishment as a remedy for the evil of which the country had to complain.[4]   To threaten to punish people by imprisoning them without an orderly procedure meant in a certain sense, it is true, the prevention of acts which they might have committed if they could have reckoned with such a procedure.   Yet Robert Owen's statement, made a few years previously in *A New View of Society*, though expressing the opposite view, remained, I think, true in a deeper sense.

Such has been our education [Owen had written] that we hesitate not to devote years and expend millions in the detection and punishment of crimes, and in the attainment of objects whose ultimate results are in comparison with insignificancy itself ; and yet we have not moved one step in the true path to prevent crimes, and to diminish the innumerable evils with which mankind are now afflicted.[5]

---

[1] John Stuart Mill in his above-mentioned speech threw this paradox into relief : " Did free speaking prevent the Six Acts ? " he asked. (*Autobiography*, World's Classics ed., p. 285.)

[2] Hansard, XXXV, pp. 638–9.   [3] Ibid., p. 1217.
[4] Twiss, *Life of Eldon*, p. 292.   [5] Second edition, London, 1816, p. 30.

But it must be admitted that the Government in its policy towards the disaffected did not restrict itself to preventive measures in the narrow sense in which they were understood by the Lord Chancellor ; measures, that is, preventing only the signs of disaffection. Knowing and appreciating one of the most important doctrines of Edmund Burke, namely, that the Established Church was one of the cornerstones of the social *status quo*,[1] they tried to prevent disaffection itself by supporting an institution which would make people imbibe views which the Government regarded as constructive. It was at the same time that Coleridge observed " the sore evil now so general alas ! only not universal, of supporting our religion, just as a keen party-man would support his party in Parliament." [2] That was why, in the winter of 1815–16, the Home Secretary, for all generations to come branded as the personification of Hypocrisy,[3] employed a good deal of his time in preparing the Government and the public for some general measure in promotion of Church extension ; [4] why, in 1818, the sum of one million pounds was voted for the building of Anglican churches [5]—though Vansittart, the Chancellor of the Exchequer, declared the whole problem to be one on which no party feelings could arise ; [6] why, for example, Owen, who desired a kind of prevention which would go more to the root of things, was called an atheist ; and why Shelley, who was anything but irreligious, went so far as to pose as an advocate of atheism.

In order to complete the enumeration of the measures taken by the Government to deal with the disaffection in the country, it must be mentioned that some of the governing men in the period immediately following Waterloo seem to have regarded

[1] See Chapter I of this book. Cf. also the following passage from James Mill's above-mentioned article in the *Edinburgh Review* : " In the composition of the aristocracy of England, the importance of its two props deserves much and careful consideration. Its two props are : the Church and the Law ; by the Law, we mean here the professional body." (Op. cit., p. 213.)

[2] *Anima Poetæ*, London, 1895, p. 264.

[3] Cf. Shelley's *Mask of Anarchy*, stanza IV :

> Clothed with the Bible, as with light,
> And the shadows of the night,
> Like Sidmouth, next, Hypocrisy,
> On a crocodile rode by.

[4] As to the fact, cf. Pellew, *Life of Sidmouth*, Vol. III, London, 1847, p. 138.

[5] Cf. the debate in the House of Commons on March 16th, 1818, in Hansard, *Parliamentary Debates*, XXXVII, pp. 1116–31.

[6] On March 16th, 1818. (Hansard, XXXVII, p. 1127.) In 1829 Carlyle wrote ironically : " Among ourselves, when it is thought that religion is declining, we have only to vote half-a-million's worth of bricks and mortar, and build new churches." (*Signs of the Times*, Edinburgh Review, No. 98.)

trade expansion as a desirable method in this connection. Contrary to the opinion of the liberal historians writing in the second half of the nineteenth century, it can be and indeed has been proved that Wellington as well as Castlereagh,[1] strong Tories though they were, were among those who in this matter showed quite a different and a much deeper understanding of prevention. But as this tendency, which was later developed by George Canning, proved to be a factor working against the Concert of Europe, it will be examined in a later chapter.

[1] The " antithesis " Castlereagh-Canning, which belonged to the stock-in-trade of liberal historians (Continental as well as Anglo-American) is well refuted by Carl Brinkmann, *England seit 1815*, 2nd ed., Berlin, 1938, pp. 23–4.

CHAPTER IV

CENTRAL EUROPE

The economic situation of the Austrian people, desperate as it had been especially towards the end of the Napoleonic Wars, hardly improved after victory had been achieved. The constant confiscations and occasional looting which the then victorious French Army had carried out on Austrian soil had indeed ceased. But so likewise had confiscation and looting by the Austrian Army itself on foreign soil. Two months after Waterloo Castlereagh had shrewdly remarked in a despatch to Lord Liverpool :

> I much suspect neither Austria nor Prussia, and certainly none of the smaller Powers have any sincere desire to bring the present state of things to a speedy termination : so long as they can feed, clothe and pay their armies at the expense of France, and put English subsidies into their pockets besides, which nothing can deprive them of, previous to 1st of April 1816, but the actual conclusion of a treaty with France, you cannot suppose they will be in a great hurry to come to a final settlement, since the war may be said to have closed.[1]

However, a settlement was eventually reached. Thereafter only about an eighth or ninth part of the Austrian army could remain in France ; the rest had to come home. These troops had noticed while abroad that they were less adequately equipped than all the other forces ;[2] now on their return they began to realize that their life abroad, in spite of its many dangers and hardships, had been—and for their luckier fellow-soldiers still was—one of comparative well-being.[3]

In the regained Italian provinces of Lombardy and Venetia an additional economic problem arose. The former Italian army was disbanded ; 40,000 to 60,000 Italians lost their places in favour of German-speaking Austrians, and became unemployed. The army of these provinces, which formerly had been supplied by products of Italian manufacture, was now provisioned with goods made in the German portion of the Monarchy.[4] To complete the misery, many of the public works projects which had

---

[1] *Correspondence, etc., of Viscount Castlereagh*, Third Series, Vol. X, p. 485.

[2] " Freiherr Anton von Baldacci über die inneren Zustände Österreichs. Eine Denkschrift aus dem Jahre 1816 ", ed. F. von Krones, *Archiv für österreichische Geschichte*, LXXIV, 1889, p. 53.

[3] Ibid., p. 54.

[4] Cf. Sir W. Napier, *The Life and Opinions of Sir Charles James Napier*, I, London, 1857, p. 278. Napier visited Milan in 1819.

been initiated under the French régime were discontinued by the Austrian rulers.[1]

A sharp setback was felt all over the Monarchy by a considerable part of the population who had not actively taken part in the wars. The suspension of the Continental blockade harmed, as we have seen, even some British industries. Its effect on Austrian large-scale industry, which had only just developed under cover of it, was much more extensive. During the wars the Government had made various concessions to the die-hard guilds ; on the other hand, inflation, which began in 1800 and gradually increased in intensity, though it had led to the financial ruin of a great many people, had also had its beneficial side. Artisans had found it comparatively easy to fill their workshops with more modern equipment, partly because machinery was still looked on with a certain distrust so that its price did not keep pace with the rise of prices in general. There had been openings for enterprising people owing to an increasing demand for the products of manufacture as well as of the newly-established industries. Eastern and south-eastern Europe too had become more interested in Austrian products owing to the Continental blockade. Another favourable aspect of this blockade for Austria had been that the cotton and woollen industries had grown considerably, for in the ordinary way they could not have competed with English goods. Since cane sugar was no longer imported from the West Indies via Great Britain, the production of sugar beet had become of the utmost importance. The glass and linen industries alone had suffered badly from the Continental blockade, because they relied almost entirely on export. In general the blockade had acted as a spur to Austrian industry. When it was removed, the newly-established industries felt the keen competition of England very acutely. Many branches were both too recently established, and too hampered by Government restrictions [2] to be able to compete successfully with British goods in Austria, let alone on the rest of the Continent. The results, translated into terms of human suffering, were analogous to those arising from the collapse of some of the British industries.

The misery was aggravated by the situation of the currency. While up to 1816 the appalling insecurity always caused by

---

[1] Cf. John Rath, " The Habsburgs and the Great Depression in Lombardy–Venetia 1814–18 ". *Journal of Modern History*, XIII, September 1941.

[2] Friedrich Engel-Janosi, " Über die Entwicklung der sozialen und staatswirtschaftlichen Verhältnisse im deutschen Österreich 1815–1848 ", *Vierteljahrsschrift für Sozial- und Wirtschaftsgeschichte*, XVIII, 1924, p. 99, n. 2.

inflation had been the chief trouble in this respect, the " tight-ness " brought about by the stabilization [1] was hardly less dis-astrous. But at the same time the effects produced by the previous inflation were to a large extent still operating. Prices had progressively increased until the stabilization took place ; but extra allowances for those with fixed salaries had not kept pace with them.[2]

In addition, the almost continuous rain during the summer of 1816 caused, as it did in England, a catastrophically poor harvest throughout almost the whole of the Austrian Empire ; even the following year's harvest was only slightly better. The result was that about 10 per cent. of the larger peasants and as many as 50 per cent. of the smaller ones were ruined.[3] While, for climatic and other reasons, the plight of some districts was especially hard, the bad state of communications [4] made it extremely difficult and often impossible to send relief in time from other quarters.

All this, of course, has to be viewed against the background of an outworn feudalism. This is true of the whole of the mon-archy, with the exception of the Alpine provinces, Tyrol and Vorarlberg, and the Italian provinces, Lombardy and Venetia. At the beginning of the nineteenth century different degrees of feudalism survived in different provinces. The crudest form existed in Hungary and Transylvania. On paper, the reforms of Maria Theresa and Joseph II applied to these parts also. Legal procedure of a sort was now available to the serf, but the seigneur remained judge in his own cause. In certain circum-stances the peasant had the right to take the case to a higher court, namely, the county court. But the members of this court, belonging exclusively to the landowning nobility, as a rule con-sidered a peasant who dared to do this as a disobedient son, and treated him accordingly, dismissing his complaint. Or, to take an example of another paper reform : any Hungarian peasant condemned to a hundred strokes with the rod, had the right of appeal to the King's Court before the punishment. To avoid this difficulty and delay, his seigneur would order him only ninety-nine strokes.[5]

People who had experience of foreign countries with a different

---

[1] Hans Pirchegger, *Geschichte und Kulturleben Deutschösterreichs von 1792 bis zum Weltkrieg*, Wien-Leipzig, 1937, p. 75.
[2] Baldacci, op. cit., p. 57.   [3] Pirchegger, op. cit., p. 73.
[4] Baldacci, op. cit., p. 61.
[5] S. Sugenheim, *Geschichte der Aufhebung der Leibeigenschaft und Hörigkeit in Europa*, St. Petersburg, 1861, p. 477.

social system, or who had seen the foreign conqueror introduce
for a time a different system brought from his own country, grew
increasingly aware of the contrasting colours of the picture : of
the contrast, for example, between the poverty of the serfs [1] who
numbered 60 per cent. of Hungary's population, and the affluence
of the Hungarian nobility who, besides many other privileges,
were completely exempt from all taxation.   Writing of Hungary
in 1811, Baron vom Stein spoke of : " A tumultuous Reichstag,
the exemption of one class from all payments, three-fifths of the
nation under serfdom of the crudest form." The most conspicuous of the other privileges which the Hungarian aristocracy
shared with the fellow-members of their class all over Austria
were a monopoly of the highest ranks in the civil service,[2] a
special jurisdiction and exemption from conscription.   After 1815,
Councillor Lehmann in Vienna worked out a scheme by which
those who until then had been conscripted for life service, had
to serve either ten years with the infantry, twelve years with the
cavalry, or fourteen years with the artillery.   In Hungary, where
recruiting was done not by officials but by the respective landowners, this comparatively humane scheme favoured by the
central Government was completely rejected by the feudal lords.[3]

In the other parts of the Monarchy, that is, in Upper and
Lower Austria, Carinthia, Carniola, Bohemia, Moravia, Silesia,
and Galicia, feudalism took somewhat milder forms.   Ruthenian
peasants had indeed to live in mud cottages together with their
cattle, and Bohemian serfs still owed half their working time and
two-thirds of the produce of their land to the landowner.   But
the reforms which had been enacted in these provinces during the
eighteenth century, had not remained a dead letter.   Ever since
the great Czech peasant revolt of 1679, *Robotpatente* had been
passed at intervals of some twenty to thirty years, limiting the
imposition of Robot (forced labour).   These decrees, unlike the
Hungarian " reforms ", had really been enforced.   The fact that
feudalism in its crudest form disappeared in Bohemia and Moravia
for example, so much more quickly than in Hungary, can be
attributed in part to the smaller numbers of the nobility in the
Slavonic provinces.   According to statistics extant for the 1830s,[4]

---

[1] In 1820 there were peasant riots at Malaczka, which were forcibly suppressed.
[2] Engel-Janosi, op. cit., p. 104.   Those leading positions at the court and in the
civil service which Joseph II had taken away from the higher aristocracy were given
back to them by Metternich.
[3] J. F. Schneller, *Österreichs Einfluss auf Deutschland und Europa*, II, Stuttgart, 1829,
pp. 406-7.
[4] Johann Springer, *Statistik des österreichischen Kaiserstaates*, Wien, 1840.

in Hungary there was one nobleman to twenty inhabitants, whereas in Bohemia and Moravia the proportion was about one to 840.

On the other hand, Karl Grünberg has shown that the institution of Robot as such had been strengthened rather than weakened by the fact that the duties it involved had been rendered more bearable.[1] This is where the famous decree of Joseph II of February 1789, which might be called the " Anti-Robot Patent ", had differed essentially from earlier legislation. Its purpose was not to limit Robot duties, but to abolish them altogether. Soon after the Emperor's death in 1790, however, his anti-robot decree as well as other parts of his reformatory legislation had been cancelled. Although some members of the landowning nobility had openly declared that serfdom as a retarding economic factor ought to be abolished, this was by no means the view of the bulk of the aristocracy. In the meantime, also, the French Revolution had broken out and was keeping all the European courts in breathless suspense. Its effect on the Austrian rulers was twofold : first of all they cancelled the major reforms that had been enacted by their predecessors ; then they decided to sit and wait. On one occasion the Emperor Francis declared : " I do not want any novelties ; all that needs to be done is to apply the laws in a fair way ; they are good and satisfactory. The present is not the time for reforms. The nations are dangerously wounded. We must avoid provoking them by touching their wounds."

Yet, however appalling the stagnation since the death of Joseph II had been, it is well to remember that Austria had been well ahead of Prussia throughout the eighteenth century. Baron vom Stein, who in 1809 visited Bohemia, Moravia and Austrian Silesia, summed up his impressions thus : " The position of the peasants in this Monarchy, with the exception of Hungary, is much more fortunate than in Prussia." His judgment may be regarded as fairly reliable, all the more since four years previously, he had signed the decrees introducing agrarian reform in Prussia.

The average Austrian aristocrat was, then, still a feudal lord, so far as his own estate was concerned. But in respect of larger units the concentration of power in very few hands was even more marked. Some of the provinces, it is true, had diets of a sort.

---

[1] Cf. also G. F. Knapp, " Die Bauernbefreiung in Österreich und Preussen ", *Schmollers Jahrbuch*, Neue Folge, XVIII, 1894.

But their function was in most cases restricted to listening to the tax-demands (*Steuerpostulate*) of the sovereign and consenting to them without even a word of discussion. The British Parliament had, as we have seen, hardly any influence on the treatment of disturbances at this period ; yet there were other matters in which, no doubt, it acted as a check on the endeavours of the ruling class to concentrate all power in their own hands. Thus much has to be said even if, as seems to be the case, it remains doubtful whether there existed at that period a decisive divergence on any point of social importance between the opinion of the British Cabinet and that of the vast majority of the unreformed House of Commons comprising all the Tories and almost all the Whigs ; in cases where Parliament was divided—as over the treatment of conquered France—so also was the Cabinet. In Austria there did not exist even such an assembly as this. Political power was thus more openly concentrated in the hands of the Emperor and a small number of ministers and counsellors. Metternich's reforms, even had they been carried out *en bloc*, would in no wise have altered this situation. What Metternich aimed at, and partly achieved, was an acceleration of the administrative procedure. From now on the Cabinet Ministers used to meet in frequent conference. Thus business was settled far more quickly than under the former cumbersome method of dealing with it *per rollam*.[1]

It is obvious that this system of more naked power had to use a cruder ideology for its justification. That is why the Emperor Francis I could openly declare : " Peoples ? What does that mean ? I know only subjects."

The more exalted the position of the few chosen aristocrats who shared this extreme degree of power with their sovereign, the more highly precarious, for that very reason, it became. An important psychological factor increased this precariousness. It is well to remember that the cultural life of the higher aristocracy towards the end of the eighteenth century was by no means uninfluenced by the ideas of the Enlightenment. Scepticism regarding the dogmas of autocratic statesmanship and the related dogmas of conservative religion had made much headway in those circles. This was the *milieu* in which men like Metternich had grown up. But as Heine put it, " the Earth could not remain quiet when Heaven was revolutionized ". When, at the

[1] Heinrich Ritter von Srbik, *Metternich, Der Staatsmann und der Mensch*, I, München, 1925, p. 460.

outbreak of the French Revolution, men like Metternich realized the extent of the threat to their own social status which it involved, they soon made up their minds to fight it ; they did not underestimate the danger. Metternich, then a man of about 20 years of age, decided even at that time to dedicate his whole life to the struggle. Yet, having eaten too profusely of the Tree of Knowledge, they were all the time serving a cause in certain aspects of which they had never believed. Metternich, for example, wrote to Comtesse de Lieven about monarchs : " If you knew what I think about the inhabitants of these lofty regions, you would take me for an out-and-out Jacobin . . . I have seen so many of those who live in this atmosphere that I know all about them ; . . . set on an altar and surrounded by the poison of error, ignorance, servility and flattery." [1]

The same can be said of the attitude of Metternich and some of his associates to religion in the narrower sense of the word ; it is well known that he strongly supported many of the claims of the Catholic Church, though he was anything but a pious Catholic. Among those who were given the highest posts in the civil service were a striking number of converts from Protestantism to Catholicism.[2] The most famous of these, the Romanticist Friedrich von Schlegel, complained in June 1816 in a letter to his wife Dorothea—the daughter of the philosopher Moses Mendelssohn—that all this Christian zeal was put on for reasons of party politics.[3] A letter written by Dorothea to her husband earlier in the year took much the same line. Describing high society life in Vienna she says : " Zacharias Werner's sermons continue to raise a furore. . . . Distinguished people dine at 6 o'clock only in order to hear the sermon. At night elegant ladies and gentlemen ask each other : ' Where were you at the sermon ? How did you like the preacher ? ' in the same way as in other places one enquires about theatres or concerts." [4] Zacharias Werner, incidentally, was also a convert. But converts, though more conspicuous, were by no means the only persons to show an exaggerated zeal in matters of religion. Pilat

---

[1] *Lettres du Prince de Metternich à la Comtesse de Lieven 1818–1819*, ed. Jean Hanoteau, Paris, 1909, p. 207. I have taken the translation of the passage from E. L. Woodward, *Three Studies in European Conservatism*, London, 1929, p. 25.

[2] This is emphasized by J. Beidtel, *Geschichte der österreichischen Staatsverwaltung*, II, pp. 218, 261.

[3] *Briefwechsel zwischen Dorothea und Friedrich Schlegel*, p. 216. It is an established fact that neither his nor his wife's conversion was the outcome of opportunist considerations. (Cf. H. Finke, *Über Friedrich Schlegel*, Freiburg, i. B., 1918, p. 44.)

[4] *Dorothea v. Schlegel, geb. Mendelssohn, und deren Söhne Johannes und Philipp Veit, Briefwechsel*, II, Mainz, 1881, pp. 339–40.

who, together with Gentz, was in charge of Austrian propaganda at home as well as abroad, had always been a Catholic. On one occasion in 1818, Gentz went to see Friedrich von Schlegel, and reporting the conversation afterwards to Pilat, he wrote : " When recently I mentioned your zeal and your activity in the interests of the Church, he laughed heartily and said that this was impossible since you had no order for it ; he made some other similar bewildering remarks." [1] Two years later, Friedrich von Schlegel, in a profound diagnosis of his time, exclaimed in despair : " Even religion, the light of God, the last gracious beam of hope, is being debased and treated like any common or earthly party affair." [2] In a poem which he called " Unsere Zeit " (1820),[3] Schlegel at first rejects political radicalism ; then he turns to the powers that be in these words :

> Und Ihr andern wollt beschwören
> Durch ein künstlich Nichts den Sturm ?
> Wen kann solch' Geweb' abwehren
> Selbst zernagt vom Lügenwurm ?
> Was nicht Gott erbaut, muss fallen
> Also ruft die Stimm uns allen,
> Nieder stürzt der Babelthurm.

How apt was John Stuart Mill's somewhat more pedestrian description of " this age, in which real belief in any religious doctrine is feeble and precarious, but the opinion of its necessity for moral and social purposes almost universal ".[4] A German author, Karl Immermann, formulated the same diagnosis in three words : " Devotion without God ".[5] Nor did Jean Paul expect much support for the spiritual rebirth of the Church from the " newer mystical poets " of whom he remarked : " They act and sing belief and disbelief to us—with the same belief." [6]

Perhaps these points could be supplemented, but even the two so far mentioned—Monarchy and the Church—were surely not minor aspects of Metternich's system. At times, indeed, the Chancellor and his paid ideologists must have felt uneasy about the cynicism of their attitude, for example, when Gentz, after 1815, remarked that he himself had grown immensely old

[1] *Briefe von Friedrich von Gentz an Pilat*, Leipzig, 1868, p. 315.
[2] *Signatur des Zeitalters*, Concordia, I, Wien, 1820, p. 51.
[3] *Sämmtliche Werke*, 2 Ausgabe, X, Wien, 1846, p. 171.
[4] *Autobiography*, World's Classics ed., p. 59.
[5] Letter to Tieck, 8th October 1832.
[6] *Über die jetzige Sonnenwende in der Religion* (1809). In a later work he asked sarcastically : " Instead of making reason the prisoner of faith, why not try for once to make faith a prisoner of reason ? " (*Überchristenthum*, written between 1817 and 1823.)

and wicked. He was, to be sure, fully justified in saying this. We have only to remember that during the second year of the French Revolution he had written to a friend :

If the Revolution should fail, I should regard it as one of the greatest misfortunes that had ever befallen the human race. It is philosophy's first practical triumph, the first instance of a form of government based on principles and on a coherent and consistent system. It is the hope as well as the consolation for so many of the old evils under which humanity groans. If this revolution should give way, all these evils would become ten times more incurable. I can vividly imagine how the silence of despair would everywhere confess, in defiance of all reason, that man can be happy only as a slave, and how all the tyrants, great and small, would make the most of this admission, in order to take revenge for the terror with which they were seized on the awakening of the French nation.[1]

Soon afterwards he had hailed and translated Burke's *Reflections on the Revolution in France*, and now, in 1815, he was well established as the chief literary hack of one of the most regressive régimes of the time. We have Wellington's testimony to the fact that Gentz was highly venal ; the Duke amongst others used to pay him.[2] From Aix-la-Chapelle Gentz reported to Adam Müller : " I have had the most instructive talks with the foremost ' puissances ' of the business world, and I have witnessed in my small room the biggest financial transactions which men have ever negotiated." One of these " puissances," Rothschild, called Gentz " the golden pen ". In 1830 Gentz, in a conversation with Prokesch von Osten, described himself as " agent for the firm of Rothschild " which paid him a yearly sum of 10,000 florins.[3] It is generally believed that Gentz gave away State secrets in return. Nor did Pilat have any particular scruples in this respect. This is what Cotta, the publisher, wrote to a friend about Pilat's methods : " As regular as the equinoctial gales there arrived towards the end of each half-year Pilat's threatening letters announcing the impending embargo [for Austria] on the *Allgemeine Zeitung*, only in order to be allayed each time with abundant payments." [4]

There had long existed in England an appreciable tendency on

---

[1] Letter to Garve, 5th December, 1790. (*Briefe von und an Gentz*, ed. F. C. Wittichen, München, 1909, I, pp. 178 seqq.)
[2] Stanhope, *Notes of Conversations with the Duke of Wellington, 1831–1851*, London, 1938, p. 226.
[3] *Aus den Tagebüchern des Grafen Prokesch von Osten, 1830–34*, Wien, 1909, p. 58. For more evidence about Gentz's financial connections, cf. Paul R. Sweet, *Friedrich von Gentz. Defender of the Old Order*, Wisconsin, 1941, pp. 218–19.
[4] *Briefe an Cotta. Das Zeitalter der Restauration, 1815–1832*, Stuttgart, 1927, p. 54.

the part of the land-owning aristocracy to come to terms with the rising bourgeoisie. This tendency, obvious in the case of Canning, can be traced even in Castlereagh. No such tendency existed in Austria. Therefore it is understandable that a great deal of Metternich's anxiety was directed towards the upper middle class, those " wealthy men, real cosmopolitans, securing their personal advantage at the expense of any order of things whatever ",[1] as he chose to put it in the famous Secret Memorandum to Alexander I entitled " Profession of Faith ". In order to handicap this social stratum which to the Central European aristocracy seemed so incongruous in the whole system, various methods were devised. The Government began once more to support the guilds [2] which had been undergoing a slow process of decay ever since the middle of the eighteenth century. The building up of a new industry was severely hampered by all sorts of restrictions, such as that new factories must be built in open country in order to impede as far as possible the growth of towns.[3] Another restriction was the prohibition for a time by the Government of the further construction of houses in order, as they thought, to check further increase of the population. Again, the Government made it almost impossible for journeymen working in Vienna to marry. Measures of this kind served two purposes at the same time. They were not only directed against the accumulation of capital in the upper middle class, in hands, that is, other than those of the high land-owning aristocracy : they also sought to prevent the aggregation of persons of the " lower orders " in a few centres.[4]

At this time the workers in the factories of the Austrian Empire consisted mainly of artisans who had at one time owned their own workshops but had failed financially, and of sons of ruined peasants. Their wives and children also worked in them. On the average every worker was out of work for three months each year. In a time of crisis large numbers were dismissed, all at about the same time. Rural home industry was fairly widespread ; a great deal of weaving was still done by peasants working in their own homes. Conditions there seem to have been particularly miserable, for these weavers were paid for a day's work of about fourteen hours only about 10 per cent. of

---

[1] *Memoirs of Prince Metternich*, III, London, 1881, p. 467.
[2] Pirchegger, op. cit., p. 74.
[3] Ibid., p. 75.
[4] Cf. E. Wertheimer, *Geschichte Österreichs und Ungarns im ersten Jahrzehnt des 19. Jahrhunderts*, II, Leipzig, 1890, p. 48.

what was received by an operative in a textile factory. According to statistical data for the year 1834, 75 per cent. of the population were living in rural districts. Just as some of these were
engaged in rural home industry of one kind or another, so also
the population of small market towns and even of towns of
medium size included a large number of farmers and cattle-
breeders, especially in Hungary and Galicia. In many of the
smaller towns, commerce and manufacture were still pursued as
secondary occupations.

To neglect industry meant, as was proved later, to renounce
one very considerable chance of raising the standard of national
well-being ; it implied that the very low standard of the poor
was denied improvement. In England, where owing to the
compromise with the rising bourgeoisie factories had grown up
in much larger numbers, the prospect of a proletariat kept per-
manently just above the starvation-level seemed to some far-
sighted conservatives and their forerunners too risky ; that is one
among other reasons why they sought an expansion of trade and,
in consequence, of the Empire. In Austria, where the industrial
proletariat was far less numerous, the ruling class, though dreading
the slightest increase in its numbers had less reason to fear it even
when its standard of living was very low, provided only that it
could be kept fairly small. " The people ", Metternich tells us
in his *Memoirs*, " let themselves be duped easily enough ; you
cannot exaggerate the goodness of the people, I might even say
of all the people ", and his predilection for moralizing made him
add : " but their ignorance is as great ; therefore they must be
led." [1]

One way of leading them was to keep them busy. " The
labours to which this class—the real people—are obliged to devote
themselves ", Metternich wrote in his profession of faith, " are
too continuous and too positive to allow them to throw themselves into vague abstractions and ambitions." [2] This applied,
of course, to the lower orders in general, not only to the not very
numerous industrial proletariat. As early as 1796, when the
problem of the forced labour services (*Robot*) of the serfs was
being discussed, Councillor Greissler had put forward an
analogous suggestion ; forced labour services should not be
abolished, in his opinion, since the subjects had to be kept constantly active and busy ; otherwise he feared they might become

[1] Translated from *Mémoires*, 2 éd., III, Paris, 1881, p. 357.
[2] *Memoirs of Prince Metternich*, III, p. 466.

a threat to the internal peace of the country ; moreover, forced labour services seemed to him a good training for obedience and humility.[1] Gentz was cynical enough to reveal, in his conversation with Robert Owen at Aix-la-Chapelle, the chief motive for the Government's attitude to the lower orders : " We do not by any means desire the great masses to become wealthy and independent ; how could we govern them ? "

So far we have investigated the Austrian Government's attitude to the upper middle class and to the lower orders. The former, we have seen, was more hampered than in Britain ; the latter, chiefly because of the comparative backwardness of Austrian large industry, was not considered so dangerous as was the British proletariat by the men then ruling in Britain. Between those two strata lay that of the lower middle class, represented especially by the intelligentsia. As to the threat which this group constituted to the preservation of the social *status quo*, unanimity existed between the British and Austrian rulers. While the aspiration of the " wealthy men " was for a share in the government of the country and the social amenities connected with it, the intelligentsia was—in some cases quite rightly— suspected of questioning the system as a whole. *Cogitat, ergo est Jacobinus*, as Gagern wittily put it.[2] These were the social groups which Metternich together with the " wealthy men " called " agitated classes "—" paid state officials, men of letters, lawyers, and the individuals charged with public education ".[3] The antipathy towards the intelligentsia is equally well marked, if rather more crudely expressed, in the words of Francis I : " I have no use for the so-called geniuses and scholars ; they always want to be cleverer than everybody else and hold up business, or everyday business displeases them. To have common sense and to stick to one's work, that's the best." [4]

The obscurantist measures which were taken in order to suppress the intelligentsia were as thorough as could be expected from a Government which suffered chronically from a great many incompetent officials. They were directed mainly against all institutions of public instruction. The Emperor told a group of teachers at Laybach : " I want not scholars, but good citizens.

---

[1] Pirchegger, op. cit., p. 73.
[2] *Mein Antheil an der Politik*, IV, Stuttgart, 1833, p. 72.
[3] *Memoirs*, III, p. 467. Metternich's distrust of the men of letters was based on a certain tradition. Cobenzl, one of his predecessors, had written to Colloredo on August 6th, 1802 : " Je n'aime pas plus que Votre Excellence la personne des auteurs."
[4] I have tried to give an impression of the slovenly Viennese style of the Emperor's actual words.

It is your duty to educate youth in this direction. Whoever serves me must teach according to my orders. Whoever is not able to do so, or starts new ideas going, must go or I will eliminate him." [1] University teachers saw themselves faced with the same alternatives. The fiction had to be upheld that there existed a kind of special Austrian truth.[2] Professors and lecturers received precise syllabuses laying down not merely the general principles decided on by the Government, but exact details for their work. There were but few professors who, concerned with subjects of obvious social implications, felt in spite of several official warnings that in a higher sense it was their duty to " start going "—to profess—new ideas. Yet there was one among them whose outstanding importance, not only in the field of mathematics and the theory of knowledge but also as the writer of a Communist utopia, will, I believe, soon be established : Bernhard Bolzano of Prague University.[3] He too, of course, lost his professorship. There was, indeed, only one outlet : music. Grillparzer enviously remarked to Beethoven in 1823 : " Censorship does not affect music." [4] On the whole, Prince Dietrichstein was not unfair in his judgment of the ministers and high officials when he remarked to Prokesch von Osten in 1822 : " Every day they are lying to the Emperor about the happiness of his subjects, and are condemning everybody who speaks the truth." [5]

The obscurantism of the Austrian Government had also, so far as education was concerned, a preventive side. It was not, apparently, that the people had to be led because they were ignorant ; but they had to be kept ignorant so that they would let themselves be led. " We cannot be surprised ", remarked John Stuart Mill in 1823, " that those who are interested in misgovernment should raise a cry against the diffusion of knowledge on the ground that it renders the people dissatisfied with their institutions." [6] For this reason even elementary education, for example, was in certain districts of the Austrian Empire accessible only to people of some wealth. It is significant that

---

[1] Pirchegger, op. cit., p. 92.   [2] Schneller, op. cit., p. 415.

[3] Bolzano's Utopia is entitled *Von dem besten Staat* and was written about 1840. The author wished that it should not be published until 100 years after his death. Actually the work was published in Münster in 1933 and in Prague in 1934. While teaching at the University, Bolzano had already anticipated some of the ideas later expressed in the Utopia ; he was therefore " eliminated ".

[4] *Grillparzer's Gespräche*, ed. August Sauer, II, Wien, 1905, p. 185.

[5] F. Engel-Janosi, *Die Jugendzeit des Grafen Prokesch von Osten*, Innsbruck, 1938, pp. 37–8.

[6] Speech on the Utility of Knowledge before the Mutual Improvement Society, *Autobiography*, p. 274.

an elementary school in Mantua which used the method of instruction devised by Bell and Lancaster was ordered by the Provincial Government to close down ; it had ventured to teach even those who could not afford to pay any fees at all. Even so harmless an institution as the Kindergarten was opposed by the Empress Caroline Augusta, Francis's fourth wife, on the ground that it might foster too much enlightenment among the lower orders. Another preventive measure was that by an Imperial order the official newspapers—there were no others—were forbidden even to mention the word " Constitution " (Staatsverfassung). Censorship and the like did not, however, greatly affect the masses ; they could say what they liked about ministers, generals, bishops and abbots so long as their criticism and abuse were directed against individuals, not against the Government or its policy.[1]

There was also complete agreement between the Austrian and British rulers as regards the rôle of the Church. In Austria as in Britain the official Church was supported at this time, for it was looked upon as the most valuable of allies in the continual struggle against the ideas of the Enlightenment, and indeed against any idea of complete social innovation. The Catholic Church, being for many reasons dependent on the favour of the Austrian Government, was therefore entrusted with the education of those of all ages in that spirit which the Emperor so bluntly prescribed. It thus held, among many other privileges, almost a monopoly of teaching. Even in the Universities the students were compelled to attend a great many lectures on the Catholic religion, however little it had to do with their special subject. The Minister of Police explained to Professor Schneller : " His Majesty desires the purely monarchical and the purely Catholic, because they essentially support and strengthen each other." [2] This too is why certain books which had been passed by the censor under Joseph II now had to be re-examined ; almost a hundred were forbidden, among them works by Voltaire, Rousseau, Helvetius, Diderot, and Bayle. Certain famous foreign books of more recent origin appeared in expurgated editions, the Government pretending that these contained the full text.[3]

Finally, the views of the Austrian and the British Govern-

---

[1] Schneller, op. cit. p. 383.
[2] Schneller's letter to his wife Gabriele, dated October 8th, 1821. (Lebensumriss, Hinterlassene Werke, I, Stuttgart, 1840, p. 211.)
[3] The technical name for this was " maskierter Nachdruck ". (Schneller, Österreichs Einfluss auf Deutschland und Europa, II, Stuttgart, 1829, pp. 417, 419.)

ments coincided as to the choice of an instrument which seemed indispensable for the policy they were carrying out. In 1793, approximately, that is, at the very time when certain London magistrates and the Home Office were collaborating to establish a systematic method of spying on the earliest radical societies,[1] the foundation of the Polizeihofstelle took place in Vienna. In both countries the climax in this respect was reached about 1817. In England the notorious Oliver was then sent out principally, as Mr. Hiley Addington explained in Parliament, with a view to gaining information about the Midlands rising in June ; [2] in Austria Sedlnitzky, who prided himself on being a pupil of Fouché, became Minister of Police. Under his régime spies were introduced even into the lecture rooms of the Universities, and according to a persistent rumour significant in itself, two of the Emperor's brothers who had shown liberal tendencies were at times watched.[3] Even Gentz complained bitterly about his correspondence being searched, and according to the *Note confidentielle sur le degré de sûreté des communications* which he sent to Prince Caradja in April 1816 by a specially reliable messenger, not even Metternich's order to the Secret Cabinet expressly forbidding the opening of Gentz's correspondence was able to stop the police in this activity.[4]

But the precariousness of a system which had to rely to such an extent on measures of this kind is perhaps best illustrated by the fact that the whole of the expeditionary force which in 1821 was sent to crush the revolution in Naples had itself to be kept under observation by the police at Sedlnitzky's order.[5] At the same time Metternich described the intervention against Naples as a police action. Never had the question *Quis custodiet ipsos custodes ?* been so topical.

We will now turn to the condition of affairs in the other States which, together with Austria, belonged to the newly-constituted German Confederation. To what extent was Capodistria right when he stated, in 1819, in a conversation with Lebzeltern in Warsaw : " The German princes have called the people to arms against Napoleon as the instigator of all their sufferings. The

---

[1] Philip Anthony Brown, *The French Revolution in English History*, London, 1918, p. 171.
[2] Hansard, *Parliamentary Debates*, XXXVI, p. 1422.
[3] Stern, *Geschichte Europas*, I, p. 223.
[4] August Fournier, " Gentz und das Geheime Kabinett ", in : *Historische Studien und Skizzen*, 3. Reihe, Wien-Leipzig, 1912, pp. 225, 228.
[5] Anton Springer, *Geschichte Österreichs seit dem Wiener Frieden 1809*, I, Leipzig, 1863, p. 289.

enemy has been defeated, and the people are now worse off than before " ?

Although we must be careful not to minimize the tremendous difference which existed between conditions in Eastern and Western Germany, it can be said that all over the country people's expectations were bitterly disappointed. The Swabian poet Uhland, commemorating the third anniversary of the Leipzig *Völkerschlacht*, wrote in 1816 :

> *Man sprach einmal von Festgeläute,*
> *Man sprach von einem Feuermeer ;*
> *Doch was das grosse Fest bedeute,*
> *Weiss es denn jetzt noch irgend wer ?*

> *Nicht rühmen kann ich, nicht verdammen,*
> *Untröstlich ist's noch allerwärts.*

Prussia, the most active among Napoleon's German enemies, had done most in the way of raising the hopes of those on whose active support the Government felt increasingly obliged to rely. After Jena, Stein and Hardenberg had initiated what the latter described as a " revolution from above ". In order to unite the nation against Napoleon they had, much to the disgust of the big landowners, especially those of East Prussia, somewhat loosened the shackles of feudalism. When popular enthusiasm no longer seemed indispensable, the revolution from above not only came to a sudden end, but soon gave way to the long-customary reaction from above.

Already, between 1799 and 1805, the crown peasants had been emancipated. In October 1807 a decree abolished serfdom altogether ; that is to say, the peasants belonging to private landowners, and not to the Crown, were emancipated also. Among the numerous comments which were made on this decree, one, I think, deserves special attention. Councillor Scharnweber of the War Ministry, who was in close touch with the Prime Minister, Hardenberg, noted that for many of the peasants concerned " freedom " meant merely that " they were being reduced from peasants to day-labourers ". No longer were they chained to the soil for their lifetime : but, in the Councillor's words, " they had to yield to being driven away ".[1]

---

[1] In the Berlin archives there is a file of documents containing a copy of the newspaper *Der Volksfreund*, dated August 3rd, 1808. One of the Cabinet Ministers had anonymously contributed a short article on the decree in question, and Scharnweber made a few marginal notes on that copy. (G. F. Knapp, " Anmerkungen zum Vortrag : Die Landarbeiter bei der Stein-Hardenbergschen Gesetzgebung ", *Schmollers Jahrbuch*, Neue Folge, XVIII, 1894, pp. 90–91).

However, it must needs be admitted that the peasants' " freedom ", which they were granted in 1807, worked both ways : they were allowed to move away and the *Fron* (*corvée*) was abolished. The spirit of the Enlightenment came into view. Prussia, it is true, had first to be utterly defeated by Napoleon before she embarked upon the path of progress in this respect, but now apparently nothing could stop her. Looking back in 1827, C. D. Grabbe wrote to a friend : " Prussia was the conqueror for seven years (1756–63), and she has suffered for seven years (1806–13). She has gained more by her seven years' suffering than by her seven years' success." [1]

The combined resistance of the Junkers did in fact stop Prussia on her progressive path. At first the more powerful of them, those of East Prussia, made in effect the following proposal. We must, they said, have labourers on our estates ; if serfdom is to be abolished, we must be allowed to take over the peasants' part of the land ; " Bauernlegen " (" putting down of peasants ") must be revived. The peasant will then have no land, and what will he be able to do but to work on our estates ? Administrative law, according to which the " putting down of peasants " was forbidden, stood in the way. But economic liberalism soon removed this restriction. Free trade became the slogan. Why not, then, free trade in the peasants' parts of the land ? In fact, between 1808 and 1816 new legislation was introduced, slowly and surreptitiously, permitting the aggrandisement of the seigneur's estate at the expense of the peasant's part. [2] It would thus seem as if the Junkers had won a total victory. This was not quite the case. After a long struggle between the more progressive elements in the higher civil service on the one hand and the Junkers on the other, a compromise was agreed upon. Two decrees were important in this connection : the first of 1811, due partly to the influence of Councillor Scharnweber, the second of 1816. A certain category of peasants, those, namely, who were capable of harnessing their own yoke of oxen, could become full proprietors of their part of the land, if they so desired ; they had, indeed, to abandon a certain portion of it to the Junker, but the rest, half or a third, they retained. The Junker could always offer to buy the peasants' land ; but now that they were proprietors they would sell only if they wished to do so. This

---

[1] Letter to Kettembeil, *Sämmtliche Werke*, IV, Detmold, 1874, p. 406.
[2] G. F. Knapp, *Die Landarbeiter bei der Stein-Hardenbergschen Gesetzgebung*, Strassburg, 1891.

privileged category of Prussian peasants had now, at last, also got rid of *Fron*. But there still remained, to the satisfaction of the Junkers, a category of peasants more or less in the same position as before : the poorest. They possessed small holdings, but could be driven away at any time by the Junker. Their holdings were, in most cases, so small that they could not possibly live on them. They thus supplied rural wage labour ; they became day-labourers on miserable wages. This category was, after 1816, no better off than the peasants of Mecklenburg. By the reforms of 1807–16 they had, in effect, gained nothing ; on the contrary, they had lost a great deal. They had gained nothing, for they still had to perform labour services under conditions allowing them to keep just above starvation-level. They had lost much, for the Junker, so long as they had been his " Roboters ", had also been in some degree their protector. Now they were free, but their freedom meant essentially freedom from this precarious yet not entirely useless protection. The question of the day-labourers was thus once more decided in favour of the landowning aristocracy. Gentz, the cynic, was right when he said : " The liberation of the fatherland amounts to nothing more than reinstating the Prussian nobility in its old rights so that it may remain untaxed."

The plight of the peasants was by no means confined to East Prussia. On the whole, it may be said that the most outrageous features of German feudalism were concentrated in Mecklenburg and Holstein. In the eighteenth century it had actually happened more than once that Junkers had played cards not for money, but for human beings : the loser paid one serf. Serfs had quite frequently been sold in Holstein as well as in Mecklenburg. But this institution was by no means a relic of the Middle Ages. On the contrary, it was introduced only after the Thirty Years' War, and became more widespread during the eighteenth century. Even after 1815 conditions in Mecklenburg and Holstein remained extremely miserable. In both Mecklenburg-Schwerin and Mecklenburg-Strelitz the free movement of the great majority of the inhabitants was restricted to such an extent that in the words of a Mecklenburg historian these people had no fatherland, but only a father-village or a father-town. In January 1820 serfdom was abolished in both Mecklenburgs. All that the reform meant in practice was that the peasant now had the right to leave the estate—the freedom to starve.

In Western Germany, the position of the peasants was far

less miserable. This was due in part to the more immediate influence of the French Revolution. But the progressive character of the legislation introduced in some of the Western German States about 1800 has been exaggerated by some authors. Of Baden, for example, all we are told is that serfdom was abolished there in 1783. But in fact this reform applied only to a part of the country. So far as the rest was concerned, the Grand Duke confined himself in the main to renaming the old institution of serfdom (*Leibeigenschaft*), which continued to exist, " hereditary obligation " (*Erbpflicht*). Similarly in Württemberg the nobility for twenty successive years obstructed the execution of the decree of 1819 by which serfdom was supposed to have been abolished. In Bavaria and Hesse, where the decrees were published in 1808 and 1811 respectively, reform seems to have been more effective.

The general agricultural situation indeed furnished sufficient reason for the deepest apprehension. The effects of the Continental blockade proved of great disadvantage to Germany. Before the blockade, Germany had exported considerable quantities of grain to England. When this export had virtually stopped, and Russian grain likewise could no longer be imported into England, Britain's agriculture had to be readjusted to meet the rapidly increasing demand. When the Continental blockade was suspended, it was no longer absolutely indispensable to Great Britain to import grain from the Continent. But it was not only the export of grain which suffered heavily from the blockade : the export of timber was hampered in no less degree. This meant, as Sartorius von Waltershausen points out, a serious decline in the activity of Germany's Baltic ports, so that they were not in a position to recover quickly enough to participate fully in the North Sea trade which after 1815 was again on the increase.

Conditions in German towns were hardly better than in the country, though it is probably true to say that the depression was of shorter duration in industry than in agriculture.[1] For a time Voltaire's prophecy that Germany was condemned to eternal poverty seemed justified. We know very little about the wages and working conditions of that time ; no one as yet has been able to overcome the innumerable and serious difficulties which hinder

---

[1] Cf. Wilhelm Treue, " Wirtschaftszustände und Wirtschaftspolitik in Preussen 1815–1825 ", Beiheft 31 zur *Vierteljahrsschrift für Sozial- und Wirtschaftsgeschichte*, 1937, p. 31.

research on this important question. Yet there exists a considerable contemporary literature on the poor.[1] The causes of poverty were manifold. Above all, the suspension of the Continental blockade had the same effects in Prussia as in Austria. On the one hand, under the blockade English competition was suspended, and this encouraged home industries. On the other, those industries which relied almost entirely on exports found their markets closed. The woollen, iron and steel industries, in which the superiority of English goods had been most marked, flourished during the blockade, and at the Leipzig Fair of 1810 it was reported that the demand for these products outran the supply ; it was the liveliest fair yet held in Germany. East of the Elbe, the only industry to profit by the exclusion of English competition was the Silesian mining industry. Exports from Eastern Germany, especially of Brandenburg cloth and Berlin silk, suffered through the blockade ; this was especially true of the linen industry of Silesia, which had already suffered badly in the preceding period of the war, and now with the closing of the port of Hamburg almost collapsed. Even after the blockade was lifted, things were no better, for England had recovered all her foreign markets with the aid of the power-looms and spinning-jennies which she had adopted in advance of her Continental competitors. She now poured her yarn and her stored-up colonial sugars into the Hanse towns.[2] The Continental industries should be smothered at birth—this saying of Henry Brougham, the prominent Whig politician, was highly significant. Even during the blockade, thirty English commercial firms maintained branch establishments on the small island of Heligoland ; small trawlers used to traffic between Heligoland and the mouths of the Elbe and the Weser ; and thus English goods had even at that time found their way into Germany. But after 1815, German markets were simply flooded with English goods.

The unemployment problem was aggravated by the great number of soldiers who had to find their way back into civilian life,[3] as well as by the peasants pouring into Berlin, who had had to pay the landowner so much for their liberation

---

[1] Cf. P. Mombert, " Aus der Literatur über die soziale Frage und über die Arbeiterbewegung in Deutschland in der ersten Hälfte des 19. Jahrhunderts ", *Archiv für die Geschichte des Sozialismus und der Arbeiterbewegung*, ed. Carl Grünberg, IX, 1921, pp. 177 and passim.

[2] J. H. Clapham, *The Economic Development of France and Germany 1815–1914*, 4th ed., Cambridge, 1936, p. 87.

[3] R. Sartorius von Waltershausen, *Deutsche Wirtschaftsgeschichte, 1815–1914*, 2. Aufl., Jena, 1923, p. 35.

that what was left of the land was no longer sufficient to feed them.[1]

The poor state of communications all over Germany increased the general depression. Bad harvests in the surrounding country-side brought much suffering to town-dwellers, as food could not easily be brought from a distance. Industry, too, was greatly hampered by transport difficulties, as coal and iron had to be brought together ; for example, a short distance of about 50 miles was considered a real barrier to the growth of the iron-smelting industry.

The survival of the guilds formed a serious obstacle to the development of the manufacture of machine-made articles ; the guilds were afraid that their prices might be undercut. In Prussia a decree of 1810 removed the obligation upon artisans to join one of the guilds. But for a long time to come the decree was nullified in practice simply by the refusal of guild members to employ journeymen who had undergone their apprenticeship with artisans not belonging to a guild, with the result that men who did not belong to a guild could not find apprentices, and their output was consequently restricted. In Württemberg a compromise was effected : guilds were not abolished, but it was no longer absolutely necessary for an artisan to belong to one. In Baden and Saxony, the guilds remained powerful until the 1860s ; entrance to them, however, was made easier, and some of the abuses which had become apparent during the eighteenth century were removed.

The slow growth of German industry had yet another cause ; the existence of numerous customs barriers. As early as the fourteenth century, an Englishman had referred to the multiplicity of customs barriers in Germany as *miram Germanorum insaniam.* In the eighteenth century, no central authority existed to check the 300 rulers in Germany in their levying of excise and customs. Duties were levied not only at the frontiers, but also on the roads and rivers, at town gates, at fairs and markets. It is estimated that there were about 1,800 customs frontiers in Germany in 1790. The territorial changes wrought by Napoleon improved matters in this respect, for they reduced the number of States. Between 1807 and 1812 the three Southern States, Bavaria, Württemberg and Baden, dropped most of their internal dues. But the adminis-tration of customs was still very confused, for few States had

[1] Franz Schnabel, *Deutsche Geschichte im neunzehnten Jahrhundert,* II, Freiburg i. B., 1933, p. 294.

A.N.W.

customs frontiers of the modern type ; most of them raised revenue by various local excise dues. As a result of all this, legitimate internal trade was seriously hampered, and contraband traffic greatly encouraged. Many suggestions were made in the years that followed the Napoleonic Wars for the formation of a Customs Union. At Carlsbad, in the summer of 1819, the question was raised officially. Metternich postponed discussion on the subject until the Ministers' Conference in Vienna which was to begin in November of that year. But no practical results were achieved by that Conference so far as economic affairs were concerned.

On the whole it may be said that the position of the German people deteriorated somewhat after 1815. If we add to this the climatic catastrophe of 1816 which brought about the worst harvest of the century, so that dwellers in some localities had to make their bread from the bark of trees, the mass emigration from Germany then beginning, mainly to the U.S.A. (20,000 in twelve months [1]) but partly also to Russia, becomes understandable.

The deterioration in the position of the common people in Germany was not absolute only ; there is enough contemporary evidence to show that it was also relative as compared with the position of the aristocracy. This tiny minority succeeded not only in preserving or regaining their immense social and economic privileges—especially in East Prussia, Saxony, Mecklenburg and Hanover—but also in extending the great amount of landed property they already possessed. The half-hearted liberation of the serfs soon turned out favourably for the big landowners, for in many cases the newly-acquired freedom, as we have seen, meant for the peasant nothing but the freedom to sell out to one who, having ceased to be his legal, still remained his economic master. In these circumstances, the German aristocracy after 1815 grew bolder from year to year. At the Congress of Vienna an association of German aristocrats was founded ; its statutes referred to the people as the " subjects of the nobility ". In Silesia, the Aristocratic Association openly proclaimed its purpose to be " the recovery of the rights and property of the German nobility, which had succumbed only to a period full of morbid political theories ". The means for achieving this " renaissance

---

[1] In large ports, such as Amsterdam, many of these emigrants had to wait for years if they were not sent back by the Dutch for they had not enough money left for the fare overseas. The greater part of their scanty possessions they had in the meantime given to agents of all kinds, swindlers in fact, who promised these desperate people anything and everything.

of the nobility " was to consist in " accustoming public opinion to the nobility's more determined appearance at the head of the nation, for as soon as the forces of opinion and custom were won over, the force of law would then obligingly stretch out a helping hand ".[1] The great classical scholar Niebuhr is our witness ; he testifies to the fact that middle-class people had not been treated with so great disfavour for the past forty years. Even so late as 1825, Varnhagen von Ense, the anti-aristocratic aristocrat, reports : " The aristocracy is gaining in strength daily : first at court, then in the army and administration. It is true, of course, that the individual aristocrat is not looked up to as much as he used to be, but the aristocracy as a whole has perhaps gained in this respect." [2] In a Protestant country, as Friedrich von Schlegel shrewdly remarked,[3] this artificial superiority of the aristocracy was bound to make itself felt especially strongly because of the lack of a genuinely higher organ.

The Saxon Immermann, who was not an aristocrat, sympathized to some extent with the aristocracy. He knew that feudalism, with its over-valuation of social prestige, would soon be replaced by industrialism with its over-valuation of Mammon, but his heart was on the side of the lost cause. He realized very clearly that in the long run the nobility was doomed. Intellectually it was no longer leading the nation. When, in 1816, Prince Radziwill in Berlin arranged a performance of Goethe's *Faust*, it was discovered that not one of the assembled noblemen knew the drama or even possessed a copy of it. In Immermann's novel *Münchhausen*, an aristocrat utters the significant words : " Too much knowledge is not decent in a cavalier." Similarly, Heine described the knights who appear in the German novels of the die-hard aristocrat *émigré* de la Motte Fouqué as consisting of iron and " Gemüt ", but lacking flesh and reason.

Immermann saw that the aristocracy was rotten to the core ; the façade alone was still standing. " The nobility of to-day ", he said, " is like a ruin." In his greatest novel he referred to them and, indeed, to all those whose function as a ruling class seemed to have come to an end, as " Epigonen ".[4] Achim von

---

[1] Paul Kampffmeyer, *Geschichte der modernen Gesellschaftsklassen in Deutschland*, Berlin, 1896, p. 121.
[2] Quoted by M. von Boehn, *Biedermeier. Deutschland von 1815–1847*, Berlin, 1911, p. 276.
[3] *Signatur des Zeitalters*, Concordia, VI, 1823, p. 393.
[4] Joseph von Eichendorff, too, in his essay *Deutsches Adelsleben am Schlusse des achtzehnten Jahrhunderts* (1857) criticized the Romantic illusions of the aristocracy and their intransigent adherence to all that belonged to a bygone age.

Arnim, the Prussian aristocratic Romanticist, though never carrying his criticism so far as Immermann, points out an essential weakness of the post-Napoleonic aristocracy in his little-known essay *Metamorphosen der Gesellschaft* (1825) : " They regard piety as a restorative for the state." [1] This is why the new court preacher Strauss, whose thundering sermons filled the Cathedral of Berlin from 1822, was welcomed there in the same fashion as was Zacharias Werner in Vienna. Among his pious listeners there were so many officers that people spoke of a new regiment of " Tartuffe dragoons ". Before long, piety without God began to influence public opinion ; its organ was called *Berliner Politisches Wochenblatt*.

An examination of the attitude of those who were most affected by the state of affairs described above shows a world of difference between town and country. Field-Marshal Gneisenau, a shrewd observer, stated in 1818 : " In all the towns everybody talks about the constitution ; in the provinces the subject is hardly mentioned at all ; all that people want there is to be freed from the fear of new taxes." Similarly, Gentz reported from the Rhineland in the same year : " It is absolutely untrue that the Prussian Government is hated here for the reason that they have not yet introduced a constitution. The immense majority does not think of this at all. They do hate the Prussian Government, very much so, and without concealing it, but for totally different reasons." [2]

The agrarian population everywhere cared as little for German nationalism as for constitutional ideals. [3] Both these movements were for a long time confined to the urban population and, within that section, to intellectuals. Perthes, a leading German bookseller of the time, in a letter written in 1819, shrewdly remarked : " Our political literature, to its great disadvantage, in contradistinction to that of England and France, is being written by bookworms." The leading part played by the University students, above all, in the national movement can, I think, be ex-

---

[1] *Sämmtliche Werke*, XV, Berlin, 1846, p. 46. Cf. also the following stanza from Chamisso's *Nachtwächterlied* :

> *Hört, ihr Herrn, so soll es werden :*
> *Gott im Himmel, wir auf Erden,*
> *Und der König absolut,*
> *Wenn er unsern Willen tut.*
> *Lobt die Jesuiten !*

[2] Letter to Pilat, 29th September 1818. Several years later Prussian officers told Varnhagen that living in the Rhineland they felt as though they were in an enemy country ; they were so hated and alien to the population.

[3] Schnabel, op. cit., p. 94.

plained as follows. In the Napoleonic Wars soldiers from many different parts of Germany had fought side by side against the French invader, but after 1815 the overwhelming majority of them went back to their narrow little sovereign States, probably never to meet their war comrades from other parts of Germany again. The students, however, were in a very different position. Following an old tradition, German students used to visit at least two or three universities before taking their degree. Thus it came about that the more famous German universities always attracted students from all over Germany. That is why the Silesian Romanticist Joseph von Eichendorff, in his autobiographical sketch *Halle und Heidelberg*, called the German universities the last resort of German unity.[1] Middle-class people —for such most of the students were—many of them with some war experiences in common, here met again, and again discovered, if indeed they had ever forgotten,[2] that the differences between the subjects of the thirty-nine sovereign princes were not nearly as great as most of these princes and their bureaucracies had, for obvious reasons, made them believe. The polished High German spoken and written in the universities must have constituted yet another factor in the direction of unification.

It may be of some interest to recall the theory which Wellington put forward as an explanation of the difference between German and British universities considered as factors in politics. " Is it not curious ", the Duke asked Stanhope in 1839, " that all the mischief in Germany seems to have its rise in the Universities ; while in this country we look to the Universities, and to the state of feeling there, as one of our main sources of security ? " The explanation, according to Wellington, could be found in two facts. In the first place, in Germany the young men did not reside in the colleges—they were removed from all moral training or control, and open only to secular instruction. Secondly, the professors and tutors were not paid fixed salaries, but received optional fees from those who attended their lectures ; consequently they were dependent on their pupils instead of their pupils being dependent on them.[3] So far as concerns Wellington's first point, the absence of a moral tutor and the lack of

---

[1] *Gesammelte Werke*, VI, p. 422.

[2] Some of them might have forgotten : the exhausting drill of the barrack-squares, unnecessary and tiring marches, unending useless parades where the cleaning of hundreds of articles, the folding of overcoats, the combing of hair, were the main items on the programme—all this proved, in some cases at least, sufficient to deaden the enthusiasm in these young hearts for any higher ideals. (Boehn, op. cit., p. 19.)

[3] Stanhope, op. cit., p. 196.

personal contact between academic teacher and pupil, it certainly
accounts for something.   Another fact, overlooked by the Duke,
goes much further, however, to explain early liberal " mischief "
in the German universities.   After a long journey through Germany in 1819, William Jacob the economist wrote :   " The
number of students in the Universities of Germany is much
greater, in proportion to the population, and to the wealth of the
country, than in England." [1]   He continues :   " Many young
men, after completing their university career with honour, are
glad to fill stations, the duties of which could be as well performed
by youths of very common qualities."   Obviously the same could
not be said of England, where the wealth of the country almost
guaranteed every graduate a satisfactory job.   This explains to
some extent why the figure of Baccalaureus,[2] " the personification
of that arrogance which is especially characteristic of youth ",[3]
was conceived in Germany and not in England.

German professors, again, were not so well off as their English
counterparts.   There is certainly a great deal of truth in Wellington's explanation for the " mischief " on their part.   The Duke's
materialist interpretation was corroborated by a man of very
different political convictions.   The Liberal professor Schneller
wrote from Freiburg-im-Breisgau to his stepson Prokesch in 1825 :
" The Liberals are Envy personified . . . I must approve the
principle, but I cannot respect the persons." [4]

A great deal has been said about the connection between
liberalism and nationalism in early nineteenth-century Germany.
Yet which was cause and which effect is still extremely doubtful.
Attempts at unification naturally met with fierce opposition from
the sovereigns as well as from the higher nobility ;   this may
account in part for the liberal attitude of some of the most outstanding apostles of unified Germany.   It would seem from this
that nationalism begot liberalism.   On the other hand, it cannot
be denied that there is also some truth in the argument of the
German historian Franz Schnabel, that the ideological situation
in post-Napoleonic Germany was just the opposite.   Those who
advocated a national State did so because they thought that a
powerful State would give them the greatest measure of protection
against the licentiousness of their respective petty tyrant-princes.
Over a hundred years have gone by since then, and it is easy to

---

[1] *A View of the Agriculture, Manufacture, Statistics and State of Society of Germany,
and Parts of Holland and France*, London, 1820, p. 231.

[2] *Faust*, second part, Act II, Sc. i.

[3] Goethe to Eckermann in 1829.   [4] *Hinterlassene Werke*, II, p. 115.

stress the fallacy of such expectations. Nevertheless, the possibility that they played an important rôle at the time cannot be excluded. After all, the petty tyrant-prince was always in sight, but the Leviathan of the future was inconceivable, especially as nineteenth- and twentieth-century technique had not then provided the instruments so indispensable to the modern monster.

The preponderance of intellectuals among the heralds as well as the followers of liberal thought in Germany had a decided and obvious effect. The value of a written constitution was more emphasized there than in any other country. The intellectual not only has a predilection for the written word ; he is also, rightly or wrongly, inclined to believe that a system of rules, once it is written down, will serve as a fairly reliable guide to people's actual behaviour, and that he thus will be able to foresee that behaviour. That is why Kant's conception of *Rechtsstaat* attained such importance in German liberalism. The idea that man is free if he has to obey not persons but only statutes, certainly makes its main appeal to intellectuals. Uneducated folk—and perhaps also those who have come to regard it as a self-deception [1] —fail to see the subtle distinction upon which Kant based his peculiar liberal ideology. There is ample evidence to show the special importance which German liberalism attached to a written constitution. Above all, it is very significant that King Frederick William III was obliged no less than five times between 1807 and 1820, to pledge his word that such a constitution would soon be introduced.[2]

It is hard to believe that such a movement, confined as it was almost exclusively to the universities, could have constituted a very serious threat to those in power. This was also Gneisenau's opinion. At the beginning of August 1819, that is at the time when Austrian and Prussian representatives were secretly at Teplitz to devise some means to crush the " conspiracy " in Germany, the field-marshal wrote in a letter : " Neither an actual conspiracy nor a society with oaths and mysteries has been discovered so far, merely a lot of silly twaddle in letters and articles, all sorts of opinions about various forms of government, a desire for a constitution and for a common Germanity ; a

---

[1] Cf. for example, Hsun-tze, quoted by Liang Chi-chao, *History of Chinese Political Thought during the Early Tsin Period*, London, 1930, p. 137 : " There are men who govern, but there are no laws that govern." Similarly, Hölderlin spoke of " Jesetzes-despolie " and of the superstition of clinging to the legal sphere. (*Hyperion*, I Band, 1 Buch.)

[2] Veit Valentin, *Geschichte der deutschen Revolution 1848–1849*, I, Berlin, 1930, p. 26.

great deal of gossip—not exactly eulogies—about officials." [1] A little later the Russian foreign minister expressed a similar judgment about the state of affairs in Germany. Nor did our English traveller Jacob think much of the chances of constitutionalism in that country : " No two that I converse with, could agree even on the preliminary step to what they all clamoured to obtain." [2]

In an earlier part of this book the conclusion was arrived at that the English Government seems to have greatly overrated the chances then existing of a revolution in England ; and this conclusion is, I think, all the more justified in the case of Germany. The German princes were terrified when the Students' Union was formed in Jena, claiming to be the personification of German unity. One of the leaders of this Union, Karl Follen, was busy initiating young men into a career of politico-religious martyrdom; he tried to establish among them a Union of Death-brethren, an idea which came to him from the horror themes of the knight and robber romances.[3] The German rulers were also shocked when they learned what had happened at the Wartburg festival on October 18th, 1817. But the greater part of the ceremonies which took place there seem to have been harmless enough. The grotesque *auto-da-fé*, which had been devised by Jahn, " the father of gymnastics ", certainly showed bad taste. But it was only a side-show, in which few of the visitors took part ; the contents of the books were practically unknown to the youngsters who posed as their judges. Besides, not only was reactionary stuff like Haller's *Restauration der Staatswissenschaften* or Kamptz's *Kodex der Gendarmerie* condemned to the flames, but also the *Code Napoléon*. Follen's folly and this narrow-minded spiritual autarky [4] were, I suggest, sure signs of immaturity.

Another symptom was antisemitism, which began once more

---

[1] Quoted by Hans Delbrück, *Das Leben des Feldmarshalls Neithart von Gneisenau*, V (the first volumes were written by G. H. Pertz), Berlin, 1880, p. 391. Delbrück's date for this letter has been corrected by A. Stern, op. cit., p. 566, n. 1.

[2] Jacob, op. cit., p. 222.

[3] Boehn, op. cit., p. 33.

[4] Another symptom : Jahn quite seriously suggested that Germany should plant a big swampy forest on her western border ; it was to be protected by double fortifications, and filled with bison, bears, and wolves, thus forming impenetrable waste land. It would be erroneous, however, to think that preposterous suggestions of this kind were specifically German. In Russia, Shishkov had gone so far as to declare that Frenchmen were a combination of tiger and ape (Masaryk, *Spirit of Russia*, I, London, 1919, pp. 115–16). Nor were *autos-da-fé* at that time confined to Germany. The Société des Missions de France held one in which the works of Voltaire and Rousseau were consigned to the flames. A few years later, " suspicious " foreign books were burned at Kazan University.

to rear its ugly head. Just at the time when, according to the decision reached at the Congress of Vienna, the Jews of Frankfurt-am-Main acquired the legal status of " Israelitische Bürger," [1] Varnhagen reported from that city : " The prejudice against the Jews has become deeply rooted, and not only do the mob display the base emotion of hatred, but some educated people stand on exactly the same level in this respect." [2] His wife Rahel, *née* Levin, who like Dorothea Schlegel, Henriette Herz, and a few other Jewesses, had done much cultural work in Germany, wrote in 1819 to her brother :

I am extremely sad ; and in such a way as I have never been before. Because of the Jews. What is this crowd of expelled people to do ? They [their enemies] want to keep them, but only in order to torment and despise them, to shout after them " Juden mauschel ", to let them practise low and petty usury, to kick them and throw them downstairs. . . . It is not hatred of their religion ; they themselves do not love their own religion, so how could they hate another ? —why all these words which I could heap up without end ; it is only wickedness in deed and motive ; and it is not the deed of the people, for they have been taught to shout " hep ".

Börne—one of those Jewish literati who might never have become one had a civil service career been open to him—to some extent explained, in an early essay, why antisemitism was increasing at the time when feudalism was fighting a rearguard action against the new forces. He wrote : " The Jews and the nobility, i.e. money and supremacy, material and personal aristocracy, constitute the last two pillars of the feudal system. They cling together. For the Jews, threatened by the people, seek the protection of the nobles, and these, terrified by Equality, seek arms and strength in money." [3] However, this theory failed to give an entirely satisfactory answer to the question why the ill-feeling was not confined to rich Jews.[4] Perhaps for this reason Börne in later years preferred the cruder psychological explanation : " Poor Germans ! Living on the ground floor and oppressed by the seven stories of the higher Estates, they feel relief from their anxiety if they can speak about men living still further below, namely in the cellar." [5] He also compared the

---

[1] Cf. Salo Baron, *Die Judenfrage auf dem Wiener Kongress*, Wien, 1920, p. 204.
[2] *Denkwürdigkeiten des eigenen Lebens*, V, 3. Aufl., Leipzig, 1871, pp. 13–14.
[3] " Für die Juden ", *Gesammelte Schriften*, IV, 2. Aufl., Hamburg, 1840, p. 180.
[4] This applied equally to Börne's *jeu-de-mots* : " Ihr hasst die Juden nicht, weil sie es verdienen ; Ihr hasst sie, weil sie—verdienen." ("Der ewige Jude ", *Gesammelte Schriften*, VI, Wien, 1868, pp. 25–26.)
[5] *Briefe aus Paris*, 7th February 1832.

German people to prison guards of the Jews, guards who themselves are not allowed to leave the prison.

The second spectacular incident (the first being, of course, the Wartburg festival and not the antisemitic scenes), which had a highly alarming effect upon the rulers, was the assassination of Kotzebue by the German student Karl Sand in March 1819 ; the third, the attempted assassination of a high civil servant in Prussia in July of the same year. The analogy with English history is again obvious : horrified though they were at these outrages, the German rulers seem to have received the news not without a certain feeling of satisfaction. They had been suspecting the darkest conspiracies all the time ; now they were almost glad to receive some sort of confirmation. Metternich spoke of the good fortune which had enabled him " to adorn " one of his diplomatic masterpieces with " the example which the exquisite Sand had provided for him at the expense of poor Kotzebue ".[1] When, a couple of weeks earlier, he had received preliminary information of the incident, he had at once decided " to draw the greatest possible advantage from the matter ".[2]

The panic which most of the German princes felt at the very idea of a written constitution was hardly more reasonable. It is well known that Metternich never forgot to warn the Prussian king whenever he feared that his royal confidant might one day fulfil one of his rash pledges. It is known also that Frederick William III was only too pleased to be warned by this well-meaning political confessor.[3] Historians have tended to overlook, however, that the written constitutions introduced in 1818–19 in three South German States (Bavaria, Baden and Württemberg) were anything but revolutionary. In fact, they contained a solemn confirmation of most of the aristocratic privileges. The only feature of them which might inspire conservative circles with apprehension belonged once again to the sphere of words

[1] Metternich to Gentz, Rome, 23rd April 1819. " Poor Kotzebue "—in this connection it is well to recall what Gentz had written to Pilat from Carlsbad on August 20th, 1818 : " As long as matters in Germany remain as they are to-day, Kotzebue is a useful and necessary ally for us. If we can achieve a radical cure for public opinion, then he may fall like other temporary instruments." (*Briefe von Gentz an Pilat*, p. 303.)

[2] Metternich to Gentz, Rome, 9th April 1819.

[3] Cf. also Gentz to Pilat, August 4th, 1818 : " I could write you a long letter about the veneration which the Prussians—the older and more distinguished ones—are feeling for everything connected with Austria : our whole position, our system, our methods, our language and so forth. The personality of Prince Metternich, as well as his kindly and well-calculated behaviour, has now altogether enchanted them. From this aspect, Carlsbad is a very useful place for us." (*Briefe von Gentz an Pilat*, p. 291.)

rather than that of deeds. That is to say, parliaments of a kind were introduced, and thus free discussion of political topics was initiated. Max von Boehn is right to remind us, in his comprehensive work *Biedermeier. Deutschland von 1815–1847*, that this achievement must not be altogether overlooked. At the same time, all necessary precautions were taken to forestall any additional interference in the more essential of these topics. Especially striking was the antinomy between the liberal letter of the constitution of Baden on the one hand, and the reactionary trend of the Grand-Duke's legislation on the other. It was this same antinomy that Gentz had in mind when he called the new Bavarian system " a royal democracy ", thus obviously magnifying its progressive side in order to give emphasis to his verbose lamentations about that sad state of affairs.[1]

If the men then ruling in Germany tended to over-estimate the danger involved for them in both the national and the liberal movements, this may partly be explained by the well-documented fact that just at that time the gulf between the aristocracy and the rest of the population grew markedly wider. This phenomenon was accompanied by a process which, in essentials, bore a close resemblance to the English social history of the time. We have noticed the existence in England of a high degree of class-consciousness in all owners of property of whatever rank ; we have observed the contrast to the lack of integration shown by the masses. In England the possessing class was composed at this time of various elements : the bourgeoisie had already made their way well inside the charmed circle. This was not the case in ·Germany ; here the comparative backwardness of industry and many other factors had worked to prolong the autocratic monopoly. The fact that, during the first half of the nineteenth century, Germany was still preponderantly an agricultural country is brought out when we compare the size of its towns with those of France. The total population of the twelve towns which in 1914 were the largest of the German Empire was in 1815 about 750,000 as against 500,000 in Paris alone.[2] The inhabitants of the smaller towns were frequently engaged for part of their time in agricultural work.

The ruling class in Germany at that time was, with negligible exceptions, identical with the possessing class. This high degree

---

[1] " Eine Denkschrift von Friedrich von Gentz über die erste Baierische Ständever-sammlung ", in : *Deutsche Zeitschrift für Geschichtswissenschaft*, X, 1893, p. 336.
[2] Clapham, *The Economic Development of France and Germany, 1815–1914*, p. 82.

of homogeneity probably favoured the growth of aristocratic class-consciousness. A tangible symptom of integration was to be seen, for example, in the relatively frequent journeys undertaken by aristocrats, and the many contacts they thus made, whereas poor and middle-class people, with the already mentioned exception of the students, mostly stayed for the whole of their lives inside a narrow province or even a still narrower district. But the most obvious symptom of the process was the uniform policy which almost all the German princes, with the approval of by far the greater part of the aristocracy, deemed it necessary to carry out in view of the actual or imagined danger. When Metternich kept admonishing them that " only the closest union among the courts " could exorcize the evil spirits, he knew perfectly well that he was not preaching to unwilling ears. There was a fairly general concurrence with his opinions as voiced in his despatch of January 10th, 1820, to Count Trautmannsdorf, Austrian Ambassador in Stuttgart, in which he drew an interesting comparison between the state of affairs in France and in Germany :

The revolution has passed over France destroying everything that existed there ; property has all changed hands ; the lower classes of society have established themselves in superior positions. In a like order of affairs the same danger no longer exists for France as for countries where everything may still be overthrown because everything is still *in situ.* Any revolution in France must necessarily limit itself to the throne, for the revolutionaries will be well aware how to secure themselves from the deprivations which they have caused to those they have replaced. In Germany, on the other hand, there is an equal threat to everything : to the thrones, to the existence and the fortune of the present owners. Also the spirit and the projects of the German demagogues are directed at the same time to the republic and to the agrarian law.[1]

Small wonder that in these circumstances the only working central authority for the whole of Germany was the Central Committee for Investigation at Mainz, whose task consisted in tracing the slightest indications of political activities other than those sponsored by the aristocracy. In a way, this Committee symbolized the whole paradoxical situation of post-Napoleonic Germany. On the one side, its authority extended right across the boundaries of the thirty-nine " sovereign " Member States of

[1] Friedrich von Weech, *Correspondenzen und Actenstücke zur Geschichte der Minister-konferenzen von Carlsbad und Wien,* Leipzig, 1865, p. 115.

THE ROYAL EXTINGUISHER,
cartoon by G. Cruikshank, 1821

From the Firth Collection in the Bodleian Library

[*face p.* 96

AUTO-DA-FÉ AT THE WARTBURG FESTIVAL, 1817

[*face p.* 97

the German Confederation ; it was aided, in each of these States, by what the people called " smellers-out of demagogues ". On the other side, it was strictly limited to this sphere of activity. Only with a view to the repression of oppositional movements did the princes and the aristocratic circles which shared power with them permit of any violation of the " sovereignty " of the State which they happened to run—and in the preservation of which they had therefore a vested interest. The Thuringian classical scholar, Jacobs, was right when in a letter written in 1817 he called the *Bundestag* a common council chamber of the nobility for the suppression of freedom. The proceedings of the *Bundestag* at Frankfurt, the official central authority of the Con- federation, bear witness to this. How difficult it was for this noble gathering of diplomats—Gentz, in a letter to Pilat, called it a comedy—to reach unanimity on matters not directly or in- directly related to repression ! People were continually being reminded of the uninspiring inaugural address made by the Austrian representative, in which he had insisted that the *Bund* was by no means a *Bundesstaat*, but only a *Staatenbund*, a distinction of which they had only just become aware. Accordingly, " all went off coolly, lackadaisically and pedantically, and public interest was very low ".[1] Pilat, in a letter to Friedrich von Schlegel, written on March 6th, 1819, cleverly summarized the situation in these words : " At the Diet, it is continuously decreed that there is nothing to decree."

One example from the overwhelming amount of evidence for the inactivity of the Bund may be mentioned here as particularly significant. The innumerable customs barriers around each of the thirty-nine States seriously hindered the exchange of even the most essential foodstuffs. In spring 1817, at a time, that is, when hunger and depression had reached a desperate level all over the country, the representative of Württemberg at Frankfurt put forward the suggestion of abolishing all extraordinary restric- tions of mutual traffic in the most indispensable foodstuffs. Even a sub-committee approved of this idea which, indeed, to many people seemed an imperative necessity. But neither Bavaria nor Austria, or, to be more precise, their rulers, were prepared for so bold a step. Francis I was simply horrified. In 1819 the question came up once more. In July, Börne, who had just become editor of the periodical *Zeitschwingen*, announced program- matically : " If we want to make people happy, we must bring

[1] Varnhagen, op. cit., p. 81.

politics down from heaven to earth. No hungry man is satisfied by a treatise on the free export of corn." He added that for this reason, in the *Zeitschwingen*, he would dwell rather on people's hardships than on their rights. The Emperor, however, was still as intransigent as ever. To him as well as to some of the other rulers the scheme seemed incompatible with the " sovereignty " of the individual Member States of the German Confederation.

Considerations of this kind did not enter the Emperor's mind at times when the most far-reaching measures against the impending " revolution " were devised. Nor, in these cases, did many of the other German rulers allow themselves to be restrained by such inhibitions ; in fact the most powerful of them, the King of Prussia,[1] may be said to have cared least about the sovereignty of his State whenever he felt that the sovereignty of his class was seriously threatened. For in 1819, if not earlier, Frederick William III gave the order that Metternich was to be shown even the most secret Prussian documents ; and even before that date, Wittgenstein, who was a member of the Prussian Cabinet, always kept Metternich well informed about questions relating to repression.

Thus it came about that whereas it seemed impossible to organize even an approximately equal distribution of food for the thirty-nine German States, it proved, at least for a time, quite practicable to organize for the same area an exactly equal distribution of political thought. The policy of the Carlsbad decrees of 1819,[2] agreed upon already in principle at the preliminary discussion at Teplitz and confirmed by the Final Act of Vienna in the following year, was an attempt at finding a universal solution to the problem created by the opposition in each of the member States. Strict censorship of almost all

---

[1] If we take into account how Görres characterized Prussia in 1819, the King's apprehensions must, indeed, seem exaggerated. In *Teutschland und die Revolution* Görres wrote : " Since everything here results in a military régime, these two parties [the followers of the old antediluvian creed, and those of the new Napoleonic ideas] are less differentiated here than anywhere else. (*Gesammelte Schriften*, XIII, Köln, 1929.) It was also significant that Prussia spent nearly half her revenue on the army, whereas Württemberg spent only one third, Bavaria one quarter, Austria one sixth, and Baden one ninth of their respective revenues. (Friedrich Meinecke, *Das Leben des Generalfeldmarschalls Hermann von Boyen*, II, Stuttgart, 1899, p. 391, n. 3.)

[2] Metternich, on his way to Carlsbad, wrote to Cardinal Consalvi on July 10th, 1819 : " Je tâcherai de mettre le plus qu'il me sera possible de l'ordre dans un pays où toutes les idées sont en confusion. La disposition des princes allemands est bonne, mais ils sont faibles." (Charles van Duerm, *Correspondance du Cardinal Hercule Consalvi avec le Prince Clément de Metternich, 1815-1823*, Louvain-Bruxelles, 1899, p. 236.)

publications ; [1] an inspector for each university ; [2] informers in most of the lecture rooms and some of the churches ; [3] no vacancy to be filled by an academic teacher who had lost his post in some other part of the Confederation for political reasons : these were the more outstanding of the points upon which the German rulers did not find it difficult to reach agreement. Börne, taking leave of his subscribers in October 1819, spoke of a " Continental blockade of ideas ".[4] In case of obstruction on the part of any member State, military intervention by an army of the Bund was envisaged at Carlsbad.[5] Gentz knew what he was talking about when, at the conclusion of the extraordinary Conference, he expressed his satisfaction at " the greatest retrograde movement which has taken place in Europe since 1789 ".

The verdict of more far-sighted statesmen emphasized the absurdity of the panic. In a letter to Stein, dated 10th October, 1819, Wilhelm von Humboldt described the Carlsbad policy as " raising to its highest pitch the idea of danger, and keeping as a deep secret (for the most part not even revealed to the Staatsministerium) what is dangerous in actual fact ".

Stein himself, though indeed far from sympathizing with the more radical elements among the German Liberals,[6] complained bitterly of " the scandal of the exaggerated and perfidious resolutions of Carlsbad and Vienna ".[7] These were the reasons which he offered for his verdict :

[1] The official paper *Allgemeine Preussische Staatszeitung* was referred to by the people only as *Gemeine Zeitung* (" Mean Newspaper "). As in Austria, ludicrous cases of censorship occurred. In Cologne, the censor would not allow an advertisement of Dante's *Divina Commedia* to be published, for, said he, things divine should not be made the subject of a comedy !

[2] The Saxon educationalist F. T. Thiersch and his son have noticed (Heinrich Thiersch, *Friedrich Thiersch's Leben*, Leipzig-Heidelberg, 1866, pp. 307-8) that soon, that is, in the twenties and thirties, obscurantism was to assume a different though no less dangerous shape. More and more the universities were transformed into training schools for the civil service ; secularization went hand in hand with specialization. The original idea of *universitas* was sacrificed.

[3] For example, Schleiermacher's sermons were taken down word for word by a policeman.

[4] Ludwig Salomon, *Geschichte des deutschen Zeitungswesens*, III, Oldenburg-Leipzig, 1906, p. 206.

[5] A convenient collection of documents concerning the Carlsbad Conference is to be found in L. K. Aegidi, *Aus dem Jahr 1819*, Hamburg, 1861, annex.

[6] For example, in a letter to Görres dated 26th July 1819, he refers to the " plans of our scholarly gymnast-jacobins " (*Briefwechsel* etc., V, p. 585). The same line was taken by his friend Niebuhr who, in a letter to Stein in April 1820, spoke of " this crude Jacobinism the existence of which one does not deny by accusing the rulers at the same time of having provoked and strengthened it " (*ibid.*, p. 625). Consequently, Niebuhr was regarded as a Jacobin by the reactionaries, and as a reactionary by the liberals.

[7] Letter to Capodistria, dated 29th December 1820. (*Briefwechsel*, etc., VI, Berlin, 1934, p. 10.)

Exaggerated, because the criminal doctrines of certain scholars, the extravagances of a number of young men can be coped with— even justified !—by the existing authorities, and do not require the scandalous setting up of an extraordinary tribunal of inquisition ; and perfidious, because Ministers enamoured of arbitrary rule and fearing for their positions have intimidated their monarchs by the phantom of revolution.

CHAPTER V

RUSSIA

Russia, though she had ceased to be the centre of gravity for the far-reaching reforms which her ruler had in mind, was nevertheless by no means entirely neglected by Alexander I during the last decade of his life. No part of the enormous empire, it is true, with the exception of the formerly Polish provinces, received a written constitution. Novosiltsev's project of transforming the whole of Russia into a federation of constitutional member states remained a project, just as did the earlier scheme of Speransky which had been much less revolutionary. Yet it is well to remember that the Tsar seems to have encouraged Novosiltsev to elaborate his scheme, and that shortly before his death he still adhered to the plan of giving a liberal constitution to the whole empire. The significance of such an intention is perhaps more obvious when compared with the horror which men like Metternich never ceased to feel at the very idea of such a constitution. It is also known that at the beginning of 1818 the Tsar ordered Arakcheev to draft a scheme for the liberation of the peasants.

But the Tsar's attempts at reform inside his country were not confined to projects during the first half of the decade following Waterloo. The appalling misery of the serfs as well as of those who had just been liberated was actually alleviated. In 1816, for example, a report was received by the Emperor to the effect that Government officials were purchasing peasants and sending them into the Cossack military lands on the river Don, thus " ruining peasant households and separating peasant families ". This practice was at once prohibited. Various minor restrictions were put upon the exercise of bondage right by estate owners ; as, for example, when in 1818 the Emperor ordered that peasants were not to be required to perform *bartchina* (= work for the landowner) on Sundays and fourteen other days of the year. A ukase in 1818 prescribed that persons who had enjoyed freedom even for a short time should not again become bondmen. Excessive punishment of the peasants was again and again prohibited ; in this respect there was considerable success in the whole of the empire.[1]

[1] James Mavor, *An Economic History of Russia*, 2nd edition, London, 1925, pp. 325–30.

All these achievements in Russia proper were, of course, minor ones compared with the earlier scheme of social reform which the Tsar does not seem even at this time to have abandoned. In the Baltic as well as the formerly Polish provinces, the Tsar went further. As to the former, we have already seen that feudal serfdom was abolished there between 1816 and 1819. As to the latter, several ukases attempted to restrict the arbitrariness of the Polish landowners. One or two examples may be worth mention. The Tsar discovered that the *pomyetscheke* (= landowners) and the renters of estate lands were disregarding the poverty of the peasants caused by poor harvests and epidemics among their cattle, by imposing among other things excessive *bartchina* upon them. The ukase of March 23rd, 1818, sharply condemned these practices. *Pomyetscheke* were required to supply their peasants with grain for consumption and for seed. Nor was this put forward merely as a pious wish. The ukase wisely provided for a sanction. Until the peasants of an estate were secured against want, the use of grain for liquor-making on the estate and the export of grain from the estate were forbidden. Moreover, the punishment for neglect of these provisions was to be the administration of the estate by a State official. The same ukase forbade excessive punishments and reminded the landowners of the ukase of Peter I which had limited the imposition of *bartchina* to three days a week. In 1820, another ukase for the same provinces was directed against the purchase of estates with peasants.

The Tsar's social reform was not only concerned with the deplorable situation of the peasants. This has been testified to in the most reliable way by Major de Clam-Martinitz in his *Mémoire* compiled in 1818 for the use of Metternich ; for Clam-Martinitz, to judge from his general opinion of Alexander I, certainly could not be suspected of being a blind admirer of the Tsar. A certain amount of his enthusiasm for the social achievements of Russia may be discounted ; during his journey through that country Clam-Martinitz was, no doubt, taken mainly to such places as left a favourable impression. On the other hand, he was not easily deceived ; his condemnatory account of the state of affairs in the military colonies is proof of this. This is what he reported about social conditions on the whole :

An impartial observer cannot fail to recognize that the Emperor is ceaselessly occupied with work for his empire, and that, anxiously concerned with the glory of his nation and his own reputation as ruler, he is seeking with energy and zeal to extend public activity to all matters which he can survey. As far as it depends upon himself much good is actually being done, though at times more attention is paid to appearance than to reality. . . . Infirmaries, hospitals, foundling hospitals, homes for poor and aged people, and lunatic asylums are established everywhere in a way fitted for the purpose, in the chief cities even with rare munificence ; they are in full use everywhere. Public education is a chief object of the Emperor. . . . The method of instruction of Bell and Lancaster is already being successfully applied in several institutes of education. Prisons are everywhere organized in a humane way. . . . Capital punishment has been abolished.[1]

The main value of the observations of Clam-Martinitz lies in the fact that he was obviously thinking in terms of comparison with his own country, Austria. This emerges especially clearly from the following passage :

Commerce enjoys the special care of the Emperor. . . . This is proved by the high degree of perfection which has been reached by the factories, by the abundance of valuable machines and inventions of all sorts and especially of steam-engines. . . . The contribution of the government towards this flourishing state of the factories is immense ; from all classes, especially Englishmen and Germans are being attracted with great skill ; the inventions of those countries are being propagated.[2]

As a matter of fact, it is known that the state of the factories at that time existing in Russia was far from flourishing. Clam-Martinitz would have arrived at a different evaluation had he compared it with conditions in Great Britain instead of Austria. For our purpose, however, it is important to note the general tendency of the régime ; in this respect the authority above quoted was undoubtedly right. Even so late as April 1823, in the midst of the period during which Metternich exerted his greatest influence upon Alexander I, Cancrin was appointed Minister of Finance. The main principle of his system, as pro-mised and to some extent, actually carried out, was the promotion of commerce and, accordingly, the encouragement of the activity of factories and productive work in general. It is known that

[1] In March 1819, the Tsar asked members of the Society of Friends who were on a visit to Russia to communicate directly to him whatever they might notice in the prisons, or other places, that they might think proper to bring before him. During a previous conversation the Quakers had acquainted him with the wretched situation of several prisons and poorhouses. (*Memoirs of the Life and Gospel Labours of Stephen Grellet*, ed. B. Seebohm, I, London, 1860, pp. 410, 414.)

[2] The *Mémoire*, written in German, is to be found in Grand-Duc Nicholas Mikhaïlowitch, *Les Rapports Diplomatiques de Lebzeltern*, St. Petersburg, 1913, pp. 36 sqq. Capital punishment had already been abolished by Empress Elizabeth ; but the knout had been introduced instead.

the Tsar gave Cancrin a free hand.[1] Cancrin's reforms, it is true, did not essentially alter the structure of Russian society. The huge estates so characteristic of Tsarist Russia, especially after Catherine II, continued to exist for a considerable time in almost complete self-sufficiency. The gentry retained to a large extent their control of such industry as existed, a control which they had exercised since the urban entrepreneur created by Peter the Great had been gradually pushed back. There were still comparatively few merchants, and they distinctly belonged to the *podly*, that is, the lower orders of society. Yet, the Tsar's support of Cancrin's reforms proves that the example set by the men who were then ruling in Austria never convinced Alexander I of the need for putting back the clock so far as industry was concerned, or of the expediency of a system so obviously dependent on foreign loans. To avoid these loans was one, and that certainly not the least important, of Cancrin's objects.

We have seen that Clam-Martinitz stressed the interest which the Tsar took in public education. Indeed, in 1816 the number of young people who frequented the schools of the " gouverne-ment " and city of St. Petersburg was more than six times as big as it had been in 1812, namely 5,000 instead of 800.[2] This could not fail to impress a diplomat coming from what then was obscurantist Austria, especially if he was aware of the strong opposition in Russia to educational reform. It had been the Tsar's intention to establish elementary schools if possible in every parish, but neither the rural parishes nor the landowners were inclined to take such a burden on their shoulders. Russian obscurantism had also very powerful foreign supporters. De Maistre, whose general political ideas have been analysed in a previous chapter, was outstanding among them. He had a particular aversion to the teaching of history. In a letter to Rasumovsky, who at that time was Russian Minister of Education, de Maistre expressed the opinion that the Russian people did not require more schools than already existed ; it was doubtful even if they would ever require more. The Minister would be well advised to seek to convince the Tsar of the important truth that only two kinds of people were necessary to him : " des gens braves et des braves gens ". Learning, so he asserted, had the

---

[1] Cf. Theodor Schiemann, *Kaiser Alexander I und die Ergebnisse seiner Lebensarbeit*, Berlin, 1904, p. 493.

[2] These figures are taken from a despatch from the French Ambassador to the Duc de Richelieu. (*Sbornik imperatorskago russkago istoricheskago obchestva*, CXIX, 1904, p. 25.)

effect of making men inactive and useless for business of any
kind, especially for large enterprise.[1] In Griboyedov's comedy
Woe from Wit (1822-3), the head of a Government department is
made to speak in a similar strain.[2]

Opposition to the Tsar's schemes of reform was not confined
to education. Something will have to be said about the obstruction he encountered while trying to carry out his other social
reforms. In this way it will, I believe, be possible to throw some
light on the presumable causes of the Tsar's inconsistency.

The Polish example is perhaps the most instructive. It is
well known that the Tsar did not abolish serfdom even in those
provinces where, as we have seen, he was experimenting in some
respects. The opposition he would have encountered if, as is
highly probable, he intended to take such a step, can be imagined
if we take into account the following fact. The Polish noblemen
—even Prince Czartoryski among them—tried to make the Tsar
believe that serfdom had been abolished in Poland years before.
In order to prove their bold assertion, they simply pointed to
Article IV of the constitution which Napoleon had given to the
Grand Duchy of Warsaw in 1807 : " L'esclavage est aboli, tous
les citoyens sont égaux devant la loi ; l'état des paysans est sous
la protection des tribunaux." In fact, the land had remained
in the possession of the masters, and in return for the use of
temporary allotments, the peasants rendered dues and services
in very much the same manner as before.[3] I do not suggest that
Alexander I believed what he was thus told. The ukases mentioned above are proof to the contrary. On the other hand, the
fact that these ukases became a dead letter, like much other
Russian legislation, shows that the Polish landowners not only
opposed each new step contemplated by the social reformer, but
that they also obstructed every single measure as soon as it had
been taken.[4]

As we have shown in a previous chapter, it cannot be said
that the ruling class in Russia proper was behaving very differently.[5] Here, too, the existing laws whose purpose it was to

---

[1] Theodor von Bernhardi, *Geschichte Russlands und der europäischen Politik in den
Jahren 1814 bis 1831*, Leipzig, 1877, III, p. 69.

[2] " You think it's a great calamity for a man to drink too much. It's education
that's the pest . . ." (Translation by S. W. Pring.)

[3] G. T. Robinson, *Rural Russia under the Old Régime*, London, 1932, p. 63.

[4] W. Alison Phillips has arrived at the same conclusion. (*Modern Europe, 1815-1899*,
London, 1915, p. 203.)

[5] One example from the overwhelming evidence : " J'ai vu que les seigneurs
appréhendent que l'Empereur ne nourisse le dessein d'abolir la servitude de leurs
paysans et d'établir une constitution plus libre en Russie." This information is

mitigate the suffering of the peasantry were openly disregarded. When, for example, an ukase of 1822 forbade the publication of advertisements offering serfs for sale without land, advertisements in future spoke of hire instead of purchase, and the result remained unchanged. This case of an ineffective ukase was not an isolated one. What was the use of their providing sanctions against obstinate landowners if practically no one could be relied upon to impose them?—neither the judges nor the officials of the administration, the vast majority of whom were either too corrupt [1] or weakminded or else too incompetent [2] to execute the laws on social reform with anything like sufficient vigour. The Tsar did not greatly exaggerate when he said to the King of Prussia in 1820 : " We are both surrounded by ragamuffins. There are many of them I should like to kick out, but unfortunately it is always persons of the same kind who come back." [3] Thus the problem " Quis custodiet ipsos custodes? " became insoluble in this respect—though not for the same reasons as in Austria. It is difficult to avoid the impression that the Westernization of Russia since Peter the Great was attempted with exaggerated haste ; as a result the effective destruction of large parts of the old Muscovite civilization does not seem to have been accompanied by a corresponding assimilation of Western institutions.

Count Arakcheev was certainly the most brutal and perhaps the most cynical of all those who obstructed social reform when he openly declared that once the peasant was rich he would begin to think of freedom and of leaving the soil—an idea, by the way, which we have met before in the case of the infinitely more cultured Chevalier de Gentz. Ordered by the Tsar to

contained in a despatch which Hegardt, the Swedish chargé d'affaires in Vienna, sent to the Ministry at Stockholm on June 25th, 1814 ; the despatch was intercepted, and appears in M. H. Weil, *Les Dessous du Congrès de Vienne, d'après les documents originaux des archives du Ministère Impérial et Royal de l'Intérieur à Vienne,* I, Paris, 1917, p. 8.

[1] Cf. Ivan Krylov's *Fables,* e.g. " Stone and Worm ". Another, called " The Peasants and the River ", ends thus :

> To win your suit against the small, despair,
> When all their plunder with the great they share.

(Trans. into English verse by B. Pares, London, 1926.)
It is important to remember that Krylov was far from holding Radical views ; cf. his fable *The Dollar.* Pushkin's letters, too, are full of bitter remarks against officials.

[2] Cf. N. Turgeniev, *Russlands Bild in politischer und sozialer Beziehung,* Grimma, 1847, p. 117.

[3] A. N. Pypin, *Die geistigen Bewegungen in Russland in der ersten Hälfte des XIX. Jahrhunderts,* I, Berlin, 1894, p. 540.

work out a plan for the liberation of the serfs, Arakcheev produced a most malicious scheme. Each year a certain amount of money was to be spent on the purchase of some of the private estates, and the serfs living on these were to be liberated. The financial means necessary for the purchase were to be found from the revenue of the vodka monopoly, which the author of this scheme expected would rise continuously. T. von Bernhardi summarizes Arakcheev's project thus : " The drunkenness of the Russian people was chosen as the means of their liberation." How it came about that the Tsar entrusted such a man as Arakcheev with ever-increasing power is one of those many puzzles of human history which modern psychology pretends in vain to solve.

Then there was Karamzin, the most learned opponent of liberalism in Russia. Just as in Austria Francis I was trying to rejuvenate the outworn ideology of unenlightened absolutism by divine right, so the Russian ideologist summarized his frequently professed arguments against a liberal constitution in these words : " Our Tsars are not representatives of the people but of Him who rules empires." According to Karamzin, Russian landlords were nothing but " vice-gerents of their great Tsar, each in the domain hereditarily entrusted to him ". In this way, as Masaryk has demonstrated, the picture is rounded off : the Tsar representative of God, the landlord vice-gerent of the Tsar. " The landlord therefore," Masaryk points out, " is co-representative of God, and the holder of this aristocratic doctrine is, consequently, perfectly logical when he defends serfdom." [1]

Others, indifferent to or at times even strongly in favour of a liberal constitution, concentrated all their oppositional zeal against the abolition of serfdom. A case in point is Admiral Mordvinov's attitude, but the most striking example is furnished by members of the Decembrist movement. The attitude of the Decembrists towards the question of serfdom was by no means unanimous. Pestel, to be sure, demanded the abolition of serfdom ; his ideas on agrarian reform were distinctly communistic. Pushkin, whose early poems were mentioned specifically at the trial of the Decembrists as having influenced some of the participants,[2] made a strong appeal for the abolition of serfdom in *The Village* (1819), one of the poems, that is, for

[1] T. G. Masaryk, *The Spirit of Russia*, I, p. 89. A similar idea had been already expressed by Madame de Staël in " Dix années d'exil ". (*Œuvres completes*, II, Paris, 1836, p. 605.)
[2] G. V. Vernadsky, " Pushkin and the Decembrists ", in *Centennial Essays for Pushkin*, Cambridge (Mass.), 1937, p. 51.

which he was " transferred " to South Russia in 1820. According to Muraviev's draft constitution serfdom was to be abolished ; but, following the Prussian example, no land was to be assigned to the emancipated peasants. Nor did Nikolas Turgeniev aim, in this respect, at anything more than the personal liberation of the serfs. Another branch of the Decembrists did not introduce the liberation of the peasants into their revolutionary statutes ; and this was in all probability more than a tactical manœuvre. On the other hand, it has to be noted that much practical help was given by Decembrists in the " gouvernement " of Smolensk to the people at the time of the famine in 1820 and 1821. On the whole, however, it might truly be said that the Russian liberalism of the time was possessed by " the superstition of liberty ". Liberals had to be reminded, by one who was himself a Liberal, that the first thing to be done was to limit their own rights over actual slaves.[1]

Last but not least there was the famous Speransky, the Tsar's collaborator during his anti-Napoleonic period. Even this man was far from advocating anything like the complete abolition of serfdom ; in fact it is known that he criticized the Warsaw speech made by the Tsar at the opening of the Polish diet in 1818 mainly on the ground that the peasants might take it as a pledge of their liberation.[2] The " people " from whom, according to Speransky, political power proceeds, were only the aristocracy and the middle class, the latter comprising merchants, burghers, peasant proprietors, and other owners of property.

If the failure of the liberal constitution in Poland was ascribed by Count Capodistria to the non-existence of a Polish middle class, the same applied to Russia as far as the liberal tendencies of her ruler were concerned.[3] Clam-Martinitz described the situation in these words : " The partisans of constitutional ideas are, if one looks more closely, confined to a few who became democrats from pride, from vanity, or from envy against the rich grandees whom they would so much like to imitate." Here too a middle class, so indispensable for the working of a liberal constitution, was to all intents and purposes non-existent.

So far we have examined only those forces of resistance to

---

[1] Pypin, op. cit., pp. 673-4.
[2] As to the fact, cf. Nikolas Turgeniev, *Denkwürdigkeiten eines Geächteten*, Grimma, 1847, p. 66.
[3] Also Alexander de Stourdza ascribes the failure of the Tsar's reforms to this fact. (*Souvenirs du Règne de l'Empereur Alexandre, Œuvres posthumes religieuses, historiques, philosophiques et littéraires*, III, Paris, 1859, p. 91.)

social innovation which came from outside. At the same time we must not overlook the inner resistance which is to be explained only by the Tsar's religious views. One of the main characteristics of that New Christianity which has been analysed in a previous chapter was the renunciation of force. Saint-Martin, Novalis, Julie de Krüdener, Saint-Simon, all preached this dogma. The Tsar's mind, highly susceptible to the new creed [1] as it was, could not have been uninfluenced by this important aspect of it. In order to carry into effect his main ideas of social innovation, the Tsar would have had at times to use brute force. He was, I suggest, reluctant to do so precisely during the period when the new creed with all its social implications meant much to him.

Besides, there would have been the difficult question of the instrument. This could obviously be only the army. The Tsar seems to have realized this, as the establishment of the military colonies in 1816 seems to suggest. True, considerations of foreign policy cannot be entirely excluded. The example of the Austrian military colonies, which, as a recent Soviet study proves, was copied by Alexander I, was undoubtedly of some importance ; so probably was the fact that Prussia had introduced her *Landwehr* system which amounted to a permanent partial mobilization of her forces. It may well have been one of the purposes of the Tsar's military colonies that they should act as a counterweight to that system. [2] On the other hand, diplomatic relations at this time with Prussia were especially cordial ; nor does the Austrian example in itself suffice to explain why it was copied in Russia. We must not forget that the establishment of the military colonies took place at a time when the Tsar's peaceful intentions were testified to by the ambassadors of both Great Britain and Austria, [3] by diplomats, that is, whose official duty it was not to overlook the slightest reason for suspicion.

In these circumstances it seems that the decisive motive for the establishment of the military colonies may perhaps have been a different one. What the Tsar probably desired was to become

---

[1] Of all the testimonies to the sincerity of Alexander's religious attitude none is more convincing than that of the great Lithuanian-Polish poet and patriot Mickiewicz who had been deported from Lithuania to Russia in 1824. In a lecture held in Paris in 1843, he said expressly : " Alexander became God-fearing from all his heart." (*Vorlesungen über slavische Literatur und Zustände*, II, Leipzig, 1844, p. 351.)

[2] P. P. Evstafiev, *Vosstanie voennjikh poselyan novgorodskoi gubernii v 1831 g.*, Moscow, 1934, p. 17.

[3] *Les Rapports Diplomatiques de Lebzeltern*, p. 110. Cf. also Cathcart's despatch to Castlereagh, dated St. Petersburg, April 4th 1816 (Castlereagh's *Correspondence*, XI, p. 241).

more independent of the landowning aristocracy whom he was supposed to govern as an autocrat. Before the establishment of these colonies, that class could not be left out of consideration so far as recruiting was concerned. This was now to cease; a large number of peasant-soldiers would be available at any moment. The new caste, itself independent of the landowning aristocracy, was meant to constitute the Tsar's chief support.

If this was the purpose of the project, its execution could hardly have been more unfortunate. To start with, the choice of the first site was a bad mistake; the soil of the district round old Novgorod produced little. In any case, the best use could not be made of it, since military drill of the worst description left too little time. If, as recent historians believe, one of the motives for the whole scheme was the idea that thenceforth the soldier should not be torn from his family, the drawback which emerged in practice was that the families of the peasant-soldiers were exposed to military chicanery to which they had never been accustomed, and that they too became to an increasing extent part of the army. But the peasant-soldiers also had to pay dearly for the advantage of being with their families. In the time between their various military duties they had to do hard agricultural labour, to which they in their turn found it difficult, if not impossible, to accustom themselves. Thus they hardly ever had the feeling of being off duty. Almost the same was true of the officers. Some of them who had been educated either in Russia or by contact with foreign culture during a campaign in Central or Western Europe must have suffered especially hardly [1] from the repulsive perversion of Arakcheev's " discipline " which allowed them no time for social recreation, let alone for intellectual stimulation. This at a time when Yakushkin, speaking of the mentality of the army in general, reported that chess had replaced cards as a pastime, and instead of banqueting officers now preferred to follow carefully political events abroad. Thus arose one of those typical situations which Thomas Moore must have had in mind when he began the last of his *Fables for the Holy Alliance*, called " The Extinguishers " with these verses :

> *Though soldiers are the true supports,*
> *The natural allies of Courts,*
> *Woe to the Monarch who depends*
> *Too much on his red-coated friends ;*
> *For even soldiers sometimes think—*

[1] *Zapiski I. D. Yakushkina*, Moscow, 1926, p. 12.

Nay Colonels have been known to reason,—
And reasoners, whether clad in pink,
Or red, or blue, are on the brink
(Nine cases out of ten) of treason.

The soldier who begins to think was also a theme of contemporary Russian literature. In Griboyedov's comedy *Woe
from Wit*—the first unexpurgated edition of which did not, however, appear until the '6os—a Colonel says of a young officer :
" He went all out for some new ideas : he was due for promotion,
but suddenly he left the service, and settled down in the country
to read books."

It is easy to understand, then, that the military colonies
tended to become a centre of unrest and disaffection. For the
reasons which I have outlined the Tsar must have felt this as a
heavy blow : all the more because, as has been proved, the
outward appearance of the settlements made a neat and altogether
favourable impression. By all sorts of tricks which can easily
be imagined, Arakcheev managed to deceive those who visited
the colonies. The Tsar, naturally inclined to believe in the
prosperity of his favourite scheme, seems for a long time to have
been kept in ignorance of the actual state of affairs. Nevertheless
he grew suspicious, as the following despatch to Arakcheev dated
8/20 September 1819 shows. A fortnight previously Arakcheev
had sent the Tsar a despatch reporting an insurrection which had
broken out in the Chuguyev settlement and the measures he had
taken against it. Two passages from the Tsar's reply are worth
quoting. The first read : " The incident is certainly a sad one,
but since unfortunately it had occurred there was nothing left
but to proceed in accordance with the severity of the law."
Alexander added, however : " Must we not ask ourselves strictly,
sincerely and impartially whether all that we have promised to
the regiment has been fulfilled ? Since I have not the regulations
and documents at hand I cannot at present decide. But I
sincerely ask you to turn your attention to the matter." [1]

Such an incident must have gone far to strengthen the Tsar's
feeling that the task he had undertaken was more than he could
possibly cope with. A few months earlier he had already spoken
to his brother Nicholas of his intention to resign. Later, in 1823,
he definitely made up his mind to resign on his 50th birthday
in 1827. This time he revealed his plan to Prince Wilhelm of
Prussia. The way in which the Tsar justified his intention was

[1] N. K. Shilder, *Imperator Aleksandr Pervyi*, IV, p. 171.

significant. He did not feel in good health, and an Emperor
of Russia who could no longer travel the distance of 300 versts
in 24 hours so as to discuss current business with the authorities
and to fulfil the local wishes, was in his opinion no longer able
to rule so immense an empire.

But the principal reason of his growing uneasiness seems to
have been the disappointment which the army caused him. At
the beginning of 1818, Prince Hesse-Homburg, who had been
sent as special envoy to the Tsar who was then residing in Russian
Poland, could still report to Metternich : " He [Alexander]
seems to have it specially at heart . . . to prove that he
possesses counterweights too powerful and that he knows how
to use them too well to allow liberal institutions to degenerate
or to become dangerous by abuse. He is seeking this counterweight mainly in the strict discipline of the army." [1] The
slightest independent movement of the counterweight, indeed,
irritated the Tsar immensely. It was in most cases not a question
of demands put forward by the officers. Up to 1820 the Tsar
was in constant touch with them ; he approved of the greater
part of their demands so far as they were concerned with constitutional reform. But the instrument had in his opinion no
right to interfere with the decision as to when one should act.
A Russian circular despatch, doubtless inspired by the Tsar,
said expressly : " Constitutions which emanate from the throne
are conservative ; when they arise out of the convulsions of
order, they create chaos." [2] In the light of what has so far been
said it emerges, I think, that not even during the later years of
his reign did " conservative " mean for the Tsar the same as for
Metternich. Vernadsky has convincingly shown how successive
historians have had to " postpone " the date of the beginning
of Alexander's reactionary period : first it was thought to be
1815, then 1819, finally 1820. And not even this last date, as
Vernadsky proves, can be taken as marking a complete overthrow
of everything that had been said and done previously. For it
was after 1820 that a serious attempt was made to introduce
some of these high-sounding constitutional principles into actual
political life. Novosiltsev's constitutional scheme thus led at
least to one practical result, that is, to the reform of local government, especially in the region round Orel and Ryazan.[3] It thus

[1] *Les Rapports Diplomatiques de Lebzeltern*, p. 28.

[2] Schwarz, *Die Heilige Allianz*, p. 180.

[3] Vernadsky, *La Charte Constitutionelle de l'Empire Russe de l'an 1820*, Paris, 1933,
pp. 41-8.

came about that in 1821 Ryleev, who a year previously had written a bold satirical poem against Arakcheev, called " To the Favourite ", still hoped that the Tsar might become the leader of European liberalism. This is shown by the poem "Alexander I " which is ascribed to him. Even so late as 1825 some members of the secret societies expected the Tsar to initiate reforms on a large scale.[1] However, the main point in this context is that Alexander I allowed no one to interfere with his schemes.

Considerations of a different kind added to his irritation. His effective power was, as we have seen, very far from being equal to his nominal power as " autocrat ", or indeed to that degree of power which for good or ill he would have liked to exercise. But this discrepancy did not hinder his subjects from putting the blame for many different things upon the Tsar as the visible symbol of power. In 1816, indeed, and probably also later, the masses seem to have realized that the Tsar was seriously trying to help them. For example, the Ambassador Cathcart wrote to Castlereagh from St. Petersburg on September 26th, 1816 : " The reception of the Emperor by the lower orders of the people has been as much marked by sincere loyalty and attachment as it is possible," and Cathcart added significantly : " the demonstrations of the same sentiments have been as great throughout all ranks and descriptions of persons, but it is not so easy to judge of the sincerity of the professions of the higher classes by outward appearance." [2] Among the higher aristocracy more than one plot was discovered against the Tsar's life or his personal freedom ; the reason for his growing unpopularity in these circles seems at times to have been the fact that his projected social reforms went much too far for the liking of some ; but in other cases it was the fact that he hesitated before following up the example he had set in Poland by granting a similar liberal constitution for the Empire.

But the Tsar's change of policy, caused partly by the growing unreliability of the higher officers and by various minor tendencies showing themselves inside Russia, could never have reached the dimensions it did apart from the influence of Central and Western European diplomacy. The more accustomed the Tsar became to thinking in terms of Europe, the more he naturally—and probably not quite consciously—accepted, if not the dominant

[1] Pypin, op. cit., pp. 677–8.
[2] *Correspondence, etc., of Viscount Castlereagh*, XI, p. 298.

political theory as a whole, at least the prevailing apprehensions and prophylactic measures of the Continent.

It seems, then, that Alexander's reign might be divided into four periods : (1) The Tsar concentrates on domestic social reforms ; (2) disappointed with his lack of success, he turns to the reform of European international relations ; (3) for a time after the victorious outcome of the War he tries to proceed on both lines ; (4) failing again in his domestic policy, Alexander now clings so desperately to his second ideal, the ideal of a peaceful if not a united Europe, that he is prepared almost entirely to abandon the ideal of his youth, all the more so since in the latter respect he had previously promised more than he now feels able to carry out under circumstances so hostile to any reform ; European unity thus gaining for him the new and additional value of an insurance against claims partly based on those past pledges.

During this fourth and last period the symptoms of social innovation in Russia were one after another disappearing. The gulf between *blagorodny* (the nobility) and *podly* (the lower classes), which in the first exhilaration of 1812 had seemed not quite unbridgeable, was again wide open. Whereas previously men of talent had had some reason to complain of the indifference shown towards them, obscurantism of the Austrian variety invaded the Universities ; [1] men who thought for themselves had to do so in their Siberian exile ; Magnitsky, once Speransky's collaborator, even conceived the grotesque idea of taking pathological specimens from the museums and burying them in the churchyard. Censorship became stricter and denunciations more frequent than they had ever been during Alexander's reign. Literature began once more to be circulated in manuscript form ; meetings of intellectuals assumed the character of small conventicles. In January 1821 a secret military police force was established. Arakcheev's influence grew menacingly. Nor was the religious sphere exempt. Baader, at one time admired and rewarded by the Tsar, was in 1823 refused permission to enter Russia. In the autumn of the following year the Bible Society, which had previously enjoyed the Tsar's special care, ceased to send out reports to the world ; it was denounced by Admiral Shishkov as a terrible conspiracy against the government and

[1] Interesting details are to be found in the Memoirs of a Baltic German who occupied a high post in the Ministry of Education : Peter von Goetze, *Fürst Nikolajewitsch Galitzin und seine Zeit*, Leipzig, 1882.

religion. Golitsyn, the Tsar's personal friend, had to resign his
post as Minister of Education because the Orthodox Church,
becoming bolder from day to day, called the new latitudinarian
Christianity which Golitsyn favoured " the creed of Satan ".
As Minister of Education he was succeeded by Shishkov
(" Minister of people's stultification ", as he was soon dubbed) ;
the Ministry of Spiritual Affairs over which he had also presided,
was abolished, and the scene was now dominated by Photius,
one of those sombre and terrifying figures who seem to foreshadow
Rasputin.

Yet there still existed a remnant of Alexander's past. Sharing
the anxiety and apprehensions of the ruling men of Europe, the
Tsar to a very large extent imitated their methods. But when it
came to the question of crushing the unrest in his own country
which later culminated in the Decembrist rising, Alexander I
hesitated and did nothing to prevent its outbreak. A list full of
names of political conspirators which Vassilchikev had handed
to the Tsar in June 1821, as well as a detailed report of General
Benckendorff on the existing secret societies, were found after the
Tsar's death in his study at Tsarskoe Selo ; he had not even
added any remarks to the two documents. When they were
handed to him he remarked to Vassilchikev : " You have been
in my service ever since the beginning of my reign, and therefore
you know that I shared and encouraged these illusions—it is not
for me to inflict terrible punishments on them." [1]   The historian,
therefore, has to modify the grave verdict which Mickiewicz
pronounced upon this last stage of Alexander's internal régime :

> *Sunk in tyranny—he who once was human*
> *Abandoned by the Lord to slow corruption.*
> *He has driven from him like an evil thing*
> *His last resource of conscience.* [2]

Thus it was not until Alexander's death that—as Herzen put it—
the plague began which was to extend throughout the whole
long reign of his brother Nicholas. For the purpose of this study,
however, we have to note that Alexander I behaved in these last
years as if he were wholeheartedly prepared to punish conspirators in whatever corner of Europe, perhaps even of the world,
they might be found.

[1] A. E. Presnyakov, *Aleksandr I*, Petersburg, 1924, p. 177.
[2] Introduction to Forefather's Eve, Part III, chapter " The Day before the
Petersburg Flood ", quoted from A. P. Coleman, " Pushkin and Mickiewicz ", in
Centennial Essays for Pushkin, Cambridge, Massachussets, 1937, p. 99.

CHAPTER VI

THE EUROPEAN MANAGEMENT AND FRANCE

In each of the four principal States of Europe, those who desired the maintenance of the social *status quo*, or who, as in the case of the Tsar, could not conceive of thoroughgoing changes except under their own guidance, had, as we have seen, some reason for apprehension so far as their own countries were concerned. But one of the distinctive features of the post-Napoleonic period can be seen in the fact that the men who then ruled in different European States came increasingly to share each other's apprehensions ; this is, from 1820 onwards, true also of the Tsar, for the reasons I have outlined.

France, fallen for a time on account of her military defeat from the rank of first to that of fifth European Power, was the most obvious common concern, so much so that, for the first time in modern European history, a congress was convoked in 1818, in the midst of all-European peace, one of whose main purposes was to deal with that highly delicate question. But France, or, to be more precise, her precarious position in which the forces working for the reconstitution of the *ancien régime* had to be warned off by their well-meaning advisers from abroad, was far from being the only point of universal apprehension. Nor was this apprehension confined to countries which, like the Netherlands, offered asylum to a new wave of French *émigrés*.

It is well known that Metternich dreaded the prospect of Prussia becoming more democratic ; of the Prussian King fulfilling the solemn promise given by him towards the end of the Napoleonic Wars to introduce *Volksdeputierte*. It is not so well known—though anyone who has read through the published *Correspondence* of Lord Castlereagh may have noticed it—that Metternich's apprehension on this point was fully shared by the British Foreign Secretary. The following passage from Castlereagh's despatch to Mr. Rose, Britain's Minister to Prussia, dated December 28th, 1815, will serve as an illustration :

. . . with all that partiality and a grateful admiration of the conduct of that nation [i.e. Prussia] and its armies in the war, I fairly own that I look with considerable anxiety to the tendency of their politics. There certainly at this moment exists a great fermentation in all orders of the State, very free notions of Government, if not principles actually revolutionary, are prevalent, and the army is by no means subordinate to the civil authorities. It is impossible to say where these impulses may stop, when they find a representative system in which they may develop themselves.

And Castlereagh adds :

I call your attention to these circumstances, not as any motive for interference on your part, but in order to impress your mind with the importance (and especially to Prussia herself) of keeping up a good understanding amongst the adjoining States on which these disorganizing principles have made less impression, till the internal state both of France and of the north of Germany is more assured than it can now be considered to be. To this view of European policy, I can venture to assure you, the Sovereigns themselves and their immediate Ministers are not insensible.[1]

Western and Central Europe were not the only causes of anxiety. Certain events in countries so remote as Naples or Spain added considerably to Metternich's and Castlereagh's uneasiness. That is why Austria, on concluding a treaty of alliance in 1815 with Ferdinand IV, King of Naples, insisted on a secret clause which prohibited the introduction of a liberal constitution in that kingdom. Six years later, when such a constitution had been forced upon Ferdinand by the revolting army of his own country, he was reinstated as an absolute monarch by the invading army of the other contracting party. Metternich tried to justify this invasion by the assertion that a constitution not yet tried out must lead to anarchy ;[2] it is piquant to hear these words from a man who had gone so far as to prohibit the trying out of the constitution in a solemn if secret diplomatic document.

In this connection one more point has to be stated. The apprehensions of the men then ruling in Europe—with the exception of the Tsar—were not confined to matters understood by everyone as belonging to the political sphere. They seem to have been equally worried about certain manifestations of that new type of Christianity which has been analysed in a previous chapter. Realizing the far-reaching social implications of that creed, Metternich, quite consistently from his standpoint, did everything in his power to suppress it. When, for example, it was feared in 1817 that Madame de Krüdener, whom Metternich

---

[1] *Correspondence, Despatches and other Papers of Viscount Castlereagh,* Third Series, XI, p. 106.
[2] Confidential letter to Count Rechberg, Foreign Minister at Munich, dated Vienna, 26th July 1820. (*Aus Metternichs nachgelassenen Papieren,* II, 1. Band, p. 382.)

described as a Jacobin, might wish to visit Austria for a time, special orders were sent from Innsbruck to bar her passage across the frontier, the police even taking the precaution to remove all boats from the Swiss shore of the Bodensee so that she might not make an unauthorized and embarrassing descent.[1] Madame de Krüdener's attitude at that time may be judged from her bold letter to the Minister of the Interior at Karlsruhe, written and published in 1817. The papers, she said, maintained that she was surrounded by a crowd of idlers. The truth was that they were unemployed through no fault of their own. Many of those with whom she prayed were too poor to show themselves in church ; their attire was not good enough. As to philanthropy, she had observed that in Swiss towns the rich cared for the rich, whereas the poor were looked after by the poor. From a great many testimonies to Madame de Krüdener's character, I quote two from very different quarters. Madame de Récamier wrote : " Sa bonté était réelle, sa charité et son désinteressement sans bornes." [2] According to Görres, all she had done to deserve persecution on the part of the authorities was to pray with the people, to announce to them the approaching Judgment Day, and to feed and rescue the starving.[3] Metternich was highly aware of the " dangerousness of Bible-reading ". Dangerousness for whom ? we must ask. Metternich himself answers this question with unsurpassable frankness, of course in a secret despatch. What he is worried about is not the Christian soul of the poor sinner who in despite of the Roman Catholic prohibition reads the Bible ; it is the social implications of such reading that Metternich dreads. Faithful to his favourite complex of metaphors, i.e. a kind of pseudo-medical terminology, he declares mysticism (in which form the new Christianity so often appeared) to be a " political malady ".[4] But he then becomes more outspoken, and writes that the tendency of Madame de Krüdener is " more dangerous than all the others, because her preachings were all intended to excite the indigent classes against the property-owners ".[5] Geographically, his misgivings went even further. He felt equally uneasy about Methodism in England and America,[6] which, for reasons beyond the scope of

---

[1] Knapton, *The Lady of the Holy Alliance*, p. 189.
[2] *Souvenirs et Correspondance*, I, Paris, 1859, p. 285.
[3] *Teutschland und die Revolution*, Coblenz, 1819.
[4] Metternich to Lebzeltern, Florence, June 28th, 1817, *Memoirs of Prince Metternich*, III, p. 59.
[5] Ibid., pp. 59–60.   [6] Ibid., p. 58.

this study, may be said to have had but little connection with the new creed, since it originated rather from a source common to both, that is, from the reorganized Moravian brethren in Saxony, and had in fact become by this time a somewhat conservative sect. But here again it would be wrong to assume that Metternich's attitude was exceptional. Wellington, for example, was highly pleased with a certain Mr. Briscoll who had " got the better of Methodism, which had appeared among the soldiers, and once among the officers ".[1] Certain ambassadors to Russia were also worried about the " religious radicalisms " which were increasingly showing themselves in that country.[2] Here, too, the real issue is almost beyond question. These ambassadors, none of whom professed the religion of the Orthodox Church, could not have been moved by religious considerations in the narrow sense of the word. What they were concerned about was clearly not the salvation of a number of Russian souls in the Orthodox way, but only the salvation of that social *status quo* which Russian orthodoxy so firmly supported.

In short, we can perhaps best visualize the depth of the concern if we remember that Metternich, in his profession of faith, spoke of " factions in all States ",[3] and that in 1819 he considered the activities of the " revolutionaries " in Germany, Italy, France and England as equally dangerous.[4] Francis I therefore, in a letter to the Tsar, urgently recommended the closest contact between the courts of the Great Powers as the only expedient to forestall " the revolution of all social institutions ".[5] A Prussian spokesman (Ancillon) also, in a circular sent to the Prussian foreign missions after the Carlsbad Conferences, reminded the Sovereigns, " the foremost lovers and protectors of

[1] R. W. Emerson, *English Traits*, World's Classics ed., London, 1903, p. 131.
[2] Karl Stählin, " Ideal und Wirklichkeit im letzten Jahrzehnt Alexanders I ", *Historische Zeitschrift*, CXLV, 1932, p. 101.
[3] *Memoirs of Prince Metternich 1815–1829*, III, p. 471.
[4] Metternich to Munarini, 5th July 1819. According to Stern (I, p. 629) this despatch is to be found in the archives at Modena. A further example is furnished by Gentz's letter to Pilat written from Aix-la-Chapelle on September 30th, 1818 : " What in the world could have moved you to have that damned address of the Manchester factory workers reprinted in the Beobachter ? " (*Briefe von Friedrich von Gentz an Pilat*, I, Leipzig, 1868, p. 341.)
[5] Cf. also the result at which Metternich arrived in his above-mentioned despatch to Trautmannsdorf : " The best means of avoiding such a great misfortune as a new upheaval in France would be, will indisputably be found in the maintenance of the relations—as intimate as they are beneficial—which exist between the leading Powers and in the reinforcement of the federative bond which, reuniting in a single group the forces which without this bond would be separate in Germany, will assure to each of the members of this great political body an immense support, both against attacks from without and against those of the revolutionaries which the German States nourish in their bosoms."

social order ", of " the existence of their common enemies " in
various parts of Europe. Similar language was used by Castlereagh, the " guest of Kings, and King of Tories ", as Thomas
Moore called him ; [1] an outspoken passage from his above-
mentioned despatch to Mr. Rose seems well worth quoting since
in its frankness it is certainly not equalled by any other passage
from his voluminous correspondence.

In the present state of Europe [Castlereagh writes on December 28th,
1815] it is the province of Great Britain to turn the confidence she has
inspired to the account of peace, by exercising a conciliatory influence
between the Powers, rather than put herself at the head of any com-
binations of Courts to keep others in check. The necessity for such a
system of connection may recur, but this necessity should be no longer
problematical when it is acted upon. The immediate object to be
kept in view is to inspire the States of Europe, as long as we can,
with a sense of the dangers which they have surmounted by their
union, of the hazards they will incur by a relaxation of vigilance,
to make them feel that the existing concert is their only perfect
security against the revolutionary embers more or less existing in
every State of Europe ; and that their true wisdom is to keep down
the petty contentions of ordinary times, and to stand together in
support of the established principles of social order.[2]

Other signs also showed that among the ruling classes of
Europe there was an increasing consciousness of their common
interests. Mallet du Pan anticipated this attitude by saying that
anyone who regarded the Revolution as exclusively French was
disqualified from judging it. It is not necessary to dwell too much
on such well-known utterances as that of Metternich : " Castlereagh . . . my second self ",[3] or the Prince Regent's : " I am an

---

[1] *The Fudge Family in Paris*, 1818.
[2] *Correspondence etc. of Viscount Castlereagh*, Third Series, Vol. XI, p. 105. C. K. Webster mentions this despatch in *The Foreign Policy of Castlereagh 1815–1822* in a footnote on p. 509 : " F.O. 146, France (Archives), 12. The despatch, to write which
Castlereagh took ' advantage of a bad day to spare the pheasants ', was in the first
instance addressed to Rose and then made circular to all Missions : C.C. XI, 104."
Professor Webster then gives the full text of the Circular Despatch of January 1st,
1816 (ibid., pp. 509–512). But to me it seems that the difference between the wording
of the two documents is so great that the earlier one, more outspoken as it is, should
no longer be neglected.
[3] The following passage is made up of extracts from Metternich's private correspondence. On August 25th, 1822, that is, a few days after he heard of Castlereagh's
suicide, he wrote : " The catastrophe is one of the most terrible which could have
occurred to me. He was devoted to me, heart and soul, not only from personal
affection, but also from conviction. Much which would have been easy with him,
will now need new efforts with his successor, whoever he may be. I had expected
him here [Verona] like my second self . . ." (*Aus Metternichs nachgelassenen Papieren*,
III, p. 523. I have translated this passage which has been omitted in the English
edition.)

Austrian body and soul " [1]—an utterance which can be fully understood only if we remember Talleyrand's aphorism : " Austria is Europe's House of Lords : so long as it is not dissolved, it will keep the Commons in check." [2]   Much more telling is the fact, for which we have Cobbett's testimony, that the French emigrant nobles and priests who had come to England during the French revolution received pensions from this country from the time of their arrival to the time of their death, or that of their return in 1814.[3]

Another sign pointing in the same direction can, I think, be seen in the striking number of cases in which either a ruler or an ultra-royalist party expressed a wish for the prolongation of the foreign occupation of their territory.   In France, Louis XVIII in 1815, his brother and the other " Ultras " in the following year and again in 1818 ; and in Naples Ferdinand IV in 1821, thus anticipated to some extent the attitude which in France Thiers was to adopt in face of the Paris Commune of 1871 and —so far as we are as yet able to judge—Pétain once more in 1940. In Stendhal's *Le Rouge et le Noir. Chronique du XIXe siècle*, published in 1830, a certain Marquis de la Mole is longing for " une heureuse occupation, comme celle que M. de Richelieu gaspilla si bêtement en 1817 ".   He goes on to explain to a noble gathering how and why this has to be achieved :

Que chacun de nous sacrifie le cinquième de son revenu pour former cette petite troupe dévouée de cinq cents hommes par département.   Alors vous pourrez compter sur une occupation étrangère. Jamais le soldat étranger ne pénétrera jusqu'à Dijon seulement, s'il n'est sûr de trouver cinq cents soldats amis dans chaque département. Les rois étrangers ne vous écouteront que quand vous leur annoncerez vingt mille gentilshommes prêts à saisir les armes pour leur ouvrir les portes de la France.   Ce service est pénible, direz-vous ; Messieurs, notre tête est à ce prix.   Entre la liberté de la presse et notre existence comme gentilshommes, il y a guerre à mort.   Devenez des manufacturiers, des paysans, ou prenez votre fusil.[4]

But the change which was taking place was visible above all in the new way in which some members of the ruling class began to look upon questions connected with war.   No longer did these people think exclusively or almost exclusively in terms of

---

[1] Stern, op. cit., I, p. 212.   The reference there given is the report of the Austrian Ambassador Esterhazy from London, dated 1st and 8th January 1816.

[2] *Aus Metternichs nachgelassenen Papieren*, III, p. 298.

[3] *Cobbett's Weekly Political Register*, XXXVII, 1815, p. 390.

[4] Stendhal [M. H. Beyle], *Le Rouge et le Noir*, II, ed. Henri Martineau, Paris, 1925, pp. 207, 209–10.

" dynastic wars " ; accessions of power and glory at the expense
of another ruler seem to have lost in importance in proportion
to their estimate of the threat involved in the French Revolution
and later events connected with it.   Francis I, for example, was
reluctant to make use of the help which a successful Serbian
rebellion would have offered him against Napoleon in 1808.   The
defeat of Napoleon, though from Francis's point of view desirable
for many reasons, was not to be bought at the cost of contagious
rebellions.   A blunt statement of the new attitude was given in
a leading article which appeared in *The Times* barely a fortnight
before Waterloo, and was joyfully exploited four days later by the
ever-vigilant William Cobbett.   It ran thus :

> The revolutionary ideas of France have already made but too
> great a progress in the hearts of men in all countries, and even in the
> very centre of every capital.   If crime be crowned with reward in
> France, every individual may hope that the subversion of order in his
> own country will provide him a situation, if not honourable, at least
> honoured.   It is not Bonaparte that at present forms the danger of
> Europe : he is unmasked.   It is the new opinions ; it is the dis-
> organization of men's minds ; it is the making revolt a calculation of
> private interest ; it is the most deadly of all contagions, the contagion
> of immorality, of false philanthropy, of a perfidious self-styled
> philosophy ; from all which the world requires to be protected.   This
> is the true hydra which must be destroyed, or it will destroy all Europe.
> The cause of morality is the cause of God ; it is the cause of all men,
> of all nations, of all thrones !

It was in the same spirit that the same journal expressed its
wish that the statue or statues of Voltaire might crumble to dust.[1]
The former statement was, so far as Napoleon was concerned,
exaggerated.   It would not be difficult to prove that Napoleon
before his ultimate defeat constituted a considerable danger to
the tangible interests of many of those for whom that leading
article was written ; a danger which the skilful journalist transformed into the hardly verifiable danger of Europe.   But the
point is that in the eyes of that journalist Napoleon was no
longer, so to speak, hydra No. 1.   And it was no mere phrase
when Wellington called the anti-Napoleonic campaign in its last
stage a police action.   What he meant to indicate, to all outward
appearances, was that one of the main purposes of the Allies
was to remove Napoleon the criminal and to restore liberty to
the enslaved French people.   So interpreted, Wellington's asser-

[1] Cf. Cobbett's Letter VII to Lord Castlereagh, *Political Register*, XXXVII, 1815,
p. 39.

tion could easily be refuted. The principal war aim, besides the removal of the conqueror, was to settle the internal state of France in a specific way. This necessarily implied keeping a police watch over France.

The relative nature of the difference between international and civil war must at that time have been obvious to a British statesman, even if he looked at the problem from the opposite side. We have seen how badly the British Government was in need of a regular police force during those agitated years 1812 and 1817. If, instead of removing the causes of disaffection, the Government chose to suppress its outward symptoms, the only way open to them in the circumstances was the use of military force, English [1] or, at times, Hanoverian. A part of the army thus being used for police duties at home, it was easy to conceive of another part fulfilling a like function abroad. The growing use which at that time, as we have seen, was being made of spies for internal purposes, was surely another symptom of this assimilation of the two spheres. For example, the " Secret Cabinet " in Vienna which had been busy during the War and still busier during the Congress of Vienna,[2] when even the waste-paper baskets of foreign diplomats were searched, remained exceedingly active in the ensuing period of peace ; the less opportunity there was of suspecting and spying upon distinguished foreigners, the more suspicion had to be aroused against the common people at home,[3] simply in order to keep an office and a machinery going. This symptom, of course, was by no means confined to Austria ; in Prussia, for example, it seems to have reached almost the same dimensions. Here the great training centre for spies was Aix-la-Chapelle at the time of the Congress ;

---

[1] The relativity referred to is borne out also in the following passage from Byron's first speech in the House of Lords : ". . . all the cities you have taken, all the armies which have retreated before your leaders are but paltry subjects of self-congratulation, if your land divides against itself, and your dragoons and executioners must be let loose against your fellow citizens." (Hansard, *Parliamentary Debates*, XXI, 1812, p. 969.) Cf. also, from a different point of view, the following passage from Wellington's Memorandum to the Earl of Liverpool respecting the state of the Guards, June 1820 : ". . . thus in one of the most critical moments that ever occurred in this country, we and the public have reason to doubt in the fidelity of our troops, the only security we have, not only against revolution, but for the property and life of every individual in the country who has anything to lose." (*Despatches*, New Series, I, London, 1867, p. 127.)

[2] Cf. M. H. Weil, *Les Dessous du Congrès de Vienne, d'après les documents originaux des Archives du Ministère Impérial et Royal de l'Intérieur à Vienne*, I, Paris, 1917. Cf. also August Fournier, *Die Geheimpolizei auf dem Wiener Kongress*, Wien-Leipzig, 1913.

[3] August Fournier, *Historische Studien und Skizzen*, 3. Reihe, Wien, 1912, p. 225. It should be noted that Kant had foreseen this development. (*Perpetual Peace*—commentary to fifth preliminary article.)

according to Gentz, who was greatly annoyed about it, the town was full of Prussian spies.[1] The consequences were the same as in Austria. About a year after the congress, Varnhagen von Ense wrote to the famous publisher Cotta, from Berlin : " I do not write you how things are here, because this is quite impossible for me ; . . . give my regards to all my friends, but tell them not to write to me, for it would be critical under present circumstances when every word can be interpreted in a bad sense ; paper is nowadays an evil treasure, at any moment it may become a red-hot coal." [2] On St. Helena Napoleon boasted that under his rule the technique of intercepting letters had tremendously improved. Now that the international War was over, such interception was still carried on, of course with all the newly learnt refinements. It is estimated that in Austria alone at that time far more than 15,000 letters were intercepted each year.[3] In certain cases the strong urge for activity felt by the police was not satisfied by spying of this or of any kind. For example, in Lyons, in June 1817, the police, acting as *agents provocateurs*, engineered bread riots. The political motive was to frighten the Government and to strengthen the "Ultras". Wild possibilities seemed open, since the Comte d'Artois, the head of the Ultra-royalists, maintained a private body of police in open opposition to their official counterparts.

In this connection it should also be remembered that Wellington once said in the House of Lords that he had passed a longer period of his life engaged in war than most men, and that principally in civil war.[4] Indeed it seems as if the great strategist had, in his later years, even developed some kind of theory of civil war, for his faithful Boswell, Lord Stanhope, reports on November 21st, 1831 : " The Duke anticipates greater horrors from a convulsion in this country—should any occur—than from that of any other European nation." And the reason, in Wellington's own words : " Our mob is not trained nor accustomed to regular direction as the French was ; once let it loose, and you will see what it will do." [5]

---

[1] Op. cit., p. 371.

[2] *Briefe an Cotta. Das Zeitalter der Restauration*, p. 25.

[3] Josef Karl Mayr, *Metternichs geheimer Briefdienst, Postlogen und Postkurse, Inventare des Wiener Haus-, Hof- und Staatsarchivs*, V 3, Wien, 1935, p. 20.

[4] Hansard, New Series, XXI, p. 46. The date of the speech is April 2nd, 1829. Cf. also Gentz in a letter to Pilat, dated 2nd September 1816 : " This so-called epoch of peace is in reality a *bellum omnium contra omnes* ". (*Briefe von Friedrich von Gentz an Pilat*, ed. Karl Mendelssohn-Bartholdy, Leipzig, 1868, p. 239.)

[5] *Notes of Conversations with the Duke of Wellington 1831-1851*, London, 1938 (World's Classics), p. 32. Cf. Coleridge, *Table Talk*, 4th July 1830 : " I sometimes fear the

Yet another factor which helped to bridge the gulf hitherto existing between what had formerly been regarded as internal and as foreign affairs can be seen in the fact that during the last two years of the Napoleonic Wars the sovereigns and leading diplomats of the Allied countries had become accustomed to very close co-operation. They travelled together for hundreds of miles, they often stayed together in small inns, they saw each other almost every day. There is evidence to show that even then they did not confine their discussions to the one subject ; how to get rid of Napoleon. The co-ordination of the various military efforts worked in the same direction. Yet they seem to have begun to appreciate each other's interests and to share each other's apprehensions even at this early stage. Moreover, they grew accustomed to dealing with foreign in much the same way as they were used to tackle internal affairs : that is to say, they held discussions with a handful of people who mattered, and followed them up by concerted action (or, alternatively, by concerted inaction) by these people—nothing more and nothing less. Metternich in his fragmentary autobiographical *Memoir* attached special importance to this interesting factor :

By a coincidence which was not only singular at the time, but without example in the annals of history, the chief personages in the great drama found themselves together in the very same place. The Emperors of Austria and Russia, the King of Prussia, and their three cabinets, were really never separated. The leader of the English cabinet had also generally been with his colleagues of Austria, Russia and Prussia. At the Congress of Vienna most of the Princes who now form the German Confederation were also present at the negotiations. Since, therefore, the European potentates and their ministers were in the same place, the forms of diplomatic business had to adapt themselves to circumstances. The most difficult affairs, and the arrangements most complicated in their nature, were, so to speak, negotiated from one room to another ; no sending of couriers, no written negotiations, no medium between the Courts : all these things, so necessary in ordinary times, had disappeared. Many a business which under any other circumstance, would have required a long time for arrangement, was concluded in the course of a forenoon. The most important affairs were always discussed in confidential conversations between the three monarchs, as well as between the heads of the cabinets. Only when the matter had reached a certain stage of ripeness did the ministers come together for regular conferences, carried on with

Duke of Wellington is too much disposed to imagine that he can govern a great nation by word of command, in the same way in which he governed a highly disciplined army. He seems to be unaccustomed to, and to despise, the inconsistencies, the weaknesses, the bursts of heroism followed by prostration and cowardice, which invariably characterize all popular efforts."

Protocols. A mere glance at these Protocols suffices to show that they contain no discussions. Where they are anything more than the mere formula of the point agreed upon, they give single statements, which show the shades of meaning in the opinions of the different persons who joined in them : shades which, however, never stood in the way of a general conclusion.[1]

After this new technique of diplomatic conferences had been tried out for three years in weekly ambassadorial conferences in Paris, Castlereagh—who at Chaumont in 1814 had already outlined the idea of a Concert of Europe—wrote to Liverpool from Aix-la-Chapelle on October 20th, 1818 :

> At all events, it is satisfactory to observe how little embarrassment and how much solid good grow out of these reunions, which sound so terrible at a distance. It really appears to me to be a new discovery in the European Government,[2] at once extinguishing the cobwebs with which diplomacy obscures the horizon, bringing the whole bearing of the system into its true light, and giving to the great Powers the efficiency and almost the simplicity of a single State.

If the high-sounding phrase " European Government " meant anything at all, it could mean only this : the Continent on the one hand, and the individual State on the other, were by certain persons no longer regarded as completely heterogeneous entities, for the simple reason that these persons had become accustomed to meeting, discussing, and deciding certain European questions in approximately the same way as their respective Cabinets used to discuss the internal affairs of their respective countries. The affairs of a Continent thus becoming to some extent manageable, Metternich hastened to transfer the newly invented method of government by diplomatic conference to a unit much smaller than Europe yet exceeding the limits of an individual State, namely the German Confederation. Not disturbed by the fact that such a procedure according to the Federal Act, was unconstitutional, Metternich called together representatives of the

---

[1] *Memoirs of Prince Metternich, 1773–1815*, Vol. I, London, 1880, pp. 172-3. Cf. also Gentz in a letter to Nesselrode, dated Paris, 22nd November 1815 : " Il faut dire encore quelques mots sur la partie technique ou diplomatique des dernières négociations. Je crois que c'est là notre côté brillant. Comparées à celles de 1814 et au congrès de Vienne, les conférences de 1815 ont certainement mérité des éloges. Nous avons beaucoup travaillé, et bien travaillé. Nous avons signé plus de cent protocols et sept traités ! " (*Lettres et Papiers du Chancelier Comte de Nesselrode 1760–1850*, tome V, Paris, 1907, p. 238.)

[2] The idea of a " Congrès perpetuel " was older ; it had been suggested as early as 1782 by the French schoolmaster Gargaz. Cf. his *Conciliateur de toutes les Nations d'Europe ou Projet de Paix Perpetuelle*, Passy, 1782 : reprinted New York, 1922, p. 11 ; and also Elizabeth V. Souleyman, *The Vision of World Peace in Seventeenth and Eighteenth Century France*, New York, 1941, pp. 176-81.

principal States of the Confederation, and began to " manage " Germany in the same way as, together with a handful of other men, he had already begun to " manage " Europe.

How did it come about that the " Great Powers "—the term had just begun to be current in diplomatic phraseology—arrogated to themselves the right to speak for the whole of Europe ? The excuse seems to have been the dimensions reached by the Napoleonic Wars. For the main obligations of the Treaty of Chaumont, concluded in March 1814, were, as C. K. Webster has pointed out, such as only Great Powers with large resources could undertake. The four powers agreed to protect Europe for twenty years against French aggression or against any attempt which France might make " to infringe the order of things resulting from such pacification ". For this purpose they promised 60,000 men, Britain reserving her right to employ foreign troops paid by her as her contribution. In consequence, the four Powers reserved to themselves, in Art. V of the Treaty, the right to concert together, on the conclusion of a peace with France, as to the means best adapted to guarantee to Europe and to themselves reciprocally the continuance of peace.

How then did Metternich—whom his opponents dubbed " cocher de l'Europe "—and these representatives of the three (or later four) other principal Powers [1] manage Europe ? What were the matters on which agreement was reached and concerted action taken ?

There was above all the problem of France herself. French domestic affairs, or at any rate what had previously been regarded as such, were the first to become the subject of regular international discussion and decision. Between the autumn of 1815 and the autumn of 1818, the Ambassadors of the four victorious Great Powers who were accredited to Paris met in that city for weekly conferences. Their interference in French domestic affairs was indeed far-reaching. Even in October 1815, before they were officially established as an organ of the Quadruple Alliance, they required that the King's speech should be communicated to them in advance.[2] Later, constituted as the Ambassadorial Conference, they were to require information from the French Government about all *projets de lois* ; to call for modifications ; to examine, among many other things, the com-

---

[1] In this concert, Great Britain was, of course, at least as important as Austria. Cf. Gentz, *Dépêches inédites aux Hospodars de Valachie*, I, Paris, 1876, p. 364 : " Angleterre —le pivot de la fédération ".

[2] Pierre de la Gorce, *La Restauration. Louis XVIII*, Paris, 1926, p. 93.

plaints of the exiles, and to obtain repatriation in the cases where they thought it suitable ; [1] above all, to try to counteract the Ultra-royalists whose bellicosity [2] they perceived to be a serious menace to the internal peace of the country. In addition to these concerted *démarches*, strong pressure was brought upon the French Government by the Allied Powers one by one. Wellington's warning despatch to Louis XVIII has already been mentioned. A few examples may illustrate the attitude of the Government which took the leading part in this respect. At the beginning of February 1816, the Russian Foreign Minister, Nesselrode, wrote in a despatch to Richelieu, the French Premier : " The discussions in the Chamber of Deputies are indeed shocking, and catastrophe is to be expected unless you succeed by means of new elections in improving the spirit of the members." At the same time, Pozzo di Borgo received instructions to draw the King's attention to the dangerous doings of the majority in the Chamber. In June of the same year, Alexander went further. This time Pozzo di Borgo had to hand to the King and to Richelieu a long list of points in which, it was said, the opinion of the Allies was summarized. It is generally assumed that this *démarche* caused or at least encouraged the King to issue, on July 17th, the decree on the organization of the National Guard ; its purpose was to lessen or to eliminate the influence which the Ultra-royalists had begun to exercise upon that body. Another prominent object of the discussions at, and behind the curtains of, the Ambassadorial Conference was to find out ways and means for France to pay the war indemnity to the Allies. The solution arrived at foreshadowed the paradoxical development of Germany's reparations after the First World War. It was Ouvrard who had the ingenious idea that France should borrow abroad in order to be able to pay off her foreign debts. Hope and Baring, rightly expecting large profits, supported the scheme ; Wellington, at first horrified, eventually consented to it.

But the most tangible interference in French affairs came, of course, from the Allied armies of occupation. Moreover, in all the many other cases of interference, the Powers could always rely on this coercive instrument, the threat of a prolongation of the occupation beyond the minimum period of three years ; or,

---

[1] Pierre Rain, *L'Europe et la Restauration des Bourbons, 1814–1818*, Paris, 1908, p. 207.

[2] Cf. Stendhal in a letter to Sutton-Sharpe, dated 15th June 1824 : " J'ai passé ma première jeunesse avec des grands seigneurs qui étaient aimables—ce sont aujourd'hui de vieux ultra méchants." (*Correspondance de Stendhal*, ed. A. Paupe, II, Paris, 1908.)

WELLINGTON

portrait by Sir William Beechey, 1814

From the Curzon Collection in the Bodleian Library

[*face p.* 128

METTERNICH

[*face p.* 129

on the other hand, the inducement of a partial reduction at an early stage—such were the weapons used for all these purposes.

In this connection it is perhaps well once more to recall the state of affairs then existing in France. For example, it should not be forgotten that when Richelieu, at the beginning of December 1815, expressed the desire that the Allies should withdraw their troops from Paris, he did so with the intention of frightening the Ultra-royalists. Although the Ambassadorial Conference by no means supported their exorbitant claims, this group seems to have felt safer under the protection of foreign bayonets. As to the general effect of the foreign occupation, the accounts given from the side of the then Allied countries, and repeated in our own time, were much idealized. This has, I think, been proved by Pierre Rain, who in his book *L'Europe et la Restauration des Bourbons 1814–1818* adduces considerable evidence to show that the foreign troops behaved in numerous cases in the most reckless manner, and also that, contrary to some reports, there was nothing to choose between the demeanour of the troops of the various nationalities : Englishmen, Prussians, Hanoverians, Saxons, Austrians and Russians—they were all alike.[1] In addition to the extraordinary vexation caused by these unruly guests, the ordinary features characterizing the Restoration period all over Europe were also present in France. There were the enormously exaggerated reports about revolts ; a skirmish which took place at Grenoble on May 4th, 1816, was reported to Paris by the General commanding the place as a battle lasting several hours which had cost several hundreds of lives ; a sure sign in his eyes of impending civil war ; all this followed by the typical panicky reaction of the central Government : twenty-one sentences of death. There were the police acting as *agents-provocateurs* and amassing an ever-increasing amount of information about thousands of individuals.[2] As for the economic situation, the harvest of 1816 was almost completely ruined by the continuous rain in France as everywhere else ; but the misery was greatly aggravated by the burden of the foreign occupation, which lasted for three years, from 1815 to 1818. This partly explains why for a long time in 1817 there was still no appreciable improvement in that country ; in fact, Russian wheat had to be imported in that year. We have Mme. de Rémusat's testimony

[1] Op. cit., p. 273.
[2] F. B. Artz, *France under the Bourbon Reaction, 1814–1830*, Cambridge (Mass.), 1931, p. 49.

to the fact that she then saw villages in the neighbourhood of
Lille in which 3,000 beggars appeared each day ; [1] for even
bread reached a price prohibitive for a large section of the
population. Comte Molé reports that in the eastern *départements*
whole villages fed on herbs and wild roots. In the *département* of
Seine-et-Marne corn markets were pillaged. The troops sent to
restore order did so with signs of reluctance. The plight was
further aggravated by the poor state of communications. Hardly
16,000 out of the total of 34,000 km. of highways were in good
repair. The improvement of the system of canals, which was
to be a great achievement of the Restoration, had only just begun.
Finally, how much disaffection was there in the country ? Even
in this respect there were far-reaching similarities between France
and the rest of Europe : general dissatisfaction (Gentz's estimate,
in November 1815, was 95 per cent.), a great deal of disaffection,
but no concerted agreement.

It is in the nature of things that we have more precise information about manifestations of disaffection among intellectuals than
among other sections of the population. [2] We know, for example,
that the economic crisis of 1817 made Saint-Simon, from 1820
onwards, emphasize the implications of charity in the framework
of his *Système industriel*. Copies of the periodical *Minerva* which
was the organ of the " Indépendants " are still preserved ; they
bear witness to the bitter feeling which existed against the nobility
and clergy. Among the students, too, especially the University
of Paris, Republicanism never ceased to live. [3] But on the whole
it could be assumed that Republicanism would prove a serious
menace to the precarious equilibrium of forces only in so far
as it was provoked by some action on the part of the extreme
Right. Such action, however, might be expected at any moment.
That is why the counsels of the Allied Powers often consisted of
suggestions, supported in the way mentioned above, for counter-
acting that special kind of disaffection which hid behind the
convenient slogan of Ultra-royalism, that is, in other words, why
" Europe " was so anxious to forestall in France excesses from the
Right. The full dose of Restoration, it was recognized, would
not be suffered by the patient, who in that case might refuse the
medicine altogether and would soon relapse into his old left-wing

---

[1] Cf. also Marquise de Montcalm, *Mon Journal pendant le premier ministère de mon
frère*, 3rd ed., Paris, 1936, pp. 261, 269–70.
[2] Yet it is well to remember that according to an estimate for the year 1819,
fifteen million out of about twenty-five million adults could neither read nor write.
[3] Georges Weill, *Histoire du parti republicain en France (1814–1870)*, Paris, 1926, p. 7.

revolutionary illness. This had to be avoided if possible, at almost any price.

There are many indications that this was in the mind of the European statesmen who " managed " France. Wellington, who used to be present at the Ambassadorial Conferences, and who in any case spoke with authority, warned Louis XVIII against the Ultra-royalists ; it is quite probable that the King would not have dissolved the " Chambre Introuvable " had he not received such a grave warning. Yet when Louis XVIII, in September 1816, disclosed to Wellington his intention of taking this bold step, the Duke, as we have seen, expressed his apprehension lest the new Chamber should have a democratic majority. Similarly, when, a few months earlier, he had agreed to withdraw the last contingent of foreign troops from Paris, it looked as if this measure had been taken mainly in order to weaken the Ultra-royalists. Be this as it may, it is significant that the Duke in conversation with Pozzo di Borgo also mentioned another motive. He intended, he said, to deprive the opposition in the English Parliament of a pretext for attacking the settlement in France by pointing to its unstable character.[1] Another example : when, during the Congress of Aix-la-Chapelle, by-elections were held for the second fifth of the Chamber, and sixteen Liberals were returned, among them Lafayette, Sir Charles Stuart, British Ambassador to Paris, is reported to have said : " The Government of France will fall into the hands of robbers."[2] This is an indication of the sympathies of the arbiters of Europe (the majority of them, at least) even while they were engaged in restraining the " Right ".

Their attitude was born of deep insight. For example, Wellington (who, to use Byron's hard words, had repaired Legitimacy's crutch),[3] wrote to the Rt. Hon. T. C. Villiers from France on January 11th, 1818 :

I entertain no doubt how this contest will end. The descendants of Louis XV will not reign in France ; and I must say, and always will say, that it is the fault of Monsieur and his adherents . . . I wish Monsieur would read the histories of our Restoration and subsequent Revolution, or that he would recollect what passed under his own view, probably at his own instigation in the Revolution.[4]

---

[1] *Correspondance Diplomatique du Comte Pozzo di Borgo et du Comte de Nesselrode depuis la Restauration des Bourbons jusqu'au Congrès d'Aix-la-Chapelle, 1814–1818*, I, Paris, 1890, p. 298.
[2] Stern, op. cit., p. 467. [3] *Don Juan*, canto IX, stanza 111.
[4] *Supplementary Despatches*, XII, p. 213.

The same view, more fully elaborated, had already been put forward by Gentz in his above-mentioned despatch to Nesselrode from Paris on November 22nd, 1815 :

. . . The present state of France is anti-natural, in direct opposition to the principles, sentiments and intentions of nineteen-twentieths of the nation,[1] and in direct opposition to the eternal laws of social development. So long as this state of affairs continues, the throne, supported by foreign arms and the fear of a mortal catastrophe, will never emerge from the storms, the internal disruptions, the tribulations and dangers which are every day the outcome of the general discontent.[2] It will be the same after three years or after five years— so long as the causes of the disorder are not utterly annihilated. Those who in 1814 thought they could establish the *ancien régime* pure and simple did France as much harm as did Robespierre and Bonaparte. But the natural order of things is too strong for men. The French Revolution must go through its full circle like the English Revolution in the seventeenth century. The revolutionary period has been as long as but much more terrible and more radical than that of 1635–1660. The restoration of absolute power will not be accomplished any more than that attempted in England. An outcome analogous to that of 1688 is the only one which can rationally and thoroughly bring the present revolution to an end. Absolute power once utterly overthrown will never rear its head again. The *old* Bourbons cannot and must not rule again.[3]

Both Wellington and Gentz foresaw with remarkable penetration that the fate of the Stuarts awaited the Bourbons. In this connection it is worth remarking that, according to Louis Blanc,[4] Thiers and Mignet recognized in 1830 that they were faced with a position analogous to that of 1688.

---

[1] A similar opinion was expressed by Gagern, *Der zweite Pariser Frieden*, I, Leipzig, 1845, p. 119.

[2] Cf. also Gentz's despatch to Prince Tanko Caradja from Paris, October 23rd, 1815 : " La haine contre le Roi et sa famille, loin de diminuer, augmente chaque jour. . . . Si la France était abandonnée aujourd'hui à elle-même, il est indubitable que, en moins de six mois, nous verrions se reproduire dans ce pays les scènes les plus désolantes, et, selon toute probabilité, un bouleversement total . . . Or, comme le Gouvernement n'a aucune force militaire à sa disposition, il est clair qu'il suffirait d'un choc sérieux pour le renverser." (*Dépêches inédites du Chevalier de Gentz aux Hospodars de Valachie*, I, Paris, 1876, pp. 187, 190, 191.)

[3] *Lettres et Papiers du Chancelier Nesselrode, 1769–1850*, tome V, pp. 236–7. (I have translated this passage from the original French.)

[4] " Cependant, quelques esprits inquiets avaient émis des idées singulières. On avait comparé les Bourbons aînés à la famille incorrigible des Stuarts, on avait parlé de Guillaume III ; de 1688, date d'une révolution pacifique, et pourtant profonde ; de la possibilité de chasser une dynastie sans renverser un trône ; du meurtre de Charles Ier, inutile jusqu'au moment de l'exil de Jacques II. Ces discours avaient circulé d'abord dans quelques salons. Le ' National ' feuille de création nouvelle, les avait divulgués en les appuyant . . . Telles idées, émises avec réserve par des écrivains habiles, MM. Thiers et Mignet . . ." (Louis Blanc, *Histoire de dix ans 1830–1840*, tome I, Paris, 1844, pp. 174–5.)

PART III

DISCORD IN THE CONCERT OF EUROPE

Every nation for itself, and God for us all.

Canning (1823).

CHAPTER VII

POST-WAR CONVULSIONS IN SOUTHERN EUROPE

A. SPAIN

The country that had been the first to offer a successful resistance to Napoleon, came to be the scene of the first serious outburst in peacetime. The character of this outburst, and others which followed in the Kingdom of the Two Sicilies and in Greece, will need to be studied before we can attempt to analyse the discord which on these occasions became audible in the Concert of Europe.

Spain, unlike any of the countries which we have dealt with in previous chapters, had been in a state of economic decay ever since the end of the sixteenth century. A certain degree of inertia,[1] probably due to the climate, had always been characteristic of the Spaniard. Thus it came about that at the turn of the Ages when man began to be increasingly interested in the things of this world, the greed for gold became the typical Spanish form of greed. Gold and still more gold : this was the chief aim of Spanish colonial expansion. Huge fertile regions lying in the west of what is now the U.S.A., regions, however, which could not be developed without great efforts, were contemptuously marked on Spanish maps as " tierras de ningun provecho " (territories of no profit). It has been rightly said that Spain was choked by her own colonies, and that she was reduced to poverty by American gold. For precious metals could be produced with comparative ease, especially since native American and imported African slaves performed the hard work connected with them. At the same time gold brought splendour and prestige. Consequently, wealth based on more exacting if less splendid achievements came to be looked down upon, more so than in any other

---

[1] Cf. G. Desdevises du Dezert, " La Société espagnole au XVIIIᵉ siècle ", *Revue hispanique*, LXIV, 1925, p. 598 : " Le far-niente est considéré comme le bien suprême."

European country at any time.   The result was that trade, after decreasing in the seventeenth century, became almost stagnant during the eighteenth.   Spanish merchants—what few there were —acted in most cases merely as agents for foreigners.   At the lowest point of Spain's economic decline in the eighteenth century, not more than a twentieth part of the goods consumed by the Spanish colonies were produced in the mother country.

The decay was by no means limited to the economic sphere. The growing inertia manifested itself, for example, in the lack of communications.[1]   Consequently Spain was highly decentralized, and thus many of the social achievements which other European States owed to the increasing strength of the central power were denied to her.   This was all the more striking since she did not enjoy the amenities usually connected with decentralization.   The nobility, that is to say, did not form small cultural centres all over the country ; on the contrary, they all assembled at and around the Royal Court of Madrid.[2]   This took place at times in a rather undignified way.   Young men of the " proudest families " were sent to Court as *pretendientes* (place-hunters).   Leucadio Doblado, in his *Letters from Spain* (1822) reports that few gentlemen destined their sons either for the Church or the law without calculating how they could be supported for three or four years at Madrid, admittedly for no other purpose than this.[3]   Corruption was thus one of the main features of Court and aristocracy.[4]   Of the pile of evidence for this assumption, the portraits of Goya, the greatest painter since Velasquez, may be mentioned.   Théophile Gautier, in his *Voyage en Espagne* (1840), correctly prophesied that Goya's " caricatures " would soon be looked upon in the light of historical documents. Nor did Goya's art expose the worldly magnates alone.   With equally strong bias, which he considered to be an essential part of all painting, he depicted the very worldly vices of those who were supposed to represent the spiritual power.   Among the " Desastres de la Guerra " there is one plate marked " Truth is

---

[1] Cf. George Ticknor's letter to his father from Madrid, dated 23rd May 1818 : ". . . roads so abominable that the utmost diligence from four o'clock in the morning until seven at night, would not bring us forward more than 21 or 22 miles.   Imagine a country so deserted and desolate and with so little travelling and communications, as to have no taverns." (*Life, Letters, and Journals of G. Ticknor*, I, London, 1876, p. 185.)

[2] Ibid., p. 461.

[3] P. 361.   Doblado, who was partly of Irish, partly of Spanish extraction, became known in England under the name of Joseph Blanco White.

[4] Cf. George Ticknor in Madrid in 1818 : " There is nothing that cannot be done by bribery." (Op. cit., p. 192.)

dead " ; it shows prelates imparting the last blessing to her body.

The moral decadence of the clergy failed, however, to produce the same effects in Spain as it did in France. For a considerable time to come Spanish priests and monks retained their leading rôle in the eyes of large sections of the population. This was due to the fact that sceptical rationalism had not spread. Moreover, in a country as decentralized as Spain then was, scepticism could not possibly grow up. As a rule, man wishes to free himself from the transcendental bond only if he is in close contact with his fellow-men. This condition was certainly not present in Spain. The printed word played a very small rôle ; [1] oral tradition was still far more important. It was a symptom of the almost unbroken power of the Church that when the Cortes, in 1812, abolished the Inquisition together with tithes, they did not touch ecclesiastical censorship. It was even more significant that the new liberal Constitution had to be read out at Mass.

The same lack of self-confidence manifested itself at the election of the provincial Juntas which in 1808 sprang up in several Spanish cities, at the time when Joseph Bonaparte established himself as King in the capital. These provincial Juntas were chosen by general suffrage, but those who were elected were mainly members of the provincial nobility and gentry, some priests, and only very few notabilities of the middle class. In September 1808, when Joseph Bonaparte had fled from Madrid before Spanish armies, a Central Junta of deputies from the provincial bodies met in that city. It sat there for two months before it had to flee to Seville, where it stayed until the beginning of 1810. The composition of the Central Junta was very similar, consisting as it did of grandees and prelates as well as high civil and military officials. This respectable assembly, in its turn, could not but acknowledge the Consejo Real, a body, composed of *abogados* (jurists), at the summit of the administrative hierarchy. We cannot be surprised that in these circumstances the Central Junta failed to break through the shackles of feudalism.[2] Its programme, of course, sounded very different. " It has seemed

---

[1] As late as 1799 Wilhelm von Humboldt on a journey through Spain noticed a considerable number of interesting works in manuscript form. (Tagebuch der Reise nach Spanien 1799–1800, *Tagebücher*, ed. A. Leitzmann, II, Berlin, 1918, p. 182.)

[2] The position of the Spanish peasants was very wretched. It had hardly changed since the last years of the reign of Charles III when Jovellanos had described it thus : " The poor peasants live without shoes, badly dressed, they feed on oatmeal and millet-bread ; meat and wine they taste but seldom. They sleep on straw, live in wretched huts, and are continually pressed down by heavy labour. They torment themselves until their old age, without hope of saving up anything, and are in constant struggle against destitution."

good to Providence "—so began one of their proclamations to the Spanish people—" that in this terrible crisis you should not be able to advance one step towards independence without advancing likewise one step towards liberty." In reality, as Karl Marx has pointed out,[1] there seems to have existed in the Central Junta " a most original division of labour : the Jovellanos party being allowed to proclaim and to protocol the revolutionary aspirations of the nation, and the Floridablanca party reserving to themselves the pleasure of giving them the lie direct, and of opposing to revolutionary fiction counter-revolutionary fact ".

Spain, moreover, was divided into two parts. In January 1810 the Junta, escaping to the Isla de León, had there resigned, appointing a Regency to arrange for Cortes representing Spain and America. The discrepancy between the territory which they claimed and that over which they ruled was tremendous ; for some time the latter covered no more than one square mile. There the Cortes met in September 1810, and there in 1812, under French bombardment, they promulgated a Liberal constitution. Marx summarized the situation in one of his beloved *jeux-de-mots* : " At the Isla de León, ideas without action, in the rest of Spain action without ideas."

The minority whose intellectual energy provided revolutionary ideas [2] was composed of inhabitants of sea-ports and commercial towns ; [3] but preponderatingly of aristocrats, priests and students. Foremost among the aristocratic Liberals were the old Melchior de Jovellanos and the young José de Quintana. The former, undoubtedly the greatest Spanish publicist of the period, advised the Church to make a generous concession with regard to its property rights ; this measure was to help to provide for the poor. The latter, poet and politician, was offered an appointment by Napoleon. He refused, and was made secretary of the Junta, whose proclamations and manifestoes were drafted by him. Among his chief concerns was education in the Western sense of the word. Unlike Rousseau, whom otherwise he admired, Quintana was much in favour of the Press. Indeed, within two years from the authorization of a free Press in 1812, more publica-

---

[1] " Revolution in Spain ", a series of articles contributed by Marx and Engels to the *New York Daily Tribune*. The article in question appeared on October 20th, 1854.

[2] Cf. Altamira, art. " Spain (1815-48) " in *Cambridge Modern History*, X, 1907, p. 229. The author attaches more importance to the first-mentioned group of Liberals. In the text, I follow a suggestion made to me by Señor de Madariaga.

[3] For example, Coruña, a commercial town, and an age-old antagonist of Santiago, the priests' town, became an important centre of liberalism.

tions were issued in Spain than in any two previous decades.[1] In appreciating Spanish liberalism we must not forget that it was by no means confined to the cause of the patriots. The poet Marchena and the scholar Meléndez Valdés are prominent examples of Liberals employed by the French.

The longer the war went on, the smaller Liberal influence became. At the first meeting of the Cortes the comparatively democratic provinces of Catalonia and Galicia had been almost exclusively represented. Later the Cortes found it difficult to carry out those Liberal reforms which their predecessors had missed. One important exception, however, must be mentioned. Under the influence of Jovellanos, a disciple of Adam Smith, steps were taken to bring about a general sale of communal property as well, ultimately, as of that of the Church. Thus the way was paved for the far-reaching, and as Gerald Brenan has recently shown,[2] disastrous Liberal reforms of 1835 and 1855–6. The second general election, in 1813, resulted in a decisive victory for the *Serviles* at the expense of the *Liberales*, Serviles being, of course, a term of abuse invented by their opponents, a Liberal poet having gone so far as to make the pun *ser-vil* (vile being). In spite of the decadence of the nobility, there obviously did not exist in Spanish society any stratum strong enough to take over the power from those who had so greatly abused it.

Whatever be said about the main work of the Cortes, the Constitution of 1812, it does not seem to have sprung from the general will of the Spanish people. Some of its chapters were literal translations of passages from the French Constitution of 1791. Other passages had to be inserted in order to compete with the French Government at Madrid, which had abolished all monastic and feudal institutions. In imitation of Joseph Bonaparte's educational reforms, the Cortes also did something to improve public instruction by creating new schools and drawing up educational plans, but all this took little root.[3] The vast majority of the people did not care for ideas imported from abroad ; all they grasped was that it was essential to drive the invader out of Spain.[4] This one idea seems to have been sufficient

---

[1] Jefferson Rea Spell, *Rousseau in the Spanish World before 1833*, University of Texas, 1938, p. 196.   [2] *The Spanish Labyrinth*, Cambridge, 1943, pp. 108 f.
[3] Altamira, *A History of Spanish Civilization*, London, 1930, p. 190.
[4] The first to interpret the Spanish struggle against Napoleon in this way was Görres, the Rhenish author and politician. Cf. *Europa und die Revolution*, Stuttgart, 1821. (*Gesammelte Schriften*, XIII, Köln, 1929, p. 246.) Coleridge, too, commented on the Spaniards' " rooted antipathy to all strangers as such ". (Table Talk, 26th June 1831.)

stimulus for them to wage war in the most determined way for several years. Yet the senselessness of this effort was obvious at least to Goya, although only in later years. One of the drawings of the " Desastres de la Guerra ", which were made in 1820, represents a corpse, half buried in the earth ; it supports itself on its elbow ; near by lies a paper which it scarcely seems to notice as it traces upon it with its bony hand the single almost untranslatable word " Nada " (nothingness).

To what a slight extent liberalism was rooted in the people was shown only too clearly by the scenes that took place on the occasion of King Ferdinand's return. When he entered Valencia in April 1814, people yoked themselves to his carriage, shouting " Long live the absolute King " and " Down with the Constitution ". Similarly, in Madrid huge bronze letters signifying " Liberty " over the entrance hall of the Cortes were removed by the mob ; as each of these letters was thrown into the street, a new wave of exultation laid hold of the spectators. Clergy and aristocrats, as we have seen, still held a kind of authority over a great many people. This much, at least, they were still able to achieve ; firstly, to persuade the masses that the Constitution of 1812 had brought them no relief, which was almost true because it had been effected so half-heartedly, and, secondly, to incite them to acts of terrorism and plunder. Here was something palpable for the masses, something quite unlike those abstract constitutional principles. Thus numbers of people were bought at the expense of others, namely of the *Afrancesados*, those, that is, who during Joseph Bonaparte's reign were supposed to have recognized the foreign ruler in one way or another.

Violent reaction ruled over Spain until 1820 ; the Inquisition, reintroduced by Ferdinand, was by no means its worst feature. Yet, when at last the outburst took place, the nature of which we shall presently have to define, not a single village or town declared itself spontaneously for Riego, the revolutionary leader.[1] Those Liberal forces that did exist, were divided by now into two camps, the Moderados and the Exaltados. The abuse of rhetoric was almost the only feature common to both. The Liberal government, which for a time gained the upper hand of the King, introduced a number of important reforms concerning public welfare, customs duties, a Penal Code, and last but not

---

[1] Cf. Michael Klapp, *Revolutionsbilder aus Spanien*, Hanover, 1869, p. 162 : " Leading a small band of faithful adherents, he moved from town to town, from village to village, one might almost say : begging the people to make a revolution."

NADA. ELLO DIRA
Drawing by Goya

Goya. *Desastres de la Guerra*, published by the Phaidon Press, Ltd., Oxford and London

[*face p.* 138

SÉPULTURE DE NAPOLÉON À ST. HÉLÈNE
Drawing by Sandoz, 1821

From the Curzon Collection in the Bodleian Library

[*face p.* 139

least, a new plan of education including a scheme for modern universities.[1]   In spite of all these reforms, the new constitutional system was never popular.   The people of Madrid, indeed, carried the " saint Codex " of the Constitution round the streets in a procession ; passers-by were made to show their reverence by kneeling down and kissing it.[2]   But exactly the same theatrical performance had been staged by the same actors in 1814, when Ferdinand's picture was pompously displayed.   Moreover, when French troops invaded Spain once more, in 1823, this time with the object of reinstating the absolute King, the country, for once exhausted and apathetic,[3] did not offer any resistance to their advance.

All the more determined had been the resistance which the Spanish people put up against Napoleon.   Looking back, in 1822, Bignon rightly emphasized this aspect :   " En Espagne, ce n'est pas avec un cabinet, mais avec une nation que la lutte est engagée ; et c'est là seulement qu'un triomphe définitif est refusé à nos armes." [4]   At the beginning of the struggle especially, it happened quite frequently that members of the aristocracy and the richer classes refrained from showing any signs of opposition to the foreign invader.[5]   The main part of the fighting had to be done by the common people under the leadership of the Church.   Many of the guerrilla bands even made it a rule that no *hidalgo* (gentleman) should belong to them, because men of property were not to be trusted in the fight against the invaders. Castlereagh's assertions to the contrary, in 1816, were completely unfounded.   The very fact that guerrilla warfare was so prominent was a symptom of the lack of organization.   The Swiss mercenary M. de Rocca, in his *Memoirs of the War of the French in Spain*, gives this horrid description :   " Like avenging vultures eager for prey, they followed the French columns at a distance,

---

[1] Pio Zabala y Lera, *España bajo los Borbones*, 3rd ed., Barcelona, 1936, p. 336.
[2] Hermann Baumgarten, *Geschichte Spaniens vom Ausbruch der französischen Revolution bis auf unsere Tage*, II, Leipzig, 1868, p. 273.
[3] Quin, *A Visit to Spain*, 1823, p. 317.
[4] " Les Cabinets et les Peuples depuis 1815 jusqu'à la fin de 1822 ", *The Pamphleteer*, XXII, p. 368.
The speculator Ouvrard commented thus on the difference between the Spanish warfare in 1808–14 and 1823 respectively :   " People defend Independence merely from a feeling of national pride which is being nourished by blind fanaticism ; but they defend inner freedom only if they comprehend and appreciate it."   (Otto Wolff, *Die Geschäfte des Herrn Ouvrard*, Frankfurt-am-Main, 1932, p. 219.)
[5] The allegations contained in *Memoria económica-política sobre los señores y grandes propietarios*, Salamanca 1813, are correct as far as the initial period of the war is concerned.   (The memorandum is reprinted in Zabala y Lera, *Historia de España y de la Civilización Española*, tom. V, Vol. II.)

to murder such of the soldiers as, fatigued or wounded, remained behind on a march." [1] According to the same testimony, women distinguished themselves by their perversity : " Women, or rather furies let loose," de Rocca reports, " threw themselves with horrible shrieks upon the wounded, and disputed who should kill them by the most cruel tortures ; they stabbed their eyes with knives and scissors, and seemed to exult with ferocious joy at the sight of their blood." [2] Warfare of this kind offered, of course, certain undeniable advantages : energies which in regular warfare might have been suppressed, could gain strength in a most unrestrained manner. We have also to take into account that the Spaniards had already gone through a very effective training-school for cruelty. In a satire called *Pan y Toros* (1796) which was meant in all bitter seriousness, Jovellanos had written :

If in cold blood a man can see a victim thrown up between the horns of a bull, split in two by a thrust from his horn, his intestines drawn out and covering the ground with blood ; a wounded horse throwing its rider, who is trying to mount it, even while the horse is wrestling with death ; its bowels gushing forth ; a group of toreros fleeing in panic before a grim beast wounded by spears ; the noisy clamour of a huge crowd, mingled with the clanging of warlike musical instruments which add to the confusion and the horror—how can such a man ever go into a duel or into battle with fear in his heart ? " [3]

The fanatical degree of resistance which the people of Spain put up against Napoleon's invasion can be explained also in a different way. We must not forget that the field army of 250,000 men formed by Napoleon in that country was the largest so far assembled in modern times. It has been pointed out that the wholesale robbery inevitable when so large an invading army lives off the country was bound to excite the hatred of the people.[4] The mass army thus caused mass resistance. Passions typical of the modern Wars of Nationality were aroused. At the same time, the passions which characterized the sixteenth- and seventeenth-century Wars of Religion had not died down in Spain as they had in other parts of Europe.

Reckless in time of war, in peace guerrillas must, as Marx has pointed out, form a most dangerous mob. Even before the struggle was over, Wellington reported to his brother Sir Henry

[1] Trans. from the French by M. Graham, 2nd ed., London, 1816, p. 192.

[2] Ibid., p. 255. For a Russian parallel, cf. Tarlé, *Napoleon's Invasion of Russia*, London, 1942, p. 251.

[3] Retranslated from the German edition by C. F. Mooyen, Minden, 1834, pp. 26–7. Even women enjoyed watching these modern *circences*. (Cf. the Duc de Laval-Montmorency's conversation with G. Ticknor, op. cit., p. 204, n. 2.)

[4] Hoffman Nickerson, *The Armed Horde, 1793–1939*, New York, 1940, p. 115.

Wellesley, on August 23rd, 1812 : "The guerrillas are getting quietly into the large towns and amusing themselves, or collecting plunder of a better and more valuable description.[1] When the invader had been driven out, habits like these could not easily be abandoned. Many of the guerrillas now became robbers. Gangs of them were strengthened by deserters from the regular army. In Aragon, for example, a gang of 1,500 men held their own against the troops ; they called themselves the army of the *agraviados* (aggravated).[2] Similar conditions prevailed in Castile, Andalusia, Valencia, and Catalonia.

The support which these gangs received from the ranks of the army and navy was partly connected with conditions in the services which, after Ferdinand's return, when the Exchequer was once more disorganized, were paid extremely badly. A decree, preposterous in the extreme, forbade soldiers to complain in case of their not receiving their pay. So far as the navy was concerned, the only relief offered for the extreme indigence of many of its officers was the permission granted them to support themselves by fishing.[3] At the same time it could not escape their notice that the King's personal guards were paid munificently. Nor could the soldiers whose sleeping accommodation in Madrid barracks was on the earth, fail to observe that more than twenty Madrid churches and convents were being restored and lavishly adorned with gold and silver. As early as September 1814, Werther, the Prussian Ambassador to Spain, reported : "If the government continues in this way, an explosion, perhaps later, is inevitable, and the army will not support the King, because it is being neglected and maltreated." In addition to the mal-treatment at home were the expeditions undertaken since 1814 for the re-subjugation of the revolted American colonies. Not without justification were they considered a means of getting rid of dissatisfied regiments.

Material discontent however, formed but one side of the picture. Even among those officers who could not be said to be impecunious, there were to be found adventurers who were not able, or did not wish, to accustom themselves to the changed conditions of peace.[4] It cannot reasonably be assumed that their

---

[1] *Dispatches (1799–1818)*, IX, London, 1837, p. 369. It was in the same dispatch that the Duke referred to the Spaniards as " this lost nation ".

[2] Baumgarten, op. cit., p. 66.

[3] Altamira, in *Cambridge Modern History*, X, p. 207.

[4] G. Pecchio reported from Spain in 1821 that almost all the officers who had taken part in the revolt were of an age at which one likes temerary enterprises. (*Sei mesi in Ispagna nel 1821. Lettre a Ledi G. O.*, Madrid, 1821, p. 29.)

only intention when they revolted was to improve the lot of their soldiers.   Examples such as the Generals Elio and La Bisbal,[1] who, like some of the notable military adventurers of the Thirty Years' War, was of Irish extraction, may be regarded as sufficient evidence.

Officers meddling in politics : the analogy to Russia is obvious, for almost all the Decembrists were officers.   Yet this analogy must not be carried too far.   For the Decembrists were intellectuals to a much higher degree than were the revolting Spanish officers.   Perhaps this difference was due to the fact that during the Napoleonic Wars the Russians, unlike the Spaniards, had many opportunities of fighting abroad, and thus, after their return, were able to compare conditions in their fatherland with those in Central and Western Europe.   Such an experience could, to a limited extent, be shared only by those Spanish officers who had been made prisoners during the War, and had been sent to France ; some of them, for example Riego, became in fact members of foreign secret societies.   Perhaps this discrepancy could also be interpreted differently.   It might be argued that Spain, in the social and economic no less than in the political sphere, was on the decline, whereas Russia was on the upgrade.   The apparent analogies could be drawn when the two met at a certain imaginary point on the scale of Western civilization.

The invasion of politics by the soldiery is so typically Spanish that the Spanish term *pronunciamento* has come into use all over Europe.   Between 1814 and 1817, officers attempted repeated insurrections.   Soon after 1817, the series of military conspiracies which was to culminate in the Carlist revolt of 1833 was resumed. The revolt of 1820, in my view, did not form an exception. Marx, I think, misjudged the position when he wrote : " As to the military insurrection, we have seen that, notwithstanding its failure,[2] the revolution proved victorious."   Here the prophet of revolution seems to have been carried away by his deep conviction that, at the decisive moment, the common people always tend towards revolution.   The facts mentioned above—most of them were, of course, known to Marx in 1854—seem to show the events in a different light, so much so that it might be said that notwithstanding the failure of the revolution, it was rather

[1] Cf. Quin, op. cit., p. 337, where the author speaks of " the arbitrary and unlawful exactions " of that general.

[2] Marx alludes here to the strange fact that Riego despaired of his cause two days before he succeeded.

the military insurrection that proved victorious for a time. The
Italian refugee, G. Pecchio, who was very friendly in his attitude
towards Spanish liberalism, in his *Sei mesi in Ispagna nel 1821* none
the less testified to the fact that it had been the army that had
made the revolution.[1] It was also very significant that Riego,
in 1822, was made President of the Cortes. Lord Grenville,
indeed, was right when in 1823 he referred ironically to " that
new instrument of freedom, a mutinous and self-governed army ".[2]

Any Liberal element which may still have existed at the
beginning of the revolt in 1820 gradually disappeared. This may
partly have been due to the fact that the revolutionary régime
did little or nothing in regard to the agrarian question. Early
in 1823, it appeared to the English traveller Quin that " the mass
of the people were indifferent with respect to the Constitution.
. . . Every day new enemies to the system rose from the bosom
of the country ; and in point of fact it was upheld only by the
army, by those enjoying public employments, and those desirous
to obtain them." [3] It became, however, more and more obvious
that the army was by no means necessarily on the side of the
Liberals, in fact that it was at everybody's disposal. Bessières,
for example, who had been one of the republican conspirators of
1821, was in 1823 leading a band called " Defenders of the
Absolute King ". Again, the monks took a leading part in
forming gangs and inciting them to the most reckless orgies.
Baumgarten, the German expert on Spain, has pointed out that
it was only then that the Church began to lose its authority over
great masses of the people.[4] It soon became hated and despised
by them to a degree unknown at that time in the rest of Europe.

If we see the Spanish outburst of 1820 as a link in the chain
of military insurrections which culminated in 1833, it is possible
to conceive of all these explosions as post-war phenomena of the
same category as the Kapp Putsch or the Fascist march on Rome
a century later. The outburst of 1820 was directed, it is true,
against an absolutionist régime, those round-about 1920 against
Liberal régimes. The point is, however, that this did not make
any difference. The army could unite with anybody against
anybody. More precisely these movements may be defined as
the usual after-effects of prolonged wars which are no longer

---

[1] On p. 51.   Cf. also Vicente de la Fuente, *Historia de las sociedades secretos antiguas
y modernas en España*, Lugo, 1870, p. 288.
[2] *Memoirs of the Court of George IV*, Vol. I, p. 473.
[3] P. 162.
[4] *Die religiöse Entwicklung Spaniens*, Strassburg, 1875, p. 21.

fought by mercenaries, but by whole nations. The greater the percentage of those who are actively taking part in warfare, the more difficult it becomes to switch back again to peace. The lion who has tasted blood—there is no reason why this metaphor should not be extended to armed nations. After all, one of the greatest soldiers of our own time, Marshal Foch, has called the period since the French Revolution " une ère nouvelle . . . des guerres nationales aux *allures déchainées* ".[1]

B. NAPLES

The development in the Continental part of the Kingdom of the Two Sicilies was in many ways similar to that in Spain. Nature has been so generous to Southern Italy that, from this point of view at any rate, there was little stimulus to strenuous efforts such as were involved in industrialization.[2] Naples, at the beginning of the nineteenth century still one of the four or five biggest cities in Europe, and the biggest city in Italy, had hardly any industry at all. Such industry as did exist was of a decentralized character ; work was given out to individuals who did it in their homes, often only as a secondary occupation. A symptom rather than a cause of industrial backwardness was the poor state of communications. Situated in the south-eastern corner of the Western world, the Kingdom of Naples had, since the decline of Venice, secured for itself some part of the trade with the Levant. As in Cadiz and two or three other Spanish ports, there thus existed in Naples a small but rising commercial bourgeoisie. In pursuits other than agriculture, however, crafts-manship was still predominant. As to the proportion between country and town all over Italy, it is estimated that round about 1800 the rural population constituted approximately nine-tenths of the whole. The methods of agriculture, too, were as yet rather primitive. Cattle-breeders enjoyed privileges which were incompatible with agricultural progress. Huge flocks of sheep were allowed to wander all over the country ; as a result the crops were often badly damaged.

In the Kingdom of Naples, as in Spain, there existed, side by side with the nomadic shepherd the nomadic brigand. Admired

---

[1] *Des principes de la guerre. Conférences faites en 1900 à l'École Supérieure de Guerre,* 4. éd., Paris-Nancy, 1917, p. 28.

[2] Cf. Amaury Duval, editor of Count Grégoire Orloff's *Mémoires historiques, politiques et littéraires sur le Royaume de Naples,* V, Paris, 1821, p. 316 : " Tels sont, ou du moins tels j'ai vu les Napolitains. Tout examiné, leur plus grand défaut est l'indolence ; et, comme le remarquait Addison, il y a plus d'un siècle, il ne faut en accuser que le climat, qui relâche les fibres de leur corps."

by the majority of his fellow-countrymen and especially country-women, the brigand living in the mountains followed the old Italian proverb : " Better a bull for two years than an ox for a hundred." Stendhal, who visited Southern Italy in 1818, noticed that the Italian brigand never parted with two things : his rifle to defend his life, a picture of the Blessed Virgin to save his soul.[1] This light-minded conception of religion was very significant, by no means only for robbers. Religion was a guarantee of eventual salvation. So far as this world was concerned, it was largely an excuse for enjoying oneself, a kind of perpetual feast-day.[2] In the words of the contemporary writer Vincente Cuoco, religion in Naples (in contradistinction to France) was more concerned with the senses and the heart than with the spirit.[3]

Bandits were to be found not only in the mountains but in the towns as well. The mob of the capital used to refer to pillage as the source of Naples' riches. The same strange blend of crime and religion was found here also. It was called *Santa Fede* (Holy Faith), and took the form of huge pillaging festivals. The raging mob of lazzaroni forced people to offer expiatory sacrifices. There was nothing spontaneous about their action, for well before the beginning of the rite they hired storehouses in all parts of the city to safeguard their holy booty in advance. The barbarous ceremony was performed under the purple banner of the Cross—itself a symbol of atonement.[4]

The lazzaroni seized their plunder also under the cloak of the modern substitute for religion—politics. The " bande di Santa Fede " sided with the King and the powers-that-be in 1799 against the Liberal innovators. Benedetto Croce, to whose profound research the present writer is greatly indebted, explains the attitude of the lazzaroni [5] by the affinity in character and habit between them and the coarse Ferdinand IV. An additional explanation may be found in a fact stated by the historian Piero Pieri. The new Neapolitan bourgeoisie behaved towards the

[1] " Les Brigands en Italie ", reprinted in : *Pages d'Italie*, Paris, 1932, p. 265.
[2] The Quaker Stephen Grellet who visited Naples in the autumn of 1819 noticed with horror : " Their funerals are in many instances very gaudy ; some have passed before the windows of my chamber, that looked more like a masquerade than a funeral ! " (*Memoirs*, II, London, 1860, p. 50.)
[3] *Saggio storico sulla Rivoluzione di Napoli*, 2nd ed., Milano, 1806, p. 182. Cf. also Duval, op. cit., p. 294 : " La religion du Napolitain est l'idolâtrie, rien de plus. Il s'occupe fort peu de Dieu, et ne s'est jamais demandé s'il existe, ni si tel culte est raisonnable et moral. Mais il invoque avec ardeur la Vierge et quelques saints privilégiés."
[4] G. F. Hofmann, *Beiträge zur Kulturgeschichte Neapels*, Aarau, 1823, p. 205, n.l. The author, a follower of Pestalozzi, was running a school in Naples.
[5] *Storia del Regno di Napoli*, 2. ed., Bari, 1931, p. 213.

proletariat in a manner which was more selfish than that of the old feudal lords. Often the *contadini* realized that they had but changed their overlords for the worse.[1] Perhaps this applied to a certain extent to the lazzaroni also. The more acute among them may have had some faint realization that liberalism would effect no improvement in their economic position. On the contrary, the comparative security without which a liberal bourgeoisie could not flourish, might put an end to their own peculiar methods of enriching themselves. Then they might have to work hard, a prospect particularly obnoxious amidst the glorious scenery which surrounded them. Whatever the explanation may be, no sympathy for the King hindered the lazzaroni in 1799 from plundering the royal palace at the moment when he had fled before the invading French army.[2]

Besides the King and the loyal part of the aristocracy, the peasants and shepherds, the brigands and lazzaroni, and those who followed commercial or industrial pursuits, a small group of intellectuals existed whose main interest lay in politics. According to Cuoco, they were two centuries ahead of the people. They were composed of aristocrats,[3] some members of the higher clergy, a few bourgeois, and a number of students. They either belonged to or tended towards Freemasonry. During and immediately after the French Revolution they became increasingly Jacobin in their outlook. Violently opposed to the old régime, they had no contact at all with the people, nor did they find any appreciable support from the new bourgeoisie for whose political rise they provided the necessary ideology. But the new bourgeoisie was not yet interested in ideologies, even in those that were of advantage to them. All they were after was money.[4] The political revolution for which these Neapolitan intellectuals longed was thus, as Cuoco wittily put it, *una rivoluzione passiva*.[5] The overwhelming majority of the nation was the patient behind whose back the operation was being decided on.

Nevertheless, the operation might never have been effected

---

[1] *Le società segrete ed i moti degli anni 1820–21 e 1830–31*, Milano, 1931, p. 41.

[2] In G. di Cresceri's *Memorie Segrete* it is suggested that the Liberals encouraged the mob to this act in order to divide them. Freiherr von Helfert, who edited the *Memorie Segrete* in 1892, points out that this interpretation is probably unsound. (*Sitzungsberichte der philosophisch-historischen Classe der kaiserlichen Akademie der Wissenschaften*, CXXVII, Wien, p. 36).

[3] Their absenteeism was extreme. Cf. Arnaldo Agnelli, " Il fattore economico nella formazione dell' unità italiana," *Il Risorgimento Italiano, Rivista Storica*, VI, 1913, p. 262.

[4] Croce, op. cit., p. 214.

[5] *Saggio storico*, p. 127.

without the surgeon from abroad. The French appeared for
the first time in 1799 ; the Parthenopean Republic was then
proclaimed. Three years later they withdrew under the terms
of the Treaty of Amiens. But they came again in 1806, and this
time they were to stay until 1814. Immediately in the former
year a decree of Joseph Bonaparte abolished feudalism. Murat,
who succeeded Joseph in 1808, enforced this decree vigorously.
Only on the question of the entailed estates did Murat have to
make a few concessions. This he considered necessary because
he feared that otherwise the nobility might allow themselves to
be stirred into revolt by King Ferdinand who had fled to Sicily,
or by the English who were trying to undermine the French rule
in Italy. His predecessor had, in 1807, abolished all existing
entails. Now, in 1809, Murat's decree envisaged the establishment of new entailed estates, to reward those who had rendered
special services to the new dynasty.

In Spain, as we have seen, feudalism was abolished only on
paper. The continuous fighting which went on there during the
whole period of the French régime made it impossible to carry
out the decrees in question. In the Kingdom of Naples the
position was very different. In spite of certain irritations,
French rule was never seriously threatened there. Consequently,
French ideas of administration and social innovation could be
put into practice. This was done under the conscientious supervision of Giuseppe Zurli, an official who had been taken over
from the old Neapolitan Bourbon régime. The system of communications, too, was considerably improved. Roads and bridges
were constructed, marshes were drained. On the whole it could
be said that under French rule agriculture was flourishing and
industry and commerce progressing. The same was true of
education : 3,000 elementary schools were founded, and
secondary schools as well as the University of Naples were
modernized. Finally, it must not be forgotten that French
domination brought about Italian unity, except for the islands
of Sicily [1] and Sardinia, which the French never succeeded in
occupying.

The attitude of the various strata of Neapolitan society towards
the French was on the whole favourable, though for different
reasons. The nobility sided with them partly from animosity
towards the King who, in 1799, had incited the lazzaroni against

---

[1] Even after 1814 Naples and Sicily, though under the same ruler, were administered in a very different way.

the possessing classes.[1] The new bourgeoisie could not fail to notice that the new régime was auspicious for them. On the other hand, they themselves gave the French ample reason for complaint, since laziness or indifference made them reluctant to assume public office.[2] All the possessing classes had an additional reason for welcoming the sober régime of the French : they found themselves protected against the worst excesses of the mob. To the peasants, too, the new régime proved beneficial.[3] What then of the adventurous types who tended towards " brigantaggio " in the mountains, and " saccheggio " (pillaging) in the town ? Did they too acquiesce ?—for we have seen that they had fought against the French invader in 1799. They too accepted the new régime, but it cannot be said that they acquiesced, at any rate in the etymological sense of the word. They did not have to sit still, since they were urgently needed to fill the ranks of the army of their satellite kingdom. A considerable number of them, indeed, fought in the Peninsular War and even in Napoleon's Russian campaign. Joachim Murat, Napoleon's ingenious cavalry general, appealed to their imagination, and soon " Gioacchino " became a very popular king with those very people who had been fervently loyal to the Bourbon monarch. There was but one aspect of the French régime that tarnished its popularity : its attitude towards the clergy. Convents were closed down, and ecclesiastical property sold. This policy could not fail to cause some displeasure in a nation for which the Church had not as yet lost much of its authority.

This fact does not of itself suffice to explain the growth of that secret society, called the Carboneria, which later, in 1820, was to assume an important rôle. A secret society of Charbonniers had originated in Franche Comté in the 1770s ; it had been organized on the lines of the " compagnonnage ", an old association of artisans. By the time it was transplanted to Southern Italy, it had become an association for mutual assistance among officers of lower rank. For this fact we have the testimony of General Giuseppe Rossetti, Murat's aide-de-camp, and military

---

[1] Jacques Rambaud, *Naples sous Joseph Bonaparte 1806–1808*, Thèse, Paris, 1911, p. 534.   [2] Ibid., p. 392.

[3] Even as late as January 1817 Stendhal noticed in Naples : " Les Français regrettés à Naples comme partout. La meilleure recommendation pour un étranger en Italie, c'est d'être un Français attaché au gouvernement de Napoléon." (*Journal*, IV, Paris, 1932, p. 315.) More general was Napier's résumé in 1819 : " In Italy they have the same adoration for him as in France, and express it openly, fearlessly and without disguise ; saying he was the only man capable of raising their country from its debasement." (Sir W. Napier, op. cit., I, London, 1857, p. 279.)

governor of the capital of the Kingdom.[1] About 1811 the
English politicians who were advising King Ferdinand in Sicily
began to realize, from the example of Spain, what even the
unorganized resistance of a nation could achieve. It was then
that contact was established with the Carbonari, whose activities
were thereafter of an increasingly political character. They were
at that time composed mainly of petty bourgeois and lower
clergy. Their political aims were very indefinite. Some of the
members, resenting the foreign régime, seem to have wished for
the return of the old monarchy, though perhaps in a somewhat
liberalized form. Others may have joined because Murat's
liberalism was not far-reaching enough for their liking. All of
them were probably attracted by the romantic secrecy of the
movement, a feature to be explained partly by the background
of the War, and partly by its very vagueness.[2] The Carboneria
did not for a moment constitute a serious menace to Murat's rule
so long as Napoleon was in power.

It was only after the Restoration of the Bourbon régime that
the Carbonari and other secret societies gained that importance
which some of them were not to lose until 1860. Politics, of
course, were still often only a convenient cloak. In frequent cases
brigands concluded formal alliances with secret societies. "Brigantaggio " as well as " saccheggio ", repressed during the French
era, became more widespread than ever. This was true of the
whole of Italy, but it was more marked in the south. J. W. Ward,
afterwards created Earl of Dudley, reported after a journey in
1815 : "As to the robbers, they infest the whole country, and
some entire districts are quite abandoned to them ; that is to
say, Apulia and Calabria, forming the largest part of the kingdom.
At a certain pass called Ponte Bovino, on the way to Bari, the
robbers are in such a force that there is no passing without an
escort of 150 men." [3] A new feature of some of the secret
societies was that they had a quasi-military organization. This
applied, for example, to the gruesome gangs under the leadership
of the brigand Annichiarico. They called themselves " Decisi ".
Their slogan was : " Grief, death, horror, sorrow ! " With a
total force of almost 50,000 men, they exercised a kind of Black
Hand jurisdiction and terrorized whole provinces. Foreshadow-

[1] Rossetti's report to Murat (June 1814) is quoted in Renato Soriga, " Gl'inizi
della Carboneria in Italia ", *Il Risorgimento Italiano*, XXI, 1928, p. 78–80.
[2] Mazzini, " Letters on the State and Prospects of Italy, No. 2 ", *Monthly Chronicle*,
June 1839, p. 518.
[3] *Letters to " Ivy "* [Helen d'Arcy Stewart], ed. by S. H. Romilly, London, 1905,
p. 286.

A.N.W.

ing another atrocious post-war phenomenon, the Ku Klux Klan movement of the Southern States (1865), the Decisi wore masks. Beneath these masks were hidden convicted criminals, adventurers —an amazingly high percentage of them from the peasantry— and men of all kinds who had strong reasons for shunning the light.[1] The Government proved extremely weak in this respect. Unable to get hold of the gangsters, it spent 2,000 florins a year in rewards to those who poisoned them. In Naples itself, the Santa Fede was revived. The Minister of Police, Prince Canosa, adopted in essentials the same policy as his sovereign in 1797 : that is to say, he encouraged the rise of a secret society, who called themselves " Calderari ", to signify that they would resist the Carboneria in the same way as the caldron resists the coal.[2] The Austrian general Frimont reported that the Calderari were composed of loafers and rascals of the most dangerous type. It was the same shifting and rootless stratum for which Marx later coined the name *Lumpen-proletariat*.[3]

Measures such as the official encouragement of the Calderari went far to alienate the possessing classes.[4] There were other reasons too for their apprehensions. Those who had profited by the liquidation of feudalism and the sale of ecclesiastical property were afraid that the Bourbon régime might reverse this policy. Certain signs in this direction were already visible, above all the concordat with the Holy See in 1818. The Neapolitan general Carascosa mentions in his *Mémoires* another complaint of the big landowners : [5] the import of grain from the Crimea, with the obvious result of keeping the price of grain lower than they

[1] Eugen Lennhoff, *Politische Geheimbünde*, Leipzig, 1931, p. 143. As to their leader Annichiarico, this is what Church, the general of Irish extraction employed at the time in the service of the Kingdom, reported about him : " He was a perfect Proteus in his disguises—as a woman, as a beggar, as a priest, as a friar, as an officer, as a gendarme." (C. E. M. Church, *Sir Richard Church in Italy and Greece*, Edinburgh, 1895, p. 89.)

[2] Canosa is even said to have gone so far as to compose lists of the lazzaroni who had taken an active part in the sanguinary scenes of 1799, and to make them members of a society which he called " Calderari del Contropeso " (Counterpoise Calderari). Cf. Orloff, *Mémoires*, II, Paris, 1819, p. 288.

[3] " A recruiting ground for thieves and criminals of all kinds, living on the crumbs of society, people without a definite trade, vagabonds, *gens sans feu et sans aveu*, varying according to the degree of civilization of the nation to which they belong, but never renouncing their lazzaroni character." (" The Class Struggles in France, 1848–1850," *Selected Works*, ed. V. Adoratsky, II, London, 1933, p. 211.)

[4] Baron vom Stein in a letter to Capodistria, Rome, 29th December 1820 : ". . . l'isolement du trône, qui, en repoussant ses vrais amis, les propriétaires, ne s'appuyait que sur des buralistes et des bayonettes." (*Briefwechsel* etc., ed. E. Botzenhart, VI, p. 9.) As to the bayonets, Stein's statement, as we shall see, has to be modified.

[5] *Mémoires historiques, politiques et militaires, sur la révolution du Royaume de Naples, en 1820 et 1821*, Londres, 1823, pp. 26–7.

wished. At the same time the commercial bourgeoisie was hampered by the high customs barriers of the Restoration period. Prince Jablonowski, Austrian Ambassador in Naples, reported to Metternich in January 1818 that the ferment of discontent was rife in all classes.[1] But on the whole it might be said that, apart from the army, dissatisfaction was strongest among the possessing classes.

It is understandable that in these circumstances the character of the Carboneria should undergo a considerable change. This secret political sect had the reputation of being a focal point for dissatisfied elements other than those belonging to the rabble. Now that discontent was reaching respectable circles to a much larger extent than during the *decennio* of French rule, the Carboneria too, I suggest, became far more respectable in its composition. It is significant that, according to Carascosa, reception into the sect became at this time the object of venal speculation.[2] The Carboneria, then, was gradually being transformed into a political instrument for bringing about a régime more friendly to the possessing classes. It was realized that this could hardly be achieved within a very short time. In the meantime, the immediate dangers of the increasing " saccheggio " and the " brigantaggio " had to be met. The possessing classes therefore decided to form militias which likewise came under the influence of the Carboneria. In this way contact was established with another dissatisfied section of Neapolitan society, the army. Collaboration proved beneficial inasmuch as several dangerous gangs of brigands were annihilated.

As far as the army was concerned, the analogy with Spain is striking. Both Bourbon rulers mistrusted the army, and treated it badly. In Naples, officers who had fought under Murat, though not dismissed, received sharp reductions in pay. The men were once more subjected to corporal punishment. Obviously the army had grown too big in proportion to the State. Carascosa reports in his *Mémoires* :

Malheureusement, il existait alors un grand mécontentement parmi la jeunesse militaire, parce qu'elle se trouvait arrêtée dans son avancement. En effet, ceux qui avaient été officiers sous Murat, ceux qui l'étaient en Sicile, ceux qui l'étaient devenus parce qu'ils avaient pris momentanément les armes pour le Roi en 1799, ou pendant la dynastie française, furent presque tous également compris dans le cadre étroit de la nouvelle armée . . . Ils [les jeunes gens] virent, qu'une quantité si enorme d'officiers était un obstacle à leur carrière,

[1] Lennhoff, op. cit., p. 136.   [2] *Mémoires*, p. 22.

et se voyant fixés pour toujours dans leurs grades, ils perdirent l'élan de l'espérance.[1]

The discontent of the army proved, as in Spain, the decisive factor in the outburst of 1820. We have assumed that military insurrections as typical modern post-war phenomena were liable to break out whatever régime happened to be in power. The post-Napoleonic development in Naples furnishes more evidence. For, unlike Spain, the Restoration in Naples was not carried out in a brutal way. Perhaps to do so would have been impossible ; perhaps the almost unimpaired régime of the French had changed conditions as well as the political outlook of the nation to such an extent that a total Restoration would have proved a total failure. However, the fact remains that the returning King showed no particular spitefulness. The Minister of Police, indeed, behaved in an appalling way. On the other hand, Ministers like Luigi di Medici were remarkably humane and of a highly cultivated standard. The corruption of the bureaucracy, according to Metternich, " an incurable evil of the Kingdom ", was terrific ; but it was mainly the army that complained about it ; and indeed, it happened quite frequently that high officials embezzled money that was meant to be part of an officer's pay.

These two forces—the possessing classes and the army— together brought about the revolt of 1820. As to the social significance of this event, let us at first hear the testimony given many years later by one of the protagonists. In his *Memoirs* (London, 1846) General Guglielmo Pepe writes : " The February 1819 had now arrived . . . I had succeeded . . . in forming ten thousand of the most wealthy landowners [2] into companies and battalions, full of enthusiasm for the sect to which they belonged, and adhering to the most rigid discipline." [3] And in another passage : " I with 10,000 landholders, well organized under the name of militia, and several bodies of the line, was ready to form the nucleus of a revolution, either in the immediate Kingdom or all over Italy." [4] The general mentions also the thrill of the uniform : " A trite Italian proverb says : *L'abito non fa il monaco*, but the elegant uniform of the militia produced a great effect by exciting their imagination." [5] We cannot but be reminded of Heine's description of the National Guard in Paris under the Bourgeois King : " Well-fed heroes with big

[1] Ibid., pp. 20–1.
[2] According to the census of 1824, the population of the Kingdom numbered just over 5½ million.
[3] Vol. II, pp. 176–7.   [4] Ibid., p. 181.   [5] Ibid., p. 177.

bearskin caps in which shopkeepers' heads were stuck."[1] In Pepe's militia shopkeepers, though no doubt represented, were in the minority ; it is a fact that his wealthy people were mainly landholders.[2] It may be remarked here that nowhere in Europe did wealthy landowners, not even those who might be regarded as *nouveaux riches*, ever succeed in bringing about a liberal Revolution. Not sufficiently elastic to make temporary but efficient alliances, they are not very clever in using the masses for their own political purposes. This is why in Italy Mazzini, who a few years later tried to broaden the basis of the secret political societies, had to overcome very great difficulties. He was writing from his own experience when he criticized the " tendency of the Carbonari to look for leaders to the heads of society, and to regard the regeneration of Italy as to be accomplished by the higher classes, and not by the people ".[3] He also said that " Carbonarism had no faith in the people, amongst whom it sought recruits rather in order to pass them in review, and to attract by that means men of rank in society at whom it aimed, than in order to lead them frankly into action ".[4] There is only one aspect which Mazzini omitted to mention in his brilliant analysis of the Carboneria ; the high percentage of *nouveaux riches* landowners among its membership in Southern Italy. This aspect, however, seems to me of some importance. It may have escaped Mazzini's notice for the reason that it was to be found mainly in the south of Italy. As a Genoese, he naturally knew Northern Italian conditions far better.

As in Spain, the rank of the officers who, on July 2nd, 1820, made the actual pronunciamento, was not very exalted. In Spain Riego and Quiroga were colonels, in Naples Morelli and Salvati were only sublieutenants. These facts provide further evidence for our assumption that " revolutions " such as these are to be regarded as phenomena following modern wars in which increasing portions of the population take part. One of the chief

---

[1] " Das Bürgerkönigthum im Jahre 1832," *Sämmtliche Werke*, V, Hamburg, 1876, p. 33.
[2] Pieri points out that the commercial and rising industrial bourgeoisie voiced their complaints much more distinctly after 1825, at a time that is when their situation had improved. They then realized more clearly the defects of the régime in power and were in a better position to achieve the necessary remedies. (Op. cit., p. 52.)
[3] *Monthly Chronicle*, June 1839, p. 517.
[4] Ibid., p. 518. Cf. also the following passage : " With respect to equality, it [Carbonarism] was silent ; or, if it was compelled, now and then, to speak of it, it did so in a manner so uncertain, so slightly conclusive, that its words might be taken, according to the individual tendencies of its members, to refer either to Christian or civil, or political equality." (Ibid., pp. 517-18.)

results of the French Revolution seems to be that anyone may at
any moment arrogate to himself the right to upset the applecart,
for good or ill. It is in this sphere that the nearest approach
has been achieved to equality of opportunity.[1] Often the overthrow of the existing régime becomes almost a purpose in itself.
In Italy this was obviously the case. Mazzini confirms that
" Carbonarism had no firm, enthusiastic and religious belief, or,
if it had, there was only inscribed on it a simple negation ; it
was a signal for overthrow and not a message of reconstruction ".
Mazzini speaks of the Carbonari even as " men of reaction ".[2]
By this he probably did not only wish to emphasize their spiritual
retrograde tendency towards eighteenth-century Voltairean
scepticism. " Reaction " describes their attitude also in the more
primitive sense of the word.

As in Spain, the movement in its initial stage could have easily
been suppressed by the forces controlled by the Government.[3]
Our protagonist Pepe hesitated for a time before he escaped from
Naples and placed himself at the head of the rebels. Shortly
before this, Nugent, the Austrian general of Irish extraction who
was employed by King Ferdinand, had suggested that Guglielmo
Pepe should be given command of the loyal troops. This was
plausible, since Pepe had strongly emphasized that the armed
possessing classes were to be regarded as the safest pillars of the
throne. The King and the Ministers, however, preferred to
entrust General Carascosa with the task of smashing the rebellion.
Now Pepe made up his mind.[4] Ambition now clearly pointed
in the direction in which, no doubt, his sympathies lay.

A further analogy to Spain was furnished by the fickleness of
the mob,[5] though the lazzaroni did not go to such extremes as
we have seen them do in Madrid. All they did in 1820 was to
refrain from fighting against the revolting forces, but this passivity
was, of course, very different from their attitude in 1799. Pepe,
on the other hand, grossly exaggerated when he argued in his
*Relation des événemens politiques et militaires qui ont eu lieu à Naples en
1820 et 1821* (Paris, 1822) : " Si toute la nation n'eût pas desiré
unanimement ce régime constitutionnel, comment aurait-on pu
l'établir sans répandre une goutte de sang ? " [6] All the available

---

[1] Cf. Napoleon's remark in 1802 : " Some of these men of the Revolution are
very able ; they are good handymen. The trouble was only that they all wished
to become master-builders."
[2] Op. cit., p. 519.
[3] Cf. Carlo Segrè, art. " Italy ", *Cambridge Modern History*, X, p. 112.
[4] Stern, *Geschichte Europas*, II, p. 105.
[5] Croce, op. cit., p. 104.   [6] P. 22.

evidence seems to indicate that a large part of the population, far from desiring a constitution, was completely indifferent about it. As to those who shouted " For God, the King, and the Constitution ! " the contemporary historian Pietro Colletta,[1] who himself believed in the untenableness of absolutism, reports about them in his *History of the Kingdom of Naples* :

> The meaning of this political watchword was only half understood by the hearers, or even, I might say, by those who uttered it, but all believed the words contained the expression of their particular desire ; those who paid taxes supposing it to mean a diminution of the rates ; the Liberals, liberty ; the philanthropist, the public welfare ; the ambitious, power ; and each that which he most coveted.[2]

Just as the Spaniards had taken over the ready-made French Constitution of 1791, so the Neapolitans in their turn adopted this very Spanish Constitution. We have Pepe's testimony to the fact that only a few of his fellow-countrymen knew anything at all about this political instrument. It might be said that the foreign constitution was the only thing which was stolen during the revolt. À Court, British Minister to the Kingdom of the Two Sicilies, reported to Castlereagh after the event : " Not a towel was stolen, no single knife was drawn in anger, not a drop of blood was shed." [3]   À Court's diagnosis of July 6th that this was " a war of poverty against property ",[4] proved unsound. So did Metternich's forecast that blood would flow ; in the Continental part of the Kingdom this did not happen. King Ferdinand having given his consent, a parliament was opened in Naples on October 1st, 1820. It was composed of lawyers, doctors, priests, and officials, with only two noblemen. Soon the members of this assembly were intoxicated with rhetoric.

Resistance to the intervening Austrian army, at the beginning of 1821, was not appreciably stronger than that which, two years later, the Spaniards offered to the advance of the Duc d' Angoulême. From documents reprinted in Carascosa's *Mémoires* it is evident that the wealthy people and many of the other Carbonari preferred to stay at home,[5] thus giving the lie to Pepe's boast of their rigid military discipline. The soldiers who were left to fight it out were embittered and ran away in a moment when the battle had hardly been joined. Soon after this inglorious defeat (" la

---

[1] According to Mazzini, " the only author who has written honestly on the Neapolitan movement ". (Op. cit., p. 521.)
[2] Trans. by S. Horner, II, Edinburgh, 1858, p. 327.
[3] Quoted by Lennhoff, op. cit., p. 151. (Not given in Castlereagh, *Correspondence*.)
[4] Castlereagh, *Correspondence*, etc., XII, p. 279.
[5] *Mémoires*, pp. 524, 530, 542–3.

rotta di Rieti ") of March 7th, 1821, feeling turned also against
Pepe. It was said that for the constitutional meal too much
" pepe " (pepper) had been used, and too little " sale " (salt).[1]

In conclusion, it must be emphasized that in spite of Pepe's
later assertions to the contrary, the movement in Naples did not
have any aspirations towards Italian unity or independence.
Pontecorvo and Benevento, cities belonging to the Pontifical
States, but surrounded by Neapolitan territory, also proclaimed
the Spanish constitution, and requested to be incorporated with
Naples. This offer, even, was rejected. Nor was contact
established between the revolutionary forces of Naples and those
of Piedmont,[2] which three days after Rieti—to be sure, before
the news of the defeat arrived—were to embark upon an insurrection which also was of a predominantly military character.

C. GREECE

The scene of the last outbreak, and the one which had the
widest repercussions, was Greece. Her war of independence
must, of course, be viewed against the background of the Ottoman
Empire in general, and the Balkan peninsula in particular.

Turkish power in Europe had been in decline since the end
of the seventeenth century. The Treaty of Karlowitz (1699)
marked a definite turning-point. In 1714 the Morea was regained from the Venetian Republic, but on the whole the Turks
during the eighteenth century were pushed back by both Austria
and Russia. Attempts by French officers to reform the Turkish
army were of little avail. Anglo-French commercial antagonism
was then at its height. Besides, the idea prevailed in this country
that the opening of the Black Sea to Russian ships would prove
of advantage to English merchants. It thus came about that
the Russian fleet which destroyed the Turkish navy at Tchesmé
in 1770 was largely under the direction of English officers.[3]

An inquiry into the main causes of Turkey's decline as a

[1] Luigi Re, La satira patriottica nelle scritti murali del risorgimento, Brescia, 1933,
p. 98. In a popular epigram quoted by Re, the whole constitutional episode was
satirized in these six lines :

> Movimento, parlamento,
> Giuramento, pentimento,
> Gran tormento e poco argento,
> Armamento e malcimento
> Fra spavento e tradimento
> Siam fuggiti come il vento.

[2] This revolt lies outside the scope of this book, for it did not affect the Concert
of Europe.

[3] William Miller, The Ottoman Empire and its Successors, 1801–1927, Cambridge,
1927, p. 14.

FERDINAND I TAKES THE OATH TO THE
NEAPOLITAN CONSTITUTION, 1820

[*face p.* 156

ALEXANDER YPSILANTI

[*face p.* 157

great European Power would go far beyond the scope of this
book. One aspect, however, cannot be omitted : the problem
created by the institution of the Janissaries. Established as early
as the fourteenth century, this large permanent body of infantry
contributed for centuries to the expansion of the Ottoman
Empire. The well-trained Janissaries, recruited at first by forced
levy, enjoyed an obvious advantage over the irregular armies
of the other Powers of the Continent. By the end of the sixteenth
century the privileges attaching to the corps were so considerable
that many parents themselves begged to have their children
enrolled. Soon, however, the two-edged character of the new
weapon became apparent. They were still brave in the field,
but were increasingly reckless against the civilian population, and
—what was worse from the point of view of the State—exceedingly
troublesome in their attitude to the Government. They often
set fire to Constantinople ; sometimes they even made away with
the Sultan. According to the Swedish chargé d'affaires at Constantinople, M. d'Ohsson, author of an exhaustive survey of the
Ottoman Empire, the chief aim of their frequent insurrections
was pillage.[1] Sometimes, however, their destructive activity
betrayed a marked anti-cultural bias, for example, during the
revolution which preceded the death of Selim III, when they
destroyed the mathematical school instituted by him.[2] While
in the two preceding chapters of this study the danger immanent
in a " levée en masse " had to be emphasized, it is only fair to
point out that large standing armies—of which the Janissaries
are the classical example—also tend to become highly disruptive
forces ; in both cases this is the price of military glory. That is
why Mustapha III and some of his predecessors decided, in case
of war, to rely increasingly on irregular troops and provincial
militiamen.[3] The reorganization of the Turkish army proceeded
for some time very slowly. To create a new force proved easier
than to get rid of one which was new only in name.[4] It is
estimated that there were still as many as 112,000 Janissaries in
1805. For the last time in 1807 they provoked a civil war in
the course of which Selim III was deposed. It was not until 1826
that this curse was finally and utterly exterminated.

It was against the Janissaries, not against the Ottoman Government, that the first Balkan rising of the century took place in

---

[1] *Tableau général de l'empire Ottoman*, III, Paris, 1820, p. 409.
[2] Robert Walpole, *Memoir relating to European and Asiatic Turkey*, 2nd ed., London,
1818, p. 27.
[3] M. d'Ohsson, op. cit., p. 399.   [4] " Yeni cheri " means new troops.

Serbia in 1804. Ottoman rule in Europe, which at that time still extended over 238,000 square miles with 8 million inhabitants, was by no means distinguished by extraordinary cruelty or vexatiousness. It is unfair to say, as European historians are fond of repeating, that the Rayahs (Christians) remained essentially slaves. Neither Christians nor Jews were hindered in their religious exercises. This was admitted even by the Greek ecclesiastical historian Kyriakos.[1] This tolerance may have been partly due to a tendency discernible in eighteenth-century Turkey towards sceptical Enlightenment. It was symptomatic that about 1750 the Pasha of Cairo, Ali ben Abdallah, worked out a plan of reform, in which he advocated the extermination of all positive religion and the abolition of all ecclesiastical authorities.[2] The fact that the Pasha dared to show this radical plan to the Sultan proves that he must have expected some response. Not only was there religious toleration, but education too was left in the hands of the subject peoples, and no censorship existed.[3] Nor were they liable for military service. A far more unpleasant discrimination was the poll-tax called *haratch*. Although the tax was not very high, it proved a heavy burden for the people of Eastern Europe with their low standard of living.

Economic freedom of a sort was granted, especially in matters of trade. But owing to this very lack of initiative on the part of the Government, the economic development of the Balkan provinces was extremely backward. There was hardly any industry. The roads, too, were constantly deteriorating. It is probable that the Turks had a shrewd reason for neglecting road repairs. Their military efficiency was in a state of gradual decline which made it all the more imperative for them to take refuge in defensive stratagems. So long as the condition of the roads continued to grow worse, it became more and more difficult for invading armies—Russian or Austrian—to use them. Brigands, known in Serbia and Wallachia under the name of Heiduks, increased the insecurity which made economic advance almost impossible. Selim III attacked the Bulgarian and Macedonian brigands, but his methods of attack were somewhat questionable. Setting the fox to keep the geese, the Government formed gangs from among the pugnacious Albanian tribes. These were called *armatoli*, and were supposed to police particularly dangerous districts.

[1] *Geschichte der orientalischen Kirchen, 1453–1898*, Leipzig, 1902, p. 164.
[2] Karl Mendelssohn-Bartholdy, *Geschichte Griechenlands*, I, Leipzig, 1870, p. 75.
[3] Cf. J. L. S. Bartholdy, *Voyage en Grèce*, trad. de l'Allemand par A. du C., II, Paris, 1807, p. 24.

In other parts of the Empire, too, the ruling nation was dreaded much less than their European vice-gerents.   In regard to Wallachia we have for this the testimony, among many others, of the Rev. G. Waddington, who visited Eastern Europe several times during the 1820s.[1]   From the beginning of the eighteenth century the secular and ecclesiastical dignitaries of Moldavia and Wallachia, who came from the Phanar, the principal Greek quarter of Stambul, had kept the native population at a distance ; the native languages were given an inferior status.   A Phanariot who aspired to become *hospodar* (governor) of one of the Danubian principalities had to support his application by a heavy bribe. Once appointed, he was anxious to get his own back with interest from his new subjects.   He had also to provide for his favourites who had accompanied him to Bucharest or Jassy.   In these circumstances it needed a great deal of optimism to assume, as did the Greek poet Rhigas in 1798, that " all the Macedonians would rise together, that Bulgarians and Albanians, Serbs and Rumanians would draw the sword for the cause of Greece and liberty ".   The Greek Orthodox Church, in the eyes of the Russians and Phanariots, was to be the strong uniting force.

Anti-Turkish feeling might never have developed in the Danubian Principalities had it not been for Russia's policy of expansion in these regions.   Russian troops did, indeed, enter the Principalities in 1806 on the pretext that both Hospodars had been deposed without Russian consent.   Another of the interminable series of Russo-Turkish wars followed.   Six years later, however, Russia, threatened by the imminent attack of Napoleon, had to be satisfied with the Peace Treaty of Bucharest, which though it made Bessarabia a Russian province, was not unbearable for the Turkish Government.   After Napoleon's downfall, Russian help went far to encourage the abortive attempt at a revolt undertaken by the Phanariot prince Alexander Ypsilantis, who had been in the Russian service during the Napoleonic Wars.   This adventurer, too, fits into our gallery of post-war politicians : a rapid military career ; fantastic schemes irrespective of the possible loss of human lives involved ; an ardent ambition to enter the political arena.   In 1820 this man invaded the Principalities with a battalion formed of young Greeks of the upper and middle classes, who had been living outside Greece but were the most enthusiastic supporters of a new Greek empire,

---

[1] *The Present Condition and Prospects of the Greek, or Oriental Church*, London, 1829, p. 21.

possibly but not necessarily under Russian control.   It can easily
be believed that the Rumanian peasants were not particularly
attracted by this ambitious Phanariot display.   Vladimirescu,
whose help the Phanariots sought, seized the opportunity to incite
several hundred peasants to revolt.   He actually announced the
abolition of forced labour services.   The Rumanian nobles, who
had at first favoured the designs of their Phanariot class-fellow,[1]
soon discovered that the best method of dealing with the threatened social revolt was to turn the agitation against foreigners ; [2]
a recipe faithfully adopted a century later in Eastern as well as
Central Europe.   As yet not willing and certainly not powerful
enough to shake off the Ottoman overlord, they contented themselves with eliminating the influence of the Phanariots, and
becoming in consequence their successors.

In Greece itself the effects of Russia's anti-Turkish policy were
very considerable.   As early as 1770 many Greeks were employed
by Russia in her war against Turkey.   In the ensuing Peace
Treaty of Kutchuk Kainardji important commercial privileges
for Russia were included.   In consequence, a number of Russian
consuls and vice-consuls, many of them Greeks, were appointed
in the Levant.   For her trade in and beyond the Mediterranean
the great land-power had to use the services of the seafaring
island communities.   The Greek islanders were already well
established in trade, though so far they had concerned themselves
with it only within the bounds of the Ottoman Empire.   From
now on Greek trading colonies sprang up in many different parts
of Europe.   Koraes, in his interesting *Mémoire sur l'état actuel de la
civilisation dans la Grèce en 1803*, mentions only those of Italy,
Holland, Germany, and Trieste.   Those, however, which proved
of the greatest importance were at Odessa, Moscow, and Astrakhan.   Among the most successful traders were the inhabitants
of the islands of Hydra and Spezia.   The former even went so
far as to arm their vessels heavily.   This precaution against
Berber piracy was to assume some importance in the War of
Independence.   Greek exports consisted of some cotton of inferior
quality, tobacco mainly from Macedonia, raisins from Corinth,
honey and oil from Athens.[3]   For some years towards the end
of the century, the dye-works of Ambelakia on the slope of Ossa
were very busy.

[1] Caradja, former Hospodar of Wallachia, as well as Soutsos, Hospodar of
Moldavia, were in touch with Ypsilantis.
[2] Miller, op. cit., p. 64.
[3] Félix-Beaujour, *Tableau du Commerce de la Grèce*, I, an VIII (1800), pp. 38–40.

Progress in commerce was not accompanied by a similar development in Greek agriculture. In Macedonia, it is true, things were not so bad, but the Morea experienced a serious decline as soon as the short-lived Venetian rule came to an end. Here, too, goat- and sheep-rearing often interfered in a tiresome way. Not only in the Morea, but all over Greece, the state of communications was appalling. At the beginning of the nineteenth century the German diplomat-traveller J. L. S. Bartholdy reports that in the whole of Greece hardly any roads were to be found suitable for vehicles of any kind.

The educational standard of the population was equally low. Greek merchants living abroad showed themselves keen to assimilate modern European civilization, and sometimes even to spread the knowledge of ancient Hellas. Ἑρμῆς κερδῷος could not fail to be followed by Ἑρμῆς λόγιος. Books in the modern Greek language, chiefly translations from Italian, French, German and English, were published in Leghorn, Venice, Trieste, and Vienna. But in Greece itself no appreciable degree of progress in this sphere had been reached by the turn of the century. In Athens with its 10,000 inhabitants,[1] Bartholdy looked in vain for a bookshop. According to his estimate, not more than twenty books in modern Greek were to be found in the city, other than works of theology, prayers and songs. Moreover, John Cam Hobhouse reports a few years later : " There is not in the Levant a library where books are sold." [2] The reading public, as far as it existed at all, was made up of merchants and members of the clergy.

The truth of the saying " In the land of the blind the one-eyed man is king " was borne out by the Greek clergy of the time. According to Kyriakos, in 1821 among 180 members of the higher clergy there were hardly ten who could claim a scholarly erudition.[3] Among the monks illiteracy was the rule.[4] In some cases naïve ignorance was supported by obscurantist argumentation, as with the theologian Nathanael Neokaissareos who, in 1802, went so far as to declare that the sciences were entirely useless to Christianity, and that it was therefore necessary to suppress the zeal for instruction. He also warned the Greeks to flee

[1] The population of Greece was estimated at 1,920,000 for 1800 (Beaujour, I, p. 23). Over one-fifth lived in the Morea.
[2] *A Journey through Albania and Other Provinces of Turkey in Europe and Asia to Constantinople during the years 1809 and 1810*, 2nd ed., II, London, 1813, p. 572.
[3] *Geschichte der orientalischen Kirchen*, p. 75.
[4] For the big monastery at Megaspilion in Achaia, Bartholdy estimated the percentage of those who could read and write at 1–2 per cent.

atheist Europe and Europeans. This part of his doctrine is particularly significant, for it shows that at that time Greece could be thought of as lying outside the European orbit. The obscurantist influence of the higher clergy was all the more powerful since they were regarded as authorities on many questions of ordinary daily life. As for the moral side, simony was widespread. The penalties imposed on those who confessed their sins consisted too often in the obligation to build new churches or to repair old ones.[1] Hobhouse, confirming the fact of the clergy's unbounded influence over their flock, writes how painful it was " to see the sacrifices which the meagre, half-starved peasants made to their priests. Besides many gifts, there are certain days when all the attendants, men and women, of the poorest class, bring loaves, and plates of sweetmeats, called a cobyva, and wax tapers, and lay them during the service, at the foot of the altar, whence they are conveyed into the sanctuary, and serve as the evening's feast for the priests." [2]

If some of the priests could be said to abuse their spiritual power, the same was undoubtedly true of the secular authority exercised by the " primates ". On the islands and in the Morea it was mostly the wealthiest and least ignorant men were elected for this job. Hardly ever did the Ottoman kadi interfere with the election. The primates had the right of collecting taxes for the Government. It frequently happened that they collected more than they were willing to give up to their overlord. Their arrogance no less than their greed made them highly objectionable.[3] Corruption on the part of the chiefs could not but infect the general public, as was so bluntly expressed in the proverb current at the time : Ἀπο το κεφαλι βρομι το ψαρι (It is from the head that the fish begins to stink). Political demoralization in all its depth was revealed in another saying : " Everyone is in debt to the brigand and to him who has power." Irregular methods of enrichment were not, indeed, confined to chiefs. In the Morea as well as on the mainland, brigandage was very widespread. Some of it was of indigenous growth, some was imported, for here, too, the Albanian *armatoli* often degenerated into mere robber bands. In most people's eyes *klephts* (robbers) and corsairs were regarded as *palikars* (heroes). Hobhouse's travelling companion, Lord Byron, though an ardent political

[1] Bartholdy, op. cit., pp. 10, 13.
[2] *A Journey through Albania*, II, p. 521.
[3] Bartholdy, II, pp. 47–8.

sympathizer of the Greeks, in *The Giaour* (1813) summed up their behaviour in these condemnatory lines :

> And callous, save to crime ;
> Stained with each evil that pollutes
> Mankind, where least above the brutes ;
> Without even savage virtue blest,
> Without one free or valiant breast,
> Still to the neighbouring ports they waft
> Proverbial wiles and ancient craft ;
> In this the subtle Greek is found,
> For this, and this alone, renowned.

How and to what degree was Greece affected by the French Revolution and its aftermath ? Greek traders came into intensified contact with France during the Revolution. Owing to the famine brought about by the disturbances of the Terror, the import of Russian grain which they controlled was most welcome in France. During the wars that followed, Greek traders were in a highly advantageous position, because Turkey's neutrality, to which she kept but for her war with Russia, enabled them to trade with all parties. The Turks even protected the Greek merchants.[1] Besides merchants, a few Greek medical students came to France during the critical years. Among them was the above-mentioned Koraes, a great expert on ancient Greece, who by translating the old authors into the modern tongue was trying to lay the ethical foundation for a renaissance of his nation. Koraes took up his residence in Paris in 1788. He lived to see the political triumph of his compatriots, but this by itself did not satisfy him any more than the analogous event of Italy's independence satisfied Mazzini thirty years later. Koraes never returned, and died in Paris in 1833.

While some Greeks thus came into contact with France, French rule at the same time advanced to the very doorstep of Greece. France occupied Dalmatia, and, on two occasions, even the Ionian Islands.[2] One of Napoleon's ambitious schemes, the control of the route to India, presupposed a weakened Ottoman Empire. Greek nationalism, which hardly existed at that time, would have been welcomed by Napoleon as a ferment. This is why he sent the two Corsicans Stephanopoli, uncle and nephew, on a mission to the Morea where they were to propagate the

---

[1] Walpole, *Memoirs relating to European and Asiatic Turkey*, 2nd ed., p. 29.
[2] The Ionian islanders had been under Venetian rule up to 1797 ; they had never been under Turkish domination. They enjoyed a higher economic standard, a fact which was known to all other Greek traders and may have provided them with some stimulus.

idea of the French as the liberators of the East.[1] For the same
reason the former successful klepht and now greatly dreaded
Pasha, Ali of Janina, received tokens of esteem from France. Ali,
for some time, played the game by posing to the French com-
mander of Prevesa as a faithful adept of the Jacobin religion.
Long after he had betrayed the French, Ali on some occasions
fell back into this unconvincing rôle, as for example when he
promised liberty to Greece, and a " charte " to Epirus. The
reason for the Pasha's interest in the Revolution is revealed in the
report of the French traveller F. C. Pouqueville, who paid a visit
to him at the turn of the century :

> La révolution française était, dans ces derniers temps, le sujet de
> toutes ses conversations, . . .[2] afin de s'entretenir de nos armées
> dont il admirait les succès. Il interrogeait les officiers français qui
> étaient ses prisonniers, et il leur demandait la cause de tant de
> triomphes, qu'il attribuait à une sort de magie, à un prestige qui
> enchaînait la victoire à nos drapeaux.[3]

The only thing which the Pasha really learned from the West
in general, and France in particular, was absolutism or political
centralization. Under his rule other klephts did not stand much
chance, unless they were under the orders of the chief robber.
And then, having lost their independence, they could be called
klephts no longer, nor as yet civil servants.

The response to the French Revolution among the Greeks
was very strong. Koraes, with many others, testifies to this fact.[4]
The idealist Rhigas was not the only prominent person to base
his hopes on Napoleon. The klepht Kolokotrones, who was to
play such an important part during the War of Independence,
writes in his *Memoirs :* " According to my judgment, the French
Revolution and the doings of Napoleon opened the eyes of the
world." He continues naïvely : " The nations knew nothing
before, and the people thought that kings were gods upon earth,
and that they were bound to say that whatever they did was well
done." [5] The klepht's disdain for legitimate rulers was exceeded
only by his admiration for the usurper. He adored Bonaparte

---

[1] Cf. *Voyage de Dino et Nicolo Stephanopoli en Grèce, pendant les années V et VI*, tome I,
Paris, an VIII, pp. 71–2.
[2] The text continues thus : " non, comme on l'a prétendu, dans la vue d'y puiser
des leçons pour s'affranchir, mais . . ." This passage was obviously inserted for
diplomatic reasons.
[3] *Voyage en Morée, à Constantinople, en Albanie, et dans plusieurs autres parties de l'Empire
Othoman pendant les années 1798–1801*, III, Paris, 1805, p. 25.
[4] *Mémoire*, p. 476.
[5] *The Klepht and the Warrior. Sixty Years of Peril and Daring. An Autobiography*,
trans. from the Greek by Mrs. Edmonds, London, 1892, pp. 127–8.

as the God of War.[1] However, he must have loved actual war even more than he loved the modern Mars, for when it suited his purpose he fought against Napoleon as a major in the English service.[2]

The Corfiot Capodistria was in every respect the direct opposite of such men as Kolokotrones. Like Koraes he was a highly educated medical man. He was consistent both in his opposition to French expansion and in his adherence to certain ideas of the French Revolution. During the Congress of Vienna, Capodistria together with Lord Guilford and other friends revived the old pro-Hellenic society called the *Hetairia*, which had been founded by the Phanariot Prince Alexander Mavrocordato towards the end of the eighteenth century. Its original aim had been philanthropic : the mitigation of Greek economic misery and the spread of European knowledge. Similarly, the scope of the revived *Hetairia Philike* was cultural and not political. The motives of its inaugurators were so pure that they could dare to canvass openly for members. As late as April 1819, during a visit to Corfu, Capodistria warned his compatriots : " It is with the moral and literary education of Greece that the Greek must occupy themselves entirely and exclusively ; every other object is a vain one, every other activity dangerous."

The purpose of the revived *Hetairia* was soon misinterpreted. Owing to the predilection for secrecy prevalent at the time, hidden political motives, especially on the part of Capodistria,[3] were taken for granted, and a secret political society under the same name was founded by Greek merchants at Odessa. Its aim was the restoration of the Greek empire at Constantinople. As in the Principalities, so in Greece itself subscribers to such far-reaching

[1] Mendelssohn-Bartholdy, op. cit., p. 72.

[2] For some time before that he had taken part as a privateer in the Russo-Turkish War.

[3] Cf. Anton Freiherr von Prokesch-Osten, *Geschichte des Abfalls der Griechen*, I, Wien, 1867, p. 7. It is remarkable that Prokesch, the admirer of Metternich, fully exonerates Capodistria, one of Metternich's arch-enemies. Stern (*Geschichte Europas*, II, p. 195) on the other hand, tends to believe that Capodistria, in spite of his later avowal to the contrary, did encourage Alexander Ypsilantis to undertake the adventurous invasion of the Principalities. The evidence adduced by Stern is unconvincing. It is based on accusations of Capodistrias made by Ypsilantis shortly before his death, and on a statement to the same effect made by Nesselrode to Lebzeltern in November 1821. Nesselrode's reliability in this particular case may be doubted, since he was Capodistrias' less gifted competitor. I suggest that Ypsilantis, having in 1827 regained his freedom after six years of confinement in Austrian prisons, and living now in Vienna, tried to excuse himself in the eyes of Metternich by putting the blame for the adventure on Metternich's enemy. Ypsilantis' version is to be found also in the work of the Greek historian 'Ιωαννης Φιλημων, Δοκιμον 'Ιστορικον περι της 'Ελληνικης 'Επαναστασεως, Athens, 1859, tome I, p. 32, a work dedicated to two members of the Ypsilantis family.

schemes were confined to the leaders of society.[1]   Constantine
Metaxa, one of the leaders in the War of Independence, reports in
his *Memoirs* : " Il n'y avait que quelques capitaines de navires et
quelques négociants, naviguant ou trafiquant le long des côtes de
la Russie et de l'Asie-mineure, qui fissent partie de l' Hétairie." [2]

Captains both on land and on sea—mostly referred to as
capitani—and merchants also had suffered somewhat from the
cessation of hostilities in 1814.   Kolokotrones and others with him
were dismissed.[3]   Like so many of the other ex-officers of the
Napoleonic Wars they were longing for the fight to be resumed.
The merchants too, at least many of them, were dissatisfied.
During the war they had made large profits under a neutral
flag.   Now, in peacetime, they felt the renewed competition of
foreign traders all the more keenly.   As early as October 1820,
Conduriotti and the other principal merchants of the islands
recalled the greater part of their vessels, which were detained in
port, and in condition for service the moment it should be required
of them.[4]   This measure threw a number of sailors into unemployment, and made a potential insurrection appear comparatively
profitable in their eyes.

When the insurrection actually broke out in April 1821,[5] no
agreement existed between the capitani on land on the one hand,
and the primates of the island communities on the other ; the
capitani themselves were far from united.   Yet the moment for
the outbreak was well chosen.   For the Turks were occupied
not only with the rebellion instigated by Ypsilantis, but also by
Ali Pasha's last bid for still more power ; and, finally, by a war
with Persia.   The revolt began in the Morea with isolated outrages on Ottoman officials, but soon assumed the dimensions of
a widespread if not general insurrection.   Among the islands,
Spezia and Psara were the first to join in.   The primates of
Hydra hesitated for some time.   Richer than the others, and
therefore running a much greater risk by throwing in their lot
with them, they had to be compelled by the very sailors who had
been unemployed for half a year.[6]

How did it come about that the movement, instigated as it

---

[1] Cf. Waddington : " The principle on which the Hetairia reposed, ensured the
respectability of a great proportion of its members." (*A Visit to Greece in 1823 and 1824*,
p. xxx.)
   [2] *Souvenirs de la Guerre de l'Indépendance de la Grèce*, trad. du Grec. par Jules Blancard,
Paris, 1887, p. 3.
   [3] *The Klepht and the Warrior*, p. 125.   [4] Waddington, *A Visit to Greece*, p. vi.
   [5] In the following pages I do not intend to give anything like a detailed study
of the War of Independence.   Only certain aspects relevant for social history will be
elaborated.   [6] Waddington, op. cit., p. 107.

was by adventurous capitani and discontented merchants, reached such dimensions in a short time ? The traditional hatred for the Moslems cannot of itself explain this phenomenon. We are, I think, getting nearer the truth by realizing, as Waddington first pointed out, that whereas in the Principalities the immediate visible rulers were Phanariots, in Greece they were Turks. That is to say, in Greece hatred for the infidel coincided with hatred for the privileged class. And privileged they were, for instance, by their exemption from the *haratch*. This tax was low, but it must be stressed once more that in a mountainous country like Greece, which was poorer than Moldavia or Wallachia, even a slight discrimination would be felt more severely than elsewhere. Moreover, mountains are very auspicious abodes for robbers, and indeed Greece was full of them. The degree of power which they attained was partly due to the administrative policy of the Turks, as is evident from this passage from Metaxa's *Souvenirs* :

Jusqu'aux temps de la puissance d'Ali-Pacha, il régna cette idée étrange que, pour obtenir de la renommée et avoir une capitainerie ou devenir Derven-Agas, il fallait avoir été chef d'une bande de brigands, c'est-à-dire avoir pillé les paisibles habitants, retenu captifs les plus riches, et les avoir tourmenté jusqu'à ce qu'ils eussent payé la rançon exigée. Les Turcs envoyaient contr'eux des corps de troupes sous certains chefs appelés Derven-Agas, qui les attaquaient ou feignaient de les poursuivre, car il leur importait peu d'exécuter les ordres des Paches. Ces derniers fatigués de méfaits commis par des bandits, en venaient à traiter avec leurs chefs, qui faisaient leur soumission les armes à la main, et étaient nommés en recompense commandants d'une province ou capitaines. Ces mesures irréfléchies des Turcs ne furent pas peu utiles à la révolution hellénique, car lorsqu elle éclata, beaucoup de ces capitaines chrétiens se trouvèrent prêts à la soutenir avec des forces bien disciplinées et aguerries, qui formèrent plus tard l'armée de la Grèce continentale. Tels furent Panourias, Diovouniotis, Odysée-Androutsos, Saphacas, Skylodimos, Condojannis, Iseos, Macris, Tsongas, Caraiscakis et d'autres, qui d'abord clephtes (voleurs) ou descendents de clephtes se trouvèrent ensuite au service indépendent des Turcs.[1]

The method of warfare followed by both parties was from the beginning unimaginably cruel.[2] Turkish frightfulness reached its peak in the ghastly massacre of Chios, depicted as well as art can depict such scenes in one of Delacroix's famous paintings.

[1] Op. cit., pp. 337–8.
[2] We do well to ponder Byron's general warning (*Don Juan*, canto VIII, stanza III) :

> History can only take things in the gross ;
> But could we know them in detail, perchance
> In balancing the profit and the loss,
> War's merit it by no means might enhance.

The tragedy was increased by the fact that the Chians, enjoying a high standard of living and a kind of political autonomy,[1] had decidedly rejected all proposals for their " liberation " by people who could claim the right to interfere only on the grounds that they happened to speak the same language. In reality, Chios was dragged into the war for two reasons. The strategic reason was that the capitani of the Morea and at Hydra wished to create a diversion from themselves ; the economic, the wealth of the island. The invasion was carried out in March 1822, in the most light-hearted way. On the approach of the Turkish fleet, three weeks later, the invaders, mainly inhabitants of Samos, fled and left the Chians to face the ordeal. Most of the families of the island aristocracy and of the educated classes managed to get away ; they dispersed all over Europe. The bulk of the population, however, remained. " Every Chian deserves death "—this sentence of the Ottoman civil governor was carried out in two stages, almost literally.[2] Before the massacre the total resident population was estimated at 120,000 ; after it, at 30,000.

Several months earlier, the Greeks had set the tune. When, in the autumn of 1821, the Turks surrendered at Tripolitsa, the prisoners, according to Consul P. J. Green's report from Patras (November 1st),

> were taken out of the town, and above 12,000 men, women and children, were put to death by their inhuman conquerors. Some were hanged, others impaled, many roasted alive by large fires ; the women outraged in the first instance, and then ripped open (many of them far advanced in pregnancy) and dogs' heads put into them ; upwards of 200 Jews, who were inhabitants of the city, were put to death, some of them by crucifixion.[3]

The islanders were hardly less cruel. S. G. Howe, an American doctor, noted on July 2nd, 1825, " the cold-blooded murder of 250 Turkish captives which took place here five days ago, has stained Hydra and her inhabitants with infamy which time cannot blot out ".[4] Howe was most depressed by the fact that 90 per cent. of the people of Hydra absolutely approved of the deed. As to the primates, " they sat in their balconies, smoking their pipes, and, knocking out the ashes, merely said : ' It is a bad thing ' and let the work of murder [which lasted for three hours] go

---

[1] Chapitre III, Mémoire sur Scio, dated 14th June 1824, addressed by the French Vice-Consul in Chios to Chateaubriand ; reprinted in P. P. Argenti, *The Massacre of Chios*, London, 1932.
[2] Op. cit., chapitre IV. [3] *Sketches of the War in Greece*, London, 1827, p. 69.
[4] *Letters and Journals*, London, 1907, p. 84.

on . . ." Treaties of capitulation, sparing the lives of the besieged, were almost invariably broken ; those of Navarino and Monemvasia were outstanding examples. The abyss of hatred was revealed in the popular song : " Away with the Turks from the Morea, away with them from the whole world."

The Phanariots Mavrocordato and Ypsilantis' brother Demetrios, who had joined the insurgent cause, were horrified by the excesses which they were not able to stop ; the real power lay undoubtedly in the hands of those capitani who in times of peace had been brigand chiefs. One of the most powerful among them had been a special favourite of Ali Pasha. By an irony of history he was known under the name of Odysseus. It needed all the well-meaning and vivid imagination of a Western Philhellene to maintain, as did Col. Stanhope, that this man was in favour of constitutional rights. Yet Stanhope himself noticed that the capitani, possessing all the power, had enriched themselves and had laid their hand on a portion of the land which, in consequence of the revolution, had become the property of the State. He mentioned this fact in a letter to Bowring on November 11th, 1823, adding : " Kolokotrones is said to be worth a million of dollars, Odysseus [he actually called him Ulysses] 400,000 dollars." [1] In an anonymous pamphlet entitled *Sketches in Greece and Turkey* (London 1833), the capitani's method of enrichment is analysed in more detail :

> Whenever a rumour was spread which, of course, was as often as he [Kolokotrones] chose to spread it, of the approach of any formidable enemy, the cunning klepht managed to persuade the people that it was highly important to place their more valuable property in a place of security, and offered his castle for the purpose. When the unthinking peasantry had fallen into the trap, and conveyed their few possessions to Caritena, and when the danger grew nearer and more pressing, he insinuated that as ere long they might be necessitated to take shelter in his castle, it was important to provision it for a long garrison and a long siege, and also to bring in all the munitions of war they were able to procure. As soon as the danger had blown over, the subtle Greek sold off the stock thus acquired . . .[2]

Robbed by the capitani and the enemy alike, many people—at least those who did not make up for it by pillaging the Turks —were in a state of destitution. Whereas the coffee-houses were " full of lazy, lousy, vain and foolish capitani, dressed out in gold jackets, with a boy to carry their pipe, and two or three soldiers

[1] *Greece in 1823 and 1824*, London, 1824, p. 27.
[2] Op. cit., pp. 197–8.

to tag round at their heels ",[1] the six places (Athens, Salamis, Egina, Micomi, Syra, and Tenos) into whose condition Wadding-ton inquired, contained over 20,000 persons reduced to extreme distress by the circumstances of the Revolution.[2]   Both Wadding-ton[3] and Prokesch[4] found it extremely regrettable that the sums subscribed in Europe for the benefit of the Greeks were being applied to political rather than to charitable purposes, and often wandered into the pockets of men like Kolokotrones.

It showed an equal lack of judgment on the part of the Phil-hellenes that they expected the new Greek Constitution, pro-claimed on the Greek New Year's Day 1822, to work miracles. The half-circle round Southern Europe through which the con-stitution had travelled came to an end in Greece, whose con-stitution was largely the work of an Italian refugee by the name of Gallina who had in his luggage a selection of recent constitu-tions.   It provided, among other things, universal equality before the law, a high-sounding phrase which meant little in a country where, in Stanhope's words, the laws were neither much known nor observed.[5]   It also provided a central government for the whole of Greece, but the disruptive social forces proved more powerful than grandiose legalistic planning.   The capitani, not satisfied with the wealth they had amassed and the executive power entrusted to them, were jealous of the influence which the primates and Phanariots like Mavrocordato and D. Ypsilantis were exercising in the newly-instituted legislature.   Kolokotrones therefore sent his son Panos to dissolve this body by force of arms. The obvious consequence was that the opponents of the capitani set up an executive of their own.   The position was well sum-marized in Trelawny's letter to Stanhope from Missolonghi on April 28th, 1824 : " . . . imbecile councils—intriguing people —greedy soldiers—and factious capitains, are the beings I have to deal with in this Ionian sand (or rather slime) isthmus."[6]

Shortly before that date, a greater man than Trelawny had almost despaired at the same place.   In October 1823, Byron had confessed in a letter from Metaxata to Col. Napier : " I can hardly be disappointed, for I believed myself on a fool's errand from the outset . . . because I do not feel confidence in any

---

[1] Howe, op. cit., p. 110.
[2] *A Visit to Greece*, p. 99.   [3] Ibid., p. 95.
[4] Letter to Schneller from Constantinople, dated 21st February 1826. (*Schnellers Hinterlassene Werke*, II, pp. 118, 307.)
[5] Letter to Bowring from Missolonghi, dated 16th December 1823, op. cit., p. 43.
[6] *Letters of Edward John Trelawny*, ed. H. Buxton Forman, Oxford, 1910, p. 76.

KOLOKOTRONES

[*face p.* 170

COCHRANE

[*face p.* 171

individual capacity for this kind of bear-taming . . ." In the meantime he had tried in Missolonghi to organize a regular corps of infantry, the nucleus of which was composed of Albanian Suliots. Soon he was to discover how right Mavrocordato had been in warning him not to trust this rabble.[1] On February 15th, 1824, Byron made this note in his Journal in Cephalonia : " I will have nothing more to do with the Suliots. They may go to the Turks, or the Devil—they may cut me into more pieces than they have dissensions among themselves, sooner than change my resolution." [2]

For some time it seemed as if Gentz's prophecy that the Greeks would break each other's necks was going to be fulfilled. The inner dissensions among them showed that the conception of their struggle as a national War of Independence was an illusion of the West.[3] Prokesch's diagnosis went right to the root of the matter : " The nation ", he wrote to Metternich in 1825, " is too young and at the same time too old for revolution. The great mass cannot yet be enticed by revolutionary ideas. The few powerful and somewhat developed men are ' overripe ', no longer capable of enthusiasm and altogether devoted to anarchy, in order to use in the basest fashion possible the misfortune of the majority as the source of their own enrichment." In these circumstances war and civil war, stratagems and intrigues, glory and plunder, became all inextricably mixed up. Indeed, realistic observers might have found it difficult to disagree with the warning of Sophocles :

$$\text{'}Aναρχίας \ δε \ μειζον \ οὐκ \ ἐστιν \ κακον.$$

[1] Cf. Harold Nicolson, *Byron. The Last Journey*, London, 1924, pp. 197–8.
[2] *Works*, V, p. 326, n. 1.
[4] Illusion and disillusionment about the case of the modern Greeks had both been anticipated as early as 1799 in Hölderlin's prophetic *Hyperion*. (E.g., 2 Band, 2 Buch, Diotima's letter to Hyperion : " Du führtest sie zur Freiheit, und sie dachten au Raub.") Shortly before his death, Byron complained about " the political jobbers, who mistake the accessories of our civilization for its cause ". He added : " They think if they only hoist the colours of freedom, they will immediately transform a crazy, water-logged bark into a man-of-war ". (Parry, *The Last Days of Lord Byron, 1826*, pp. 190–1.) Two months after Byron's death, Pushkin, who knew many Greeks in Odessa, wrote to Prince Vyazemsky : " I have become disgusted with Greece. One can discuss the fate of the Greeks, like that of my brothers the negroes. One can wish both liberation from the unbearable slavery, but this enthusiasm of all cultured nations for Greece is unforgivable childishness. The Jesuits have told us all that twaddle about Themistocles and Pericles, and so we imagine that the shabby nation of robbers and traders are their legitimate successors and heirs of their school-glory." Sochinenia i pisma A. S. Pushkina, VIII, St. Petersburg, 1906, pp. 66.

CHAPTER VIII

THE CONCERT OF EUROPE DISSOLVED

The military revolts that shook Southern Europe soon found a powerful echo in France. Opposition to Louis XVIII, like that towards the Bourbons in Spain and Naples, was decidedly concentrated in the army. Riego's, Quiroga's, and to a lesser extent even Pepe's, achievements seemed encouraging to their French counterparts or would-be counterparts, such as Fabvier and Lafayette.[1] Much more important, however, than these foreign examples was the indigenous tradition of " military Jacobinism ", as Metternich had called it during his stay in Paris in 1815.[2]

The Jacobin attitude to military matters in general and war in particular had varied at different stages of the Revolution and its aftermath. Here we must once more cast a backward glance at that earlier period. In the very beginning many French revolutionaries were opposed to war, or at any rate to war as they knew it, namely Dynastic War. Since the end of the seventeenth century, the time, that is, when the religious wars had ceased, the ruling classes of Europe had been accustomed to regard foreign policy in terms of the Balance of Power. For this purpose Europe was their chess-board. By the famous manifesto of November 19th, 1792, the French National Convention invited, as it were, the Balance of Power pawns all over Europe to unite and upset the cynical old game. No longer were wars to be waged as the " Sport of Kings ". War, the new dogma proclaimed, was the concern of all peoples, and why on earth should people fight each other? It was in the speeches of Cloots and the Abbé Grégoire that this cosmopolitan idealism reached its idealist peak.

It lies obviously outside the scope of this book to describe how this attitude was gradually narrowed down and transformed into a nationalist mentality.[3] Even so, a community as large

---

[1] Cf. A. Debidour, *Le Général Fabvier. Sa vie militaire et politique*, Paris, 1904, p. 159.

[2] Cf. Adam Müller to Gentz, Leipzig, 19th September 1820. (*Briefwechsel zwischen Friedrich Gentz und Adam Heinrich Müller, 1800–1829*, Stuttgart, 1857.)

[3] A. Toynbee has pointed out that this trend could already be observed in the American War of Independence. Rights of Man at the beginning, in the end ruthless persecution of the Loyalist minority. (*A Study of History*, IV, pp. 166–7.)

as a nation might perhaps be expected to avoid unnecessary wars. True, this assumption, which Montesquieu had formulated in the words " L'esprit de la république est la paix ", did not remain unchallenged in the French Assembly. On May 20th, 1790, Mirabeau himself warned : " Voyez les peuples libres ; c'est par des guerres plus ambitieuses, plus barbares qu'ils se sont toujours distingués ". His warning was drowned in the general enthusiasm. Hardly anyone then realized that whereas Dynastic War as a sport, cynical though it was, had been waged according to certain rules and with some moderation, Nationalist War as the deadly serious occupation of whole nations would hardly recognize any limits whatsoever. Few people then knew that the abolition of Dynastic Wars would, in effect, mean the end of restricted warfare which, in the opinion of a recent historian, constituted one of the loftiest achievements of the eighteenth century.[1]

The ominous word " conscription " was heard for the first time in the revolutionary parliament in October 1789. On December 12th, Dubois-Crancé, expert in military matters, proclaimed that in his view every citizen should be a soldier and every soldier a citizen. But it was not until August 1793, the time, that is, when the Revolution was menaced from without, that the National Convention passed the law devised by Carnot, ordering the " levée en masse ". Thus it was originally an emergency measure when the revolutionaries decided to send against the rigidly trained professional armies of their enemies masses inexperienced in the field.[2] Seen from this angle, the war which they were waging appears indeed as " a national war without the vices of nationalism ", as J. M. Thompson describes it in his recent study of the French Revolution.[3] The numbers of these unprofessional warriors were to make up for their lack of skill ; but this was not sufficient. The margin had to be filled by violent passions.[4] Amateurs as they were, they had to live up to the literal meaning of that word ; they had to love their occupation ; and the surest way of securing this was to make them hate and despise the enemy. These passions in their turn undoubtedly helped to bring about the switch-over from defensive

---

[1] Guglielmo Ferrero, *Peace and War*, trans. by Berthe Pritchard, London, 1933, p. 63. Cf. also Toynbee, op. cit., p. 147.
[2] Lord Acton has suggested that the general levy was facilitated by the slaughter going on at home which made people readier to face the slaughter at the front. (*Lectures on the French Revolution*, London, 1910, p. 323.)
[3] Oxford, 1943, p. 425.
[4] Cf. Foch, *Des Principes de la Guerre*, 4me éd., 1917, p. 25.

to aggressive nationalism.[1] Originally, on August 23rd, 1793, it had been envisaged that the " permanent requisition of all Frenchmen for military service " would come to an end the moment the enemies had been chased from the territory of the Republic. Not only did this fail to happen, but Napoleon's military despotism—the rise of which had been foretold by Burke —carried conscription even further than Carnot. By now requisition had actually become permanent. At the same time, the passion of the " levée en masse " had in many cases degenerated into ruthlessness. This feature was not confined for long to the French armies. Burke, it is true, observed that while the Jacobins never pardoned, the allies treated the most bloody and merciless offenders as prisoners of war instead of calling them to strict account. Such leniency seemed monstrous to him. However, with the spread of mass democracy this difference soon disappeared, for mass democracy, the heritage of the French Revolution, became inextricably bound up with mass armies, and consequently with certain unmistakable aspects of barbarism, as Taine has forcibly pointed out.[2]

During the almost twenty years of French nationalist aggression there grew up a generation of Frenchmen who have been described by Alfred de Musset as " conçus entre deux batailles . . . Ils étaient nés au sein de la guerre, pour la guerre ". Another sensitive witness, Alfred de Vigny, spoke of " cette génération née avec le siècle, qui, nourrie de bulletins de l'Empereur, avait toujours devant les yeux une épée nue ".[3] Relating his experiences at the lycée, de Vigny wrote : " Nos précepteurs ressemblaient à des hérauts d'armes, nos salles d'études à des casernes, nos récréations à des manœuvres, et nos examens à des revues." And the result : " La guerre nous semblait . . . l'état naturel de notre pays." After Waterloo,

[1] Cf. this passage, written in 1805, from Wordsworth's *Poem* (later called *The Prelude*) :

> *And now, become oppressors in their turn,*
> *Frenchmen had changed a war of self-defence*
> *For one of conquest, losing sight of all*
> *Which they had struggled for ; and mounted up,*
> *Openly, in the view of earth and heaven,*
> *The scale of Liberty.*

(Edited from the manuscript by E. de Selincourt, Oxford, 1926, pp. 404, 406.)

[2] *Origines de la France contemporaine*, I, 1891, p. 288 : " Universal, conscript, military service ! . . with its twin brother universal suffrage . . . has mastered all continental Europe, . . . with what promises of massacre and bankruptcy for the Twentieth Century ! " Cf. also the recent American study of Hoffmann Nickerson, *The Armed Horde, 1793–1939*, New York, 1940, p. 14 and passim.

[3] *Servitude et grandeur militaires*, Paris, 1835, ch. I.

this lost generation could not believe in a durable peace. In de Vigny's own words : " Chaque année apportait l'espoir d'une guerre." The régime of the Restoration and the strata of society which supported it failed for a long time to provide an outlet for these aggressive, or, to say the least, ambitious inclinations of the young generation. Musset's famous passage puts it in a nutshell : " Quand les enfants parlaient de gloire, on leur disait : ' Faites-vous prêtres ' ; quand ils parlaient d'ambition : ' Faites-vous prêtres ' ; d'ésperance, d'amour, de force, de vie : ' Faites-vous prêtres ! ' " [1] On the official scale of values, military glory had lost its place to respectable piety. The place of honour previously held by " la grande armée " was now officially reserved to the Congrégation de la Vierge.

The humiliation of " la grande armée " was not only relative. It suffered also directly and absolutely. As to the top, eighteen Napoleonic generals were court-martialled in 1815. Nearly all the new commanders were lieutenant-generals drawn from the ranks of the old aristocracy. At the beginning of 1818, as many as sixteen thousand Napoleonic officers were on half-pay,[2] and, what may have seemed to them even more annoying, were tied down to a fixed abode from which they were not allowed to move without permission from the authorities. In addition, a considerable number of " sous-officiers " had been relegated to the ranks. Some of these degraded and dissatisfied officers and ex-officers took refuge for outward purposes in bourgeois occupations such as commercial travelling, which in fact enabled them to keep in touch with many of their comrades in misfortune. Others sat in the cafés of the Palais Royal, where they indulged in wild reminiscences and wilder schemes of a comeback.

The army as a whole had been reduced in 1815 to 150,000 men. Three years later Gouvion Saint-Cyr's Army Bill increased it to 240,000.[3] But after the assassination of the Duc de Berry by an isolated fanatic in February 1820, the Ultra-royalists, exploiting this event in the same way as Metternich had done with Sand's crime, brought about first the fall of the Decazes cabinet, and next began to threaten Saint-Cyr's Army Bill. The

---

[1] *La confession d'un enfant du siècle*, ch. II.

[2] Ed. Bonnal, *Les Royalistes contre l'armée (1815–1820)*. *D'après les Archives de Ministère de la Guerre*, I, Paris, 1906, p. 324.

[3] In the same year the historian P. E. Lémontey thus characterized the modern system of large standing armies : " C'est une lèpre attachée aux états modernes, qui use et corrompt leur substance, et oppose un fatal obstacle au bonheur privé, à l'économie publique et au perfectionnement de toute bonne civilisation." (*Essai sur l'établissement monarchique de Louis XIV*, Paris, 1818, p. 373.)

new War Minister, Latour-Maubourg, was preparing to re-organize the infantry in such a way as to be able to put 2,000 more officers on half-pay. This was the time when news of Riego's progress was filling the hearts of his French admirers with new hope. Besides, Napoleon was still alive, and some of the ex-officers and disbanded soldiers toyed with the idea of his return from St. Helena. Disturbances first broke out in Paris in June 1820. Discontented officers gathered bands of insurgents from the suburbs and marched on the Palais Bourbon. This was soon followed by the conspiracy of the Bazar français, a huge storehouse where officers and rankers had been plotting for months under the cloak of an art exhibition. Both these disturbances were crushed fairly easily. In the following year and especially in 1822-3, unrest in the army reached more dangerous dimensions. Louis Blanc in the illuminating introduction to his *Histoire de dix ans* offers a sound explanation : " While Napoleon lived, all other pretensions besides his were impossible : when he was dead, pretenders rushed thick upon the field of conspiracy. There was a party for Napoleon II, a party for Joseph Bonaparte, a party for the prince Eugène ; and the crown was set up to auction by a multitude of obscure and subaltern ambitions." [1] Prominent among them were the Four Sergeants of La Rochelle, led by a non-commissioned officer named Bories. Other places where risings either took place or were planned to take place were Poitiers, Niort, Colmar, Neuf-Brisach, Nantes, Béfort, Bordeaux, and Toulouse. In the east, where hostility to the Restoration was much fiercer, the centres of conspiracy were Alsace and Marseilles. In the west, where interest in political matters was feebler, the centre of unrest was Saumur. In the latter place a ruined Napoleonic general by the name of Berton took a leading part.

Just as in Naples, the military conspirators were helped as well as hampered by other members of the secret Charbonnerie ; many of them themselves belonged to this society. Several regiments organized " ventes ", and on the other hand it was the duty, if not always the custom, of the civilian charbonnier to have in his possession a gun and fifty cartridges, and thus to be prepared for the great event. Charbonniers other than ex-soldiers or half-pay officers were members of the intelligentsia— among them numerous students—and some wealthy bourgeois. As in Naples, this motley crowd could not but aim at very different things. Besides republican, Orleanist, and Bonapartist

[1] Eng. trans., London, 1844, I, p. 47.

" ventes " there were others which were lacking in any political colour. Many a symptom justified the diagnosis of Pasquier, who spoke of a contagious mania for conspiracy. As in Naples, the charbonnerie did not descend into the lower strata of society.[1] Nor did it show any concern for the problems and worries facing the growing industrial proletariat. Liberals supported the charbonnerie for different political reasons. The Press law of March 1820 had subjected all political writings to censorship whatever their channel of publication. A lesser degree of restriction of the Press was among the aims of the Liberals, but they were conscious of the danger of its becoming an instrument by which the masses could be swayed too easily. Similarly they desired an extension of the franchise, and it is worth remembering that in 1830, before the Revolution, only 90,878 Frenchmen had the vote out of a total population of over 30 millions. But here too the Liberals were not in too great a hurry, for in their view voting for the good of the community was possible only on the basis of a certain standard of education.

The charbonnerie, as we have seen, was by no means unified in its political outlook. In fact, the programme—if such it could be called—of the " vente suprême " was as vague as the *Charte* which Louis XVIII had granted to his subjects. On the one hand this vagueness enabled the secret society to throw its doors open to so many subscribers. But on the other hand it was a symptom of weakness and must have contributed to its collapse. An additional cause of its inglorious failure was, again as in Naples, the timidity of the respectable members.[2]

The continually recurring army disturbances and the abortive attempts of the charbonnerie had very important after-effects. Government and Ultras both felt themselves threatened and decided therefore jointly to pursue a plan which was to rid them of all embarrassment. The solution they had in mind was military intervention against the Spanish revolt. Two birds were thus to be killed with one stone. The campaign would furnish an outlet for the exuberant energy of the army, and at the same time the prestige of the Government and of the right wing would be enhanced.[3] Chateaubriand's boast that the scheme was his is generally taken at its face value. No doubt this man, whose

---

[1] Louis Blanc, op. cit., I, p. 57.   [2] Ibid., I, p. 54.

[3] Cf. the following passage from Maréchal Marmont's *Mémoires* : " La maison de Bourbon avait une bonne occasion de faire un essai de l'armée. Le baptème de sang est nécessaire à des nouveaux drapeaux, à des nouvelles couleurs ; jusque— là des troupes n'offrent que peu de garantie." (VII, Paris, 1857, p. 293.)

vanity was equalled only by that of his arch-enemy Metternich, did everything in his power to get the scheme going. Legitimacy had in his view been reduced to a mummy because after the triumphs of the usurper it had failed to gain victories. In later years he proudly confessed to having sent the Prime Minister Villèle in the autumn of 1822, an untrue account of the wishes of the European Congress at Verona.[1] He knew that his own prestige and that of his country could be considerably increased only if France were to act as an independent Great Power, or at any rate not in complete concert with the other Powers. But this idea was in the air ; indeed, we have Louis Blanc's testimony to the fact that the French chamber desired the Spanish war with the utmost fervour.[2] The scheme was seriously opposed only by business men who feared trade would suffer. The Paris Rothschild refused to finance the campaign, and even Ouvrard, prototype of the modern war profiteer, who thus got another chance, hesitated [3] before stepping in to usurp the post of food commissary for the invading army.

It was highly significant that the last of this series of army disturbances took place by the river Bidassoa. For some time past, unrest in this frontier region had been due to discharged French officers and charbonniers as well as to Italian refugees from the unsuccessful revolts of Naples and Piedmont, some of whom had been collected by the untiring Fabvier from their exile in London. Now, on April 6th, 1823, the approaching French army of intervention was greeted by Fabvier and his two hundred followers who stood on the Spanish bank of the river, by the Tricolor and the Marseillaise. The reply to this was a few volleys from the guns ; they proved decisive. On the following day, the French army under the Duc d'Angoulème crossed the river. A disquieting after-effect of the Napoleonic Wars was thus quelled by another war. Though this campaign was, from a military point of view, a walk-over, it contributed much to the disruption of the Concert of Europe : this for two reasons. Firstly, France had alienated the Tsar by rejecting his proposal to send a European, rather than a French, army of intervention into Spain.

---

[1] " Nous disons au président du conseil que le vœu très prononcé des puissances est pour la guerre . . ." (" Congrès de Verone ", Œuvres complètes, XII, p. 85.)
[2] Op. cit., p. 58.
[3] Ouvrard had certain claims against the Spanish crown since 1806. He would therefore have preferred to negotiate a huge loan on the Spanish monarch's behalf. Cf. Otto Wolff, Die Geschäfte des Herrn Ouvrard, Frankfurt-am-Main, 1932, p. 206 ; and A. Nicolle, Ouvrard and the French Expedition in Spain in 1823, in : Journal of Modern History, XVII, September 1945.

Secondly, the rift between Great Britain and the Continental Powers which, so far as the Occident was concerned, had made itself felt as early as 1818 at Aix-la-Chapelle, was seriously deepened. It is to the causes of this rift that we now have to turn.

Great Britain was in the fortunate position of not being in need of a war in Europe as an outlet for her disbanded or dissatisfied soldiers and sailors. Several other outlets stood at her disposal. Prominent among them was Latin America. Disbanded veterans of the Peninsula and of Flanders went over in very large numbers to join the cause of the revolting colonies. C. K. Webster has pointed out that no other country supplied so many men to the forces of the insurgents.[1] Before the end of 1818, Bolívar's army was strengthened by the advent of at least 6,000 Britishers. Higher British officers were the only foreigners on Bolívar's personal staff. Between 1818 and 1820, two expeditions sailed in fully-armed ships from London for New Granada, and six for Venezuela. As to the war in Colombia, Wellington, in a letter to Canning from Verona, maintained that the conquest from the Spaniards had been made by " our deserters "[2] as he chose to call the dissatisfied elements. The afflux from the Navy was equally considerable. The case of Lord Cochrane, though outstanding for many reasons, was typical in the sense that after a highly eventful past he had been obliged to leave the British Navy and had decided to offer his services to the Latin American revolutionaries. Soon some British captains and numerous British sailors were serving under his command. Nor must it be forgotten that Britain, in contradistinction to the Continental Powers, could fully avail herself of this outlet because of the very fact of her great naval strength.

Adventurers from the Old World who went over to fight in the Spanish American revolt, certainly found congenial company. Whereas during the preceding two and a half centuries of Spanish rule the soldier's trade had been abhorred in these regions,[3] it was now becoming very popular. Confusion of authority enabled vagabonds, smugglers, and cattle-raiders to arrogate to themselves surprisingly high positions. A case in point was the gangster who awakened Uruguayan nationalism. Warfare in these circumstances was of course unlimited. Prisoners were

[1] *Britain and the Independence of Latin America, 1812–1830. Select Documents from the Foreign Office Archives,* Oxford Univ. Press, 1938, I, p. 77.
[2] *Despatches,* New Series, I, London, 1867, p. 384.
[3] *Cambridge Modern History,* X, p. 256.

slaughtered either on capture or after victory had been achieved. In 1823, William Cobbett received a letter from a person in Mexico who said that the question there was now not one of liberty or slavery, but one of life or death.[1]

That part of the population which was most cruelly oppressed, namely the Indians, took little part in the revolt. Legally classed as " gente misérable ", many of them terribly exploited in mines and cloth factories, above all decimated by epidemics and alcohol imported by the white man, they did not lack reasons for complaint ; and indeed inthe 1780s something like an Indian revolt had taken place. But this time they were, most of them, royalist, because they realized that the Creoles, to whose jealousy of the Europeans the revolt was mainly due, were their worst exploiters. The outcome of the struggle was to justify the grave apprehensions of the oppressed. Captain Basil Hall, who visited South America at the beginning of the 1820s, noticed that in Chile the peasant's station in society had not been materially changed by the subversion of Spanish authority, while that of his landlord was essentially altered in almost every point.[2] The establishment of the Latin-American Republics, hailed by Bentham as the triumph of enlightenment, had in actual fact much less elevating aspects. This is true even of Brazil, of whose Government it has been said, with some justification, that it was " more mild, more enlightened and more just than that of any surrounding state ".[3] On the other hand, J. H. Clapham has pointed out that in Brazil, as in Cuba, the demand of Europe for tropical produce directly encouraged the consolidation and extension of a society based on slavery.[4] Indeed, millions of African negroes, many of them in U.S. ships, operated by English capital,[5] were imported into Bahia ; and it was only in 1888 that Brazil ceased to be a slave-holding state.

The essential factor in Britain's attitude towards the Latin-American revolts was business, that is to say a peculiar combination of trade and speculation. Suggestions of such a policy go back as far as the first half of the eighteenth century. According to the terms of the Treaty of Utrecht, the sovereigns of Spain and of England each received one-quarter of the profit from the trans-

[1] *Cobbett's Weekly Register*, November 22nd, 1823.
[2] *Extracts from a Journal written on the Coasts of Chili, Peru and Mexico*, 2nd ed., Edinburgh, 1824, vol. I, p. 24.
[3] Harold Temperley, *The Foreign Policy of Canning 1822–27*, London 1925, p. 224.
[4] *Cambridge Modern History*, X, p. 761.
[5] Donald Pierson, *Negroes in Brazil. A Study of Race Contact at Bahia*, Chicago, 1942, pp. 29–31 and 36.

actions of the English South Sea Company which undertook to send to Spanish America 4,800 pieces—as the negroes were styled —of proper height and age annually for thirty years. Possibilities for a contraband trade offered themselves ; for goods were frequently introduced under pretext of clothing and feeding the negroes. In 1739, when Great Britain declared war on Spain, 250 Spanish smugglers on the Isthmus were supplied with arms and ammunition by the English enemy. Two years later, one Stephen Deveros suggested to the British Government that it should instigate and support a revolution in Spanish America for the reason that " we shall thereby greatly increase our own Riches which is the end of all conquests : and we shall do it without raising the just envy of our neighbours ".[1] In 1762, during the Seven Years' War in which Spain decided to throw in her lot with France, British forces occupied Havana, which they held for just over a year. The booty was of the value of £3,000,000.[2] Havana's trade increased considerably during this short period. A few years later, Aranda, President of the Council of Castile, warned his government emphatically of the danger of British interference with Spanish colonial possessions.[3] Indeed, before the end of the century the British Government contemplated extensive operations in these regions. Much was done to foster these plans by Picton, the military governor of the islands of Trinidad, which the British had seized in 1797. He recommended on several occasions that the British Government should send an army to the coast of Venezuela and declare its intention of giving the South Americans independence and free trade ; this would make them rise against their corrupt oppressors.[4] Vast preparations were made in 1804–5, and again in 1807 ; and actual operations, such as the capture of Montevideo, took place in 1806. But on the whole, Castlereagh, who was then Secretary for War and the Colonies, carried the day with his memorandum of 1807 in which he maintained that Britain could not undertake " the hopeless task of conquering this extensive country ". In the meantime the gradual development from contraband to legal

---

[1] " Some Thoughts relating to our Conquests in America ", *American Historical Review*, IV, January 1899, p. 327.
[2] According to Col. de Lacy Evans's first memorandum to Canning relative to the question of a seizure of Cuba by the British Government. (*Some Official Correspondence of George Canning*, ed. E. J. Stapleton, London, 1887, Vol. I, p. 116.)
[3] Richard Konetzke, " Die Politik des Grafen Aranda. Ein Beitrag zur Geschichte des spanisch—englischen Weltgegensatzes im 18. Jahrhundert ", *Historische Studien*, Heft 182, Berlin, 1929, p. 51.
[4] J. Fred Rippy, *Latin America in World Politics*, rev. ed., New York, 1931, pp. 33–4.

A.N.W.

trade was somewhat accelerated, especially in the Caribbean.[1]
The British Government showed great interest in the trade with
Spanish America, for as early as 1811–12, throughout the negotia-
tions for mediation between Spain and her colonies, the British
Cabinet adhered to the essential condition that the Spanish-
American ports should be opened to greater freedom of com-
merce.[2] Unless this condition were fulfilled, even a peaceful
mediation was out of the question.

To secure and, if possible, to increase trade with Latin
America, became of additional importance to Great Britain two
or three years after Waterloo. By then it had become evident
that the Continental countries of Europe, impoverished as they
were after the long struggle, could not provide as favourable
markets for British goods as had been expected. Nor was this
disappointment due only to their incapacity to purchase ; to
some extent it was caused by restrictive tariffs imposed by these
countries for the protection of their newly developed industries.
The same tendency was shown by the United States. As to
West Indian trade, it had lost some of its importance owing to
the introduction of beet sugar in Europe during the Continental
blockade. Canada was as yet too sparsely populated to offer
immediate hopes for British oversea trade. Finally, Eastern trade
showed no signs of rapid development. In consequence of all
this it proved impossible for Great Britain to relieve herself fully
of the excessive quantities of goods [3] which had been accumulated
during the war period in expectation of further government con-
tracts. The value of the colonial produce alone that had been
piled up in Great Britain between 1807 and 1814 is estimated by
Tooke to have been nearly £15,000,000.[4] In 1818, the British
merchants found themselves left with stocks of a market value of
over £10,000,000 still on their hands.[5] In the following year
the situation was worse. In 1820, a member of the late Parliament contributed an article on " Restrictions on Foreign Commerce " to the *Edinburgh Review*. He wrote : " When the former
sources of our wealth and channels of our commerce have been
either dried up or shut against us . . . it becomes the imperative
duty of Ministers to endeavour to open new markets for our

---

[1] From an economic point of view, the situation was not very different from the
situation in Brazil where trade was open to British shipping since 1808.
[2] Dorothy Burne Goebel, " British Trade and the Spanish Colonies 1796–1823 ",
American Historical Review, XLIII, January 1938, pp. 314, 430.
[3] Cf. a contribution to the *Tyne Mercury*, 23rd July 1816, Place Collection, vol. 29.
[4] *A History of Prices*, I, London, 1838, p. 108.
[5] L. H. Jenks, *The Migration of British Capital to 1875*, New York, 1927, p. 41.

manufactures, and to stimulate the natural demand for labour." [1]
An appreciable improvement in British trade began early in
1821–2 and continued during the boom year 1824 into the first
half of 1825. There is little doubt that this prosperity was partly
due to the rising trade with Latin America. The declared value
of total exports of British manufactures to Central and South
America in the four years ending 1825 was just over £19,000,000,
as compared with little over £12,000,000 for the years from 1818
to 1821. [2] Exports to these regions, which consisted chiefly of
cotton goods, woollens, linen and silk, could not fail favourably
to affect employment in Yorkshire and Lancashire. In exchange
Britain imported among other things coffee, cocoa, hides, sugar,
cotton, and tobacco. When imports failed to keep balance with
exports, British merchants were in many cases willing to lend their
goods abroad, because this was the only practicable way in which
these products could be disposed of commercially. [3]

British economic interest in Latin America was not confined
to the export of commodities. British capital, too, found its way
into South America. In an unpublished London thesis of 1928,
J. S. Jones has shown that these two interests were by no means
in close connection with each other ; in some cases capital loans
were accompanied by increased exports, but this was not the
rule. [4] Here it is well to remember that Britain had assumed her
rôle as moneylender to the world comparatively recently. Napoleon's invasion of Holland had caused the removal of the leading
money market from Amsterdam to London. After the Wars,
as in the case of commodities, the cessation of the Government's
demand for capital set free a huge amount for investment in other
channels. [5] The Hope-Baring loan which enabled France to pay
her reparations was the first important foreign loan contract by
a British house. Before long, lending abroad became something
of a passion with many people who were in a far less secure
position than the Barings. This tendency was strongly condemned by Alexander Baring, who attributed it to a large extent
to the alarm which had been created by the disturbances in
industrial parts of England in the autumn of 1819. Speaking in

---

[1] Vol. XXXIII, p. 350.
[2] G. R. Porter, *The Progress of the Nation*, London, 1851, p. 359. A further illustration : in 1825 Buenos Aires took one half its imports from Great Britain.
[3] C. K. Hobson, *The Export of Capital*, London, 1914, p. 99.
[4] *English Foreign Trade in the first half of the Nineteenth Century, together with some
observations on the war period of 1793–1814*, pp. 266, 268.
[5] Hobson, op. cit., pp. 96–7.

the House of Commons on December 9th, 1819, on Mr. Bennet's motion on the state of the manufacturing districts, Baring said :

There never has been a period when so much of the capital of the country was withdrawn for the purpose of being invested in foreign securities, as during the last three weeks. A sort of panic has seized the public mind. There is a general *sauve qui peut* amidst moneyed men, each endeavouring to outrun the other in removing capital from the kingdom.[1]

Loans to various Continental countries negotiated after 1817 brought, for some time, regularly paid and fairly high dividends [2] which compared favourably with the 3 per cent. to 4 per cent. interest to be derived from consols. Investors who were prepared to risk their money in overseas transactions were promised between $5\frac{1}{2}$ per cent. and 8 per cent. This difference, inviting though it was, would not of itself have sufficed to create the mania for overseas investment which actually broke out. The contractors who could pull the strings and manipulate the money market were thus able to pocket disproportionately high profits. To whet their victims' appetites, they engaged pamphleteers to prepare elaborate studies of Latin-American resources, topography and customs in much the same way as the newspaper readers' interest in Africa was aroused during the scramble for that continent half a century later. One of these pamphleteers, writing anonymously, was young Benjamin Disraeli. He was engaged for this job by John Diston Powles, the head of a financial house which had profited largely from such transactions as the establishment of mining companies in Latin America, and whose credit was in a high degree based on their continuance.[3] Disraeli's pen was enlisted to avert the danger of government interference with the speculations ; for the newly-founded companies, many of which were on a joint-stock basis, were accused of aiming at monopolies.[4] Disraeli set out to write *An Enquiry into the Plan, Progress, and Policy of the American Mining Companies* (1825), and actually arrived at the conclusion he had been asked to reach, namely that the mining companies' promise had been performed. This piece of work ran through several editions, and was soon followed by a second under the title *Lawyers and Legislators, or*

---

[1] Hansard, XLI, p. 906.
[2] William Smart, *Economic Annals*, II, London, 1917, p. 187.
[3] W. F. Monypenny, *The Life of Benjamin Disraeli, Earl of Beaconsfield*, I, London, 1910, p. 56.
[4] Smart, op. cit., p. 296. The total number of companies that sprang into brief life after the year 1823, was calculated to have been 532 with a subscribed capital of over £440,000,000. (Th. Doubleday, *The Political Life of Sir Robert Peel*, I, London, 1856, p. 327.)

Notes on the American Mining Companies. Its aim was to destroy Eldon's fitting parallel between the present state of affairs and that which preceded the South Sea Bubble.[1] The climax was reached in Disraeli's third pamphlet, which he dedicated to Canning. In it he advertised Mexico in these words : " The ancient kingdom of Montezuma is now an object of interest, not merely to the statesman, in relation to the abstract principles of government, but to every Briton, as connected with his most important interests." He also maintained that all the rich mines of Mexico's richest districts were at work.[2]

Precious metals became once again the chief magnet of people's cupidity. They readily believed that silver was so plentiful in South America that the meanest utensils were made of it.[3] Captain Basil Hall, who published *Extracts from a Journal written on the Coasts of Chili, Peru, and Mexico in the Years 1820, 1821, 1822,* felt obliged to include an appendix giving a list of minerals collected on the shores of South America and Mexico.[4] In this connection it was also significant that Southey's *History of Brazil* (1810–19) was the only instalment ever published of his long projected *History of Portugal.*

With all these appetizing prospects before their eyes, the public threw themselves into all kinds of wild speculative schemes, some of which were utterly fantastic. Between February 1824 and September 1825 as many as twenty-nine mining companies were floated to work foreign mines, mainly in Mexico and Peru. In 1822 a fictitious political entity on the Mosquito coast, calling itself the " Kingdom of Poyais ", under the command of a Scottish adventurer, sought a loan in Britain. In no time £160,000 was raised by eager subscribers.[5] The contractors' business was already specialized to the extent that firms such as Goldschmidt or Barclay contracted for most of the loans to minor—and rather

---

[1] Towards the end of 1825, over-speculation caused a serious economic crisis. To quote Baring, " it seemed as if all Bedlam had broken loose on the Royal Exchange ". In one week in December three London banks and sixty-three banks in the provinces failed. On Christmas Eve, the Bank of England nearly collapsed. Disraeli's own speculations proved disastrous. He incurred a debt of several thousand pounds which he finally liquidated nearly thirty years later. (Monypenny, op. cit., p. 56.) Most of the Mexican mining companies, so far from satisfying the investor's expectations, simply absorbed all the capital before closing down. (Smart, op. cit., pp. 297–8.) Loans to South American governments proved equally unprofitable in the long run.

[2] *The Present State of Mexico, as detailed in a report presented to the general Congress by the Secretary of State for the Home Department and Foreign Affairs, at the opening of the Session in 1825,* London, 1825, pp. 17, 51.

[3] Smart, op. cit., p. 294.

[4] Second edition, Edinburgh, 1824, Vol. II.   [5] Jenks, op. cit., p. 101.

revolutionary—states, whereas other firms, above all Rothschild and " his fellow-Christian " Baring,[1] concentrated on " legitimate government loan making ".   Between 1821 and 1825 loans contracted for South America reached the amount of £22,000,000.[2] All these loans were, of course, so much support for the revolt against Spanish rule, or to quote Byron :

> Every loan
> Is not a merely speculative hit,
> But seats a nation or upsets a throne.[3]

For, a large part of the capital which was lent to Chile, Peru, Buenos Aires, Mexico, Guatemala, or Colombia, was used for the supply of their respective armies and the construction of their miniature navies.

Although British oversea trade and speculation was thriving during and partly in consequence of the hostilities between Spain and her colonies, it was to the interest of British merchants in the long run that the actual state of independence of Latin America should be officially recognized and thus brought nearer to stabilization.   Then, it might be hoped, piratical activity in South and Central American waters would come to an end.   This explains why 113 London business houses signed a petition to be presented to the House by Sir James Mackintosh on June 15th, 1824, asking for recognition of those South American colonies " which had in fact established independent governments ".[4] Eight days later, an analogous petition signed by leading Manchester business men was presented, and this was followed by one from Birmingham.[5]   These petitions would be sure of a powerful backing in the House of Commons.   For, as W. R. Brock has pointed out in a recent study, nearly a hundred Members of Parliament were intimately connected with commerce.[6]

There also was in existence the Parliamentary Committee on Foreign Trade which sat continuously from 1820 to 1826 to explore means whereby British commerce might be extended. As to the Cabinet, nearly half its members sat in the House of Commons, as compared with under a quarter in 1815.[7]   William

---

[1] Byron, *Don Juan*, canto XII, stanza V.   [2] Smart, op. cit., p. 187.
[3] *Don Juan*, canto XII, stanza VI.
[4] Hansard, new series, XI, pp. 1344, 1475.
[5] Cf. also Arthur Redford, *Manchester Merchants and Foreign Trade*, Manchester, 1934, p. 100.
[6] There were 33 bankers and financiers, 22 general merchants, 6 brewers, 6 manufacturers, and 9 members each representing the interests of the West and East Indies. (*Lord Liverpool and Liberal Toryism 1820 to 1827*, Cambridge, 1941, pp. 83 and 287-9.)
[7] Alexander Brady, *William Huskisson and Liberal Reform*, Oxford, 1928, p. 10.

Huskisson, the new President of the Board of Trade, was M.P. for Liverpool. Canning, his predecessor in the representation of that great commercial centre, had recommended him to the constituency as " the best man of business in England, and one of the ablest practical statesmen that could engage in the concerns of a commercial country ". This description was, indeed, well founded.[1] As to the new Foreign Secretary himself, who maintained that he was unable to contend against the city-trained bands, he was bound to the mercantile interest by more than one tie. For example, he gained great advantage from the support of the family of Ellis who were leaders of the " West Indian interest ".[2] He was greatly obliged also to the firm of John Gladstone,[3] father of the future Prime Minister, for the rich merchant had brought him to Liverpool as a candidate in 1812 by personally offering to guarantee his expenses. Canning in his turn strongly supported a petition signed in 1814 by forty-five Liverpool firms of planters and merchants—among them John Gladstone—who asked the Government not to relinquish the former Dutch colonies of Demerara, Essequibo, and Berbice in South America where in the meantime much English money had been invested. In a letter to Castlereagh of June 9th, 1814, Canning drew attention to the merchants' argument that the possession of these colonies would render Great Britain independent of foreign supplies in the essential article of cotton, since the produce of Demerara alone was estimated to reach in normal years as many as 30,000 large bales.[4] By the Convention of London of 13th August, 1814, the settlements in question were formally ceded to Great Britain. The traditional opinion that they were purchased from Holland was due to some extraordinarily clever machinations of the Foreign Secretary. It has been convincingly disproved by William Robson's article " New Light on Castlereagh's Diplomacy." [5] Coleridge's general verdict was well justified : " The stock-jobbing and moneyed

---

[1] Cf. G. S. Veitch, " Huskisson and Liverpool ", *Transactions of the Historic Society of Lancashire and Cheshire*, 1929, p. 38.

[2] C. W. Crawley, *The Question of Greek Independence. A Study of British Policy in the Near East, 1821–1833*, Cambridge, 1930, p. 49, n. 16.

[3] John Gladstone's firm had formerly been mainly an East India house, but in the meantime John Gladstone had also become owner of plantations in the former Dutch colony of Demerara. His veneration for Mr. Canning was profound and, to quote W. E. Gladstone, " almost semi-idolatrous ". (*The Life of Mr. Gladstone told by himself*, London, 1893, p. 11.)

[4] F.O. Holland 75, quoted by H. T. Colenbrander, *Gedenkstukken der algemeene geschiedenis van Nederland van 1795 tot 1840*, Vii, s' Gravenhage, 1914, pp. 142–6.

[5] *Journal of Modern History*, III, 1931.

interest," he said on July 4th, 1830, " is so strong in this country that it has more than once prevailed in our foreign councils over national honour and national justice."

So far as Britain's trade with Spanish America was concerned, Castlereagh showed equal understanding. The commercial treaty between Great Britain and Spain in 1814 purported indeed to accept the Spanish eighteenth-century theory of a closed trade. On the other hand Castlereagh's memorandum to the Cabinet of August 20th, 1817, mentioned, as one of the conditions of mediation between Spain and her colonies, free commercial intercourse with South America. A week later, the British point of view was communicated to the other Great Powers. In the autumn of the following year Castlereagh refused to consent to the Spanish envoy being admitted to the discussions at Aix-la-Chapelle. Spain was not to be encouraged in her attempts to keep hold of her Empire. Another obligation arising out of the 1814 treaty with Spain was openly violated. Great Britain had undertaken to prevent her subjects from furnishing arms, ammunition, and war-stores to the insurgents. Now whole regiments were formed on British soil, and officers were wearing Venezuelan uniforms in public. Lord Cochrane, who in 1819 went so far as to blockade ports held by the loyalist viceroy of Peru, was officially threatened with prosecution according to the letter of the Foreign Enlistment Act,[1] but there was no indication that such measures were seriously contemplated. In October 1819, Castlereagh intimated to Spain that if she should attempt to recapture Montevideo, she could no longer rely on British mediation in her differences with Portugal.[2] The next important step was taken in the summer of 1822, before Castlereagh's death, when Robinson and Wallace, as President and Vice-President of the Board of Trade, obtained Parliament's consent to relaxing the navigation laws in order to attract Latin-American trade. The privilege, hitherto granted only to European countries and the U.S.A., of transmitting goods to Great Britain in their own ships, was now extended to these regions.

Thus it may be said that all Canning had to do was to complete the course taken by his predecessor. On November 15th, 1822, he recommended to the Cabinet the early recognition of the Spanish colonies.[3] In April 1823 the traffic in munitions was made legal. By the end of that year British consuls and

---

[1] Thomas Cochrane, Earl of Dundonald, *Narrative of Services in the Liberation of Chili, Peru, and Brazil, from Spanish and Portuguese domination*, I, London, 1859, p. xx.
[2] Cf. *Diary of Philipp von Neumann*, trans. by E. B. Chancellor, I, London, 1928, p. 6.
[3] *Some Official Correspondence of George Canning*, I, pp. 56–7.

consular agents were appointed to the principal places in Mexico, Chile, Colombia, and Buenos Aires. The Chilean Senate hailed Canning in July 1824 as the " Redeemer of Chile ". On December 17th, 1824, he penned the often quoted words : " Spanish America is free, and if we do not mismanage our matters sadly, she is English." [1] A month later, Great Britain recognized the independence of Buenos Aires, Colombia and Mexico. The commercial treaties signed on these occasions were, as C. R. Fay has recently pointed out, exceptionally favourable to Great Britain. [2] As a result, in 1827 British trade with Latin America was nearly four times that of the U.S.A.

So far we have investigated only the relations between Great Britain and the Latin-American colonies. But all this has to be seen against the background of world politics. Above all, it must be emphasized that Britain had to act with determination and speed, if she did not wish to be forestalled by the U.S.A. As early as 1817–18 that country had sent Commissioners to Spanish America. One of these agents, by the name of Worthington, had warned Adams on January 15th, 1818, that only extreme care would prevent England from getting " a footing in South America, too firm to be displaced ", with the result that " our countrymen would lose all the glory and profit to be derived from this great contest ". Soon afterwards U.S. consuls were appointed to places in South America, and in 1822 the U.S.A. had recognized the independence of Colombia, Chile, Buenos Aires, and Mexico. That this development was anxiously watched by the British Cabinet emerges from a letter written by C. W. W. Wynn to the Duke of Buckingham. On October 29th, 1824, Wynn—President of the Board of Control with a seat in the Cabinet—wrote :

With respect to South American independence, though I am perfectly aware that a treaty will not create trade, it may prevent its being interrupted, and I am convinced that if Buenos Ayres were to-morrow to impose duties on the ships and produce of every country except that which has recognized it—viz., North America—you would be compelled, by the outcry of the country, to recognize them in six months ; and it would in the meantime further the views of North America in favour of a closer connection. In truth, the trade already carried on with South America is too important an object to be hazarded. [3]

[1] A. G. Stapleton, *George Canning and his Times*, London, 1859, p. 411.
[2] *Cambridge History of the British Empire*, II, p. 398.
[3] Duke of Buckingham and Chandos, *Memoirs of the Court of George IV*, London, 1859, Vol. II, pp. 144-5.

A month later, on November 30th, 1824, Canning in a memorandum to the Cabinet argued in the same way : " It cannot be doubted that if we provoke the New States of America to give a decided preference in their ports to the people of the U.S. over ourselves, the navigation of these extensive dominions will be lost to us, and will in a great measure be transferred to our rivals." [1]

Just as the U.S.A. employed agents in various Latin-American countries to intrigue against potential British expansion, so Britain used the same method against her chief rival in these regions. For example, in 1823, H. G. Ward was sent to Mexico to stimulate Mexican apprehensions with respect to North American ambitions.[2] Another prominent object of Anglo-American rivalry was the island of Cuba. As early as 1808 Jefferson's Cabinet had intimated to influential persons in Cuba and Mexico : " We should be extremely unwilling to see you pass under the dominion or ascendancy of France or England." On the other hand, Wynn wrote to the Duke of Buckingham towards the end of 1822 : " We have no wish ourselves to take Cuba, but are inclined to give her the fair option of either continuing Spanish, becoming independent, or uniting with Mexico, positively resisting, however, even if necessary with arms, her occupation by any third power, i.e. North America." [3] When, on April 16th, 1823, Canning was asked in the House of Commons whether or not England would occupy Cuba, he replied that " considering the emergencies arising out of the state of war [in Europe] it was impossible to give a direct answer on this point ". The U.S.A., too, still coveted the island, for when Canning on March 31st had asked Rush what he thought his Government would say to going hand-in-hand with England in an attempt to prevent France from expansion in Spanish America, this move was interpreted by Adams as a device to trap the U.S. into a renunciation of Cuba.

In a challenging study on *The United States and Europe 1815–23* (Berkeley 1936), E. H. Tatum, Jr., has shown that the proclamation of the Monroe Doctrine on December 2nd, 1823, was intended to warn off England rather than France or Russia. It is true that differences had arisen out of somewhat pretentious claims of the Russian American Fur Company which had had some

---

[1] Wellington, *Despatches*, New Series, II, p. 358.
[2] Cf. J. F. Rippy, *Latin America in World Politics*, New York, 1928, pp. 80, 84.
[3] *Memoirs of the Court of George IV*, Vol. I, p. 398. The letter was written between November 22nd and December 7th.

backing from the Tsar. But several months before the President announced his message to the world, the conflict was practically settled.[1] Above all, Adams was comforted by the idea that Russia neither had nor apparently aspired to have a powerful navy or a great merchant marine. The same consciousness of the paramount importance of naval matters emerges from Canning's above-mentioned memorandum to the Cabinet of November 30th, 1824 :

> The views and policy of the North Americans seem mainly directed towards supplanting us in navigation in every quarter of the globe, but more particularly in the seas contiguous to America. Let us recollect that as their commercial marine is augmented their military marine must proportionally increase. . . . Let us remember that peace, however desirable, and however cherished by us, cannot last for ever. Sooner or later we shall probably have to contend with the combined maritime power of France and of the U.S.[2]

This leads us on to the investigation of Anglo-French relations, with special regard to the Iberian Peninsula and Latin America. As to the latter, the French Government, supervised by the Quadruple Alliance, did not show any aspirations before 1819. It was only then and at the beginning of the following year that plans were made, and to some extent followed up, for the establishment of independent Bourbon monarchies in Spanish America. They had to be abandoned, owing to strong opposition from Great Britain as well as the U.S.A. By 1822 France seemed once more resigned as far as South America was concerned. With the approach of the war against Spain, the old designs were immediately revived ; so were the old apprehensions on the other side of the Channel. On February 10th, 1823, Sir Charles Stuart, British Ambassador in Paris, wrote to Canning that " French intervention in Spain might result, as was predicted at the secret session of the Chamber two days previously, in rendering France the protectress of Spain, with Cuba as a new Jamaica, and an enfranchised South America as her grateful client ".[3] Canning brought strong diplomatic pressure to bear upon Chateaubriand in order, if possible, to prevent the campaign altogether.[4] On

[1] Tatum, op. cit., pp. 138–9.

[2] Cf. also Wynn's letter to the Duke of Buckingham, of November 11th, 1824, in which the event of a rupture with North America was envisaged. (*Memoirs*, II, p. 150.)

[3] F.O. France, No. 42, quoted in *Cambridge History of the British Empire*, II. (W. F. Reddaway's article on Anglo-French Colonial Rivalry, 1815–48.)

[4] Cf. the reports of Vicomte de Marcellus, French chargé d'affaires in London, to Chateaubriand. (Printed in Georges Teissier, *Un duel diplomatique. Canning et Chateaubriand. Documents inédits*, Paris, 1934.)

the other hand, the campaign itself was never regarded as a *causa belli*. After all, it gave Canning the possibility, which he had outlined in a despatch to Bagot the Ambassador to Russia on January 3rd, of " holding a shield before them [the Spaniards] with one hand, and punishing them with the other ".[1] Just before the French started their invasion of Spain, the Foreign Secretary in unmistakable terms threatened France with war in case of French intervention in the New World.[2]

The official reason for the French intervention against Spain was the support of legitimate government. This principle, enunciated from the European point of view at the Congress of Laybach, sounded well in the ears of many people who connected it with stability and peace. To be able to attack the French attitude, Canning had to argue from the European standpoint by showing that France was acting selfishly,[3] and in addition he had to produce some equally high-sounding counter-principle. This he found in Castlereagh's so-called principle of " non-intervention " which he himself extended to the formula " non-intervention and peace ". But just as the French, as we have seen, had in reality quite different and more decisive reasons for going to war with Spain, it could be shown that neither Castlereagh nor Canning consistently adhered to the principle of non-intervention.[4] Talleyrand once again hit the nail on the head with his remark that " non-intervention " was much the same thing as intervention. Moreover, not only was non-intervention not a general principle of British foreign policy at the period with which we are concerned, but it was not even applied equally to the whole Iberian Peninsula. So far as Portugal was concerned, the principle did not work.

During the first dozen years after the Napoleonic Wars, Portugal, like Spain, was continuously either on the brink or in the midst of military revolts. In the course of a revolt which

---

[1] Josceline Bagot, *George Canning and his Friends*, II, London, 1909, p. 152. Cf. also Canning's Plymouth speech of October 23rd in which he stressed that the interest of British commerce lay not in Spain, but in the Spanish colonies.

[2] Cf. Canning's despatch to Sir Charles Stuart, March 31st, 1823. (*British and Foreign State Papers 1822–1823*, p. 69.)

[3] In his speech in the House of Commons on April 30th, 1823, Canning emphasized that the question respecting Spain had been described by Chateaubriand as " toute Française et toute Européenne ". (Hansard, New Series, VIII, p. 1496.)

[4] Cf. the following passage from George Canning's discourse on General Politics, delivered to Stratford Canning at the end of 1824 : " She [Great Britain] will be no party to a general interference in the concerns of other States ; though prepared to interfere on special concerns in her opinion justifying such interference." (F.O. 352/9. Strat. MSS., quoted by Harold Temperley, *The Foreign Policy of Canning*, London, 1925, p. 458.)

BUBBLES FOR 1825, OR FORTUNES MADE BY STEAM

Cartoon

From the Firth Collection in the Bodleian Library

[face p. 192

CANNING

[*face p* 193

broke out at Oporto and Lisbon in August 1820, British officers
were deprived of their posts in the army ; among them was the
powerful Lord Beresford, who two years previously had suppressed an attempted pronunciamento in a severe manner. In
1821, Castlereagh seems to have been prepared to intervene in
Portugal,[1] no doubt on behalf of Great Britain and not of Europe,
for his representations led the Continental Powers to disclaim the
application to Portugal of their legitimist principles of intervention. In this respect, too, Canning followed in Castlereagh's
footsteps. His opinion of the Portuguese revolutionaries was low.
Men whose counterparts on the other side of the Atlantic—
counterparts but for their different attitude to England—were
constantly referred to as " patriots ", were described by the
Foreign Secretary in a private letter to Bagot as follows :
" Revolutionists in Portugal . . . the scum of the earth and the
Portuguese earth—fierce, rascally, thieving, ignorant ragamuffins,
hating England, and labouring with all their might and cunning
to force or entrap us into war." [2] France, of course, was not
to be allowed to deal with the " ragamuffins ". In a later
despatch to Bagot, Canning said expressly : " French troops into
Portugal. That one point would be fatal to the repose of
Europe." [3] The reason was clearly formulated in his letter to
Lord Grenville of January 21st, 1825 : " Portugal has been and
always must be English, so long as Europe and the world remain
in anything like their present state." [4] One way of assuring this
was to send to Portugal, at the end of 1826, a force of 5,000
Hanoverian troops of intervention. Although there was some
talk of old treaty obligations, not even international lawyers have
gone as far as to claim that the intervention was undertaken to
fulfil article 3 of John of Gaunt's treaty of 1386 which bound
England to aid in suppressing revolts in Portugal. In the meantime Sir Charles Stuart had mediated between Portugal and
Brazil, which had been in revolt since 1821. The result was that
the colony acquired her independence on condition of assenting
to receive a Braganza ruler, and at the price of paying a debt
of £1,400,000, contracted by Portugal with Great Britain in 1823.
We left the story of Anglo-French differences over Spanish

---

[1] This statement must rest on the authority of C. R. Fay, who in his *Life and
Labour in the Nineteenth Century* (Cambridge, 1920, p. 8, n. 2) refers to unpublished
records. From the historian's point of view it is deplorable that the Londonderry
Archives are still inaccessible.
[2] The date is July 14th, 1823. (Bagot, op. cit., II, p. 183.)
[3] The date is May 5th, 1824. (Bagot, op. cit., II, pp. 240–1.)
[4] Stapleton, *George Canning and his Times*, p. 509.

America at the stage when France had just embarked on the Spanish War. Under strong diplomatic pressure from Great Britain and the U.S., the French Government did not dare wholeheartedly to pursue any schemes of intervention in these regions. Canning indeed used all his skill to deter Chateaubriand. For example, in his conversation with the French Ambassador, Polignac, on October 9th, 1823, to which he gave immediate and wide publicity, he purposely exaggerated the danger of French moves in the ominous direction.[1] Chateaubriand, however, still toyed with the idea of placing Bourbon princes in separate Spanish-American principalities.[2] Perhaps he was hoping to achieve this goal through the decision of a general European Congress for which the French Government clamoured in vain in October and November 1823.[3] In 1824–5, after the successful conclusion of her military display in the Peninsula, the Government and certain individuals in France grew somewhat bolder. French commercial agents were officially sent to Mexico and Colombia by the vice-admiral commanding the squadron in the West Indies.[4] At the same time French naval forces there and off Brazil were strengthened ; moreover, early in 1826 a large French naval force appeared in Cuba. Private enterprise, too, was feverishly interested in the Spanish colonies. Ouvrard worked out a detailed scheme for a so-called " Compagnie armée espagnole au Nouveau Monde ", on which privileges similar to those held by the British East India Company were to be conferred. Thirty thousand Spanish and Swiss mercenaries were to be employed for the job of reconquering the Spanish colonies. A joint-stock company, no doubt mainly with French capital, was to finance the expedition.[5] British reaction to all these moves was unequivocal. As to the last-mentioned, the Ambassador in Madrid, Sir William À Court, did all in his power to counteract it.[6] Also France was again informed in the summer of 1825 that no plea whatever would

---

[1] Cf. Webster, *Britain and the Independence of Latin America 1812–1830*, I, p. 70 ; and also Temperley, " French Designs on Spanish America in 1820–5 ", *English Historical Review*, XL, 1925, p. 50.

[2] Cf. Chateaubriand to La Ferronays, French Ambassador in St. Petersburg, November 1st, 1823. (E. Beau de Loménie, *La carrière politique de Chateaubriand de 1814 à 1830*, thèse, Paris, 1930, II, p. 90.)

[3] Cf. Wynn to the Duke of Buckingham, 29th October 1823, and 24th November 1823. (Op. cit., II, pp. 12, 15.)

[4] Christian Schefer, *La France moderne et le problème colonial (1815–30)*, Paris, 1907, p. 371.

[5] Wolff, *Die Geschäfte des Herrn Ouvrard*, pp. 228–9.

[6] Ibid., p. 232.

justify in the eyes of the British Government the introduction of any French force into the Spanish-American islands.[1] Obviously it was feared that trade might follow the flag.

The rift between Britain and the Continent with regard to the New World becomes even more obvious if the British attitude is compared with that of the Tsar. In Alexander's view, which he intimated through his envoy Poletitsa to Adams in November 1819, the Spanish-American colonies were to remain under Spanish control. To grant them complete independence seemed to him premature. On the other hand the Tsar proposed that some scope should be given to their national interests. It seems noteworthy in this connection that Jefferson, who could not be suspected of blind admiration for legitimate government, was of a similar opinion. This is what he wrote to his old friend Lafayette on May 14th, 1817 :

As their [the South Americans'] sincere friend and brother . . . I do believe the best thing for them, would be for themselves to come to an accord with Spain, under the guarantee of France, Russia, Holland, and the U.S., allowing to Spain a nominal supremacy, with authority only to keep the peace among them, leaving them otherwise all the powers of self-government, until their experience in them, their emancipation from their priests, and advancement in information shall prepare them for complete independence.[2]

The Russian envoy also explained to Adams that the great and paramount object of the Tsar's anxiety was the maintenance and preservation of the general peace, and to secure to the world a long period of the repose which it so much needed. The Tsar

would, therefore, see with peculiar concern the breaking-out of any war, which, from the existing state of Europe, the smothered flames of passions everywhere burning under the embers, and the multitude of reduced military men scattered abroad everywhere, and eager to burst open anew their avenue to wealth and honour, there was so much reason to fear could terminate no otherwise than by a general war.[3]

Alexander's anxiety as to the latter eventuality proved unjustified ; yet it is remarkable how clearly the post-war crux of the " reduced military men " was in his mind. Here a few concluding remarks

---

[1] F.O. France No. 148. (Quoted by Reddaway.)

[2] *The Letters of Lafayette and Jefferson*, ed. G. Chinard, Baltimore, 1929, p. 390.

[3] *Memoirs of John Quincy Adams*, IV, Philadelphia, 1875, p. 447. The Tsar's apprehension with regard to the Spanish-American revolts was shared by Friedrich von Schlegel who wrote to his brother August Wilhelm on August 21st, 1818 : " It may be possible to exorcise the American thunderstorm for a while, but it is inevitable that it will overtake us in the end." (*Friedrich von Schlegels Briefe an seinen Bruder August Wilhelm*, ed. O. Walzel, Berlin, 1890, p. 603.)

have to be made with regard to the social consequences of the successful Spanish-American revolts ; for in South America that fateful problem has remained unsolved to the present day. Jefferson proved far-sighted indeed, when he prophesied in the above-mentioned letter that " our southern brethren will fall under military despotism and become the murderous tools of their respective Bonapartes ". At the beginning of 1824, Chateaubriand, obviously despairing of ever realizing his own schemes, drew this gloomy comparison : " La France a mis trente années à revenir de la Convention à la légitimité, en passant par Robespierre, le Directoire, et Bonaparte : les colonies espagnoles iront-elles plus vite ? " [1] A few years later, at the end of the twenties, Bolívar, himself in mortal danger from his ambitious and unruly captains, described the aftermath of the successful revolt in these utterly disillusioned words : " There is no faith in [Latin] America, either between men or nations. Treaties are paper, constitutions books, elections combats, liberty anarchy, and life a torment." All the republics which he had helped to liberate had by then sunk into indescribable chaos with the constantly recurring military *coup d'état* as its only regular feature.

The Tsar's proposal that Europe and the U.S.A. should mediate between Spain and her colonies was rejected by the U.S.A. It was likewise rejected by Great Britain. The first clash between the Tsar's and the British conception occurred at Aix-la-Chapelle. The official Austrian policy coincided on this point with that of the Tsar, and this explains why Gentz, in a later despatch to Metternich, described the end of 1818 as the turning-point. " During the first epoch [1813–18] ", he wrote, " England was with us . . . during the second [1819–23] England was either not with us or else more or less against us." [2] In the same year, 1823, Wellington remarked to Princess Lieven that every day England's separation from the great Alliance was becoming more noticeable. The Princess, reporting this to Metternich, added that the Duke deplored this " misfortune for England ". Besides, there were other influences at work in England against Canning's policy ; among them George IV and Lord Hertford. [3] The latter went so far as to raise Metternich's unrealistic hopes that " with the support of all the high aristocrats

---

[1] *Some Official Correspondence of George Canning*, I, p. 143.
[2] The date is October 4th, 1823. (*Briefe von und an Friedrich von Gentz*, ed. Wittichen, II, pp. 73–4.)
[3] Cf. Lord Broughton, *Recollections of a Long Life*, III, p. 53.

and country gentlemen who were feeling threatened in their property ", it might be possible to force Canning to resign.[1]

In the meantime, Canning had argued on November 30th, 1824, in his above-mentioned memorandum to the Cabinet, as follows : " Have Austria, Russia and Prussia any interest which should induce them to consider the question even impartially ? Have they ever had a ship in the seas contiguous to Spanish America, or are they likely to have one ? They have positively no national interest, not the slightest, in the matter." [2] This statement was significant for two reasons. In the first place it fallaciously implied that to be impartial one must be materially interested. This, however, may have been only a display of Canning's elegant wit. The second part was meant all the more seriously. It postulated that the Continental Powers should have no say in matters concerning regions to which Britain, owing to her naval superiority, had almost exclusive access. It was in the same vein that he stated on another occasion : " We ought never to forget that the field of our native glory is that sea, which disjoins other countries from each other, but which unites them to England."

This leads us on to the second half of our concluding chapter, in which after a short summary of Britain's and Russia's acquisitions during the Napoleonic Wars, an investigation will be made into the causes and symptoms of the rift between these two World Powers as it showed itself in the Old World. Here too the story finishes towards the end of 1825, for by that date it had become obvious that the Concert of Europe, not to mention the Holy Alliance, was a thing of the past.

With regard to the colonial conquests which Britain had made during the Napoleonic Wars, Canning's predecessor had already adopted the same high-handed attitude. The Continental Powers, as C. K. Webster has recently emphasized,[3] had no say in the distribution of the colonies captured from France and Holland. Great Britain herself decided the issue—by no means a minor one—in bilateral treaties with France and the Netherlands.[4] Apart from the acquisitions in America, almost all the

---

[1] Draft to Metternich's letter of August 23rd, 1826, probably to Gentz. (*Aus Metternichs nachgelassenen Papieren*, IV, p. 311.)

[2] Wellington, *Despatches*, New Series, II, p. 357.

[3] " Peace-Making : Vienna, Paris, and To-day." (*Agenda, a Quarterly Journal of Reconstruction*, II, May 1943, p. 100.)

[4] During the wars British politicians had used the conquered colonies as an important lever. Canning, for example, declared on repeated occasions in 1807

rest could be regarded as so many safeguards of the two routes to India. Malta was a typical case. Brougham, in 1817, contemptuously referred to it as a " barren rock ", but had to admit its " high military importance ".[1]   So great an expert as Nelson had considered Malta a most important outwork to India. Similarly, the Ionian Islands were useful for watching the overland route to India. The longer route overseas, too, was strongly fortified by the acquisition of Gambia, Ascension, the Cape of Good Hope, Mauritius, Seychelles, and Ceylon. Castlereagh was well justified in saying that Britain had acquired " what in former days would have been thought romance—the keys of every great military position ".[2]

In the same speech Castlereagh explained : " Our policy has been to secure the Empire against future attack." This tremendous task, though greatly facilitated by the new acquisitions, was of course far from being accomplished. Above all, British possessions in India had to be consolidated. To achieve this, it seemed necessary to Lord Hastings, the Governor-General of Bengal and commander-in-chief of the forces in India, to annihilate all great military states in Central India.[3] As has happened in other cases, a large empire proved the best of all reasons for a larger one. Sir John Malcolm, in *A Memoir of Central India* (1823) characterized the campaign of 1817–21 as " order contending anarchy ".[4] But, as Edward Thompson has pointed out, it was the conquests of the East India Company that had first broken up the polity of Central India.[5] Now there did not seem to be a way back ; the conquest had to be pushed further and further. This seemed an inescapable necessity. Malcolm, who was himself one of the protagonists, put it thus : " We have been compelled, by events far beyond our power to control, to assume the duties of Lord Paramount of that great Continent." [6] He also wrote : " Victory must, on any terms, be obtained, for we cannot long exist if our strength be even doubted." [7]   Marvell's warning to Cromwell was thus again proved sound :

his willingness to use the colonial conquests for the amelioration of Europe. (Cf. H. Butterfield, *The Peace Tactics of Napoleon, 1806–1808*, Cambridge, 1929, pp. 159, 210–11.)

[1] Hansard, XXXV, 1817, p. 118.
[2] Hansard, XXXII (1816), p. 1104.
[3] *Dictionary of National Biography* : article " Francis Rawdon Hastings ", by G. F. Russell Barker.
[4] Vol. II, p. 233.
[5] *The Making of the Indian Princes*, Oxford Univ. Press, 1943, p. 222.
[6] Op. cit., II, p. 264.   [7] P. 267.

The same Arts that did gain
A Pow'r must it maintain.

For, as another of our witnesses, Metcalfe, wrote in 1814 : " That insuperable separation which exists between us and our subjects renders it necessary to keep them in subjection by the presence of a military force, and impossible to repose confidence in their affection or fidelity for assistance in the defence of our territories." [1] Nor could the enormous duties on the import of Indian manufactures into England be expected to increase the Company's popularity, for millions of Indian weavers and artisans were affected by these measures. [2]

Since expansion for consolidation's sake seemed thus inevitable, it could not be difficult to find suitable occasions such as frontier incidents which arose indeed from time to time [3] through the activities of pugnacious Gurkhas or Pindaris. The campaigns were hard-fought but uneven contests. In the memorandum already mentioned, Metcalfe urged : " We have on our side the science of Europe, and we ought to bring it into play.". This was done, no doubt, to a considerable extent. [4] The conquerors' success was further facilitated by the prevailing feudalism ; for, to obtain the armed support of the people, it often sufficed to win over their Jagirdars or feudal lords, to whom they yielded unswerving allegiance. [5] By the end of the campaign, British rule embraced about two-thirds of the Indian peninsula. [6] The lines from Bombay to Calcutta and Madras respectively were in British hands. Indeed, India was completely changed since the time when Arthur Wellesley had won his first laurels there. [7]

Soon afterwards, in 1824, the Burma campaigns were to begin. Here the reason could hardly be the consolidation of possessions

[1] J. W. Kaye, *Selections from the Papers of Lord Metcalfe*, London, 1855, p. 144. Cf. also the following passage from Lieut. Col. de Lacy Evans's pamphlet, *On the Designs of Russia*, London, 1828, p. 23 : " A maxim which can never, of course, be lost sight of with impunity, namely that the defence of dependencies, held by the sword rather than by the affections of the inhabitants, can only be advantageously made, in advance of their frontiers."

[2] Romesh Dutt, *The Economic History of India under Early British Rule (1757–1837)*, 2nd ed., London, 1906, pp. 294 (with tables), 300.

[3] Sometimes it was the other way round. In February 1814, the Governor-General wrote of " the wanton provocations which we have been giving on trivial subjects to all the States around us ". (Quoted by E. Thompson, op. cit., p. 211.)

[4] Cf. Byron's satirical comment (*Don Juan*, canto I, stanza CXXXII) :
  This is the patent age of new inventions
  For killing bodies and for saving souls,
  All propagated with the best intentions.

[5] Mohan Sinha Mehta, *Lord Hastings and the Indian States*, Bombay, 1930, p. 254.

[6] Hon. J. W. Fortescue, *A History of the British Army*, XI, London, 1923, p. 250.

[7] Cf. Elphinstone to Wellington, Bombay, August 3rd, 1820. (Wellington, *Despatches*, New Series, I, p. 142.)

previously acquired. Nor was there much prospect of prize-money, which in those days was the great attraction of warring in India.[1] In vain did Archibald Campbell make a desperate search for treasures in the great pagoda of Rangoon.[2]

Consolidation however, was not confined to the British possessions in India. In Ceylon three campaigns were needed for this purpose ; the last, in 1817–18, occupied sixteen months. The Cape of Good Hope had been taken over by Britain from Dutch slave-owners ; but the heritage included continuous difficulties with the Kaffirs who had been dispossessed of much territory. Several times in 1818–19 they had to be repelled. Similarly, in 1824–6, the Ashantis in West Africa had to be dealt with.

All these various campaigns furnished outlets for British soldiers who could not find their way back into civilian life after Waterloo. To some extent this applied also to officers. Generals had to be given appointments, and the colonies offered convenient berths.[3] Some of the colonies were useful also for emigration purposes. It was only for the first few years after 1815 that emigration was officially discouraged. Things improved from about 1819, and especially after 1822, when Robert Wilmot Horton became Parliamentary Under-Secretary of State for the Colonies.[4] He welcomed emigration as a remedy for unemployment.

In turning now to the expansion of the Russian Empire during the Napoleonic Wars, it is convenient to deal separately with each of the two Russian drives towards the Indian Ocean and the Levant respectively, though both of course had been made possible by the Russian command of Caucasian territories. Another feature common to both drives, as also to the British successes in India, was their superiority in the art of war as a result of " the science of Europe ". Asiatic city walls did not offer sufficient protection against Russian siege guns ; nor Asiatic cavalry against their movable artillery.

Russia was first brought into direct contact with Persia in the reign of Tsar Paul I, who annexed Georgia in 1800. During the early years of Alexander's rule it seemed possible that that

---

[1] Fortescue, op. cit., p. 350. During the short Bhurtpore campaign in Central India (December 1824–January 1825), the army divided prize-money to the sum of £480,000, of which £60,000 fell to the share of Field-Marshal Viscount Combermere.

[2] Ibid., p. 368.

[3] Paul Knaplund, art. " Colonial Problems and Colonial Policy, 1815–37 ", *Cambridge History of the British Empire*, II, p. 304.

[4] In 1820, some 3,000 persons were sent to the Cape. The average annual emigration from the U.K. for the years 1820–4 was just over 12,000, the greater part of whom, it is true, went to North America.

acquisition might be abandoned. The Tsar's unofficial committee was unanimous in favour of such a policy. As for the
Tsar himself, the Imperial Council was told that he did not wish
to receive Georgia under Russian sovereignty, since he was of the
opinion that it was not right to annex a foreign country.[1] But
by the end of 1803 Alexander had changed his mind. As in the
case of the British Empire, the new policy necessitated armed
measures of consolidation. In January 1804, the Russian General
Tsitsiainov took Gandsha, which was christened Elizavetpol
after the Tsar's wife. The Shah now grew apprehensive, and
demanded that the Russian troops should be withdrawn from
Grusinia to the other side of the Caucasus. Tsitsiainov's reply
was the invasion of Persian territory in June 1804. The ensuing
campaign was to last nine years. Few people in Russia, even
among the higher classes, realized what was going on in Transcaucasia. The distance of the provinces which were being fought
for made it difficult to grasp, let alone keep in mind, their great
significance. Finally, by the treaty of Gulistan, in 1813, Persia
ceded to Russia Derbent, Baku, Shirwan, Shaki, Karabagh, and
part of Talish, and abandoned all pretensions to Georgia, Dag-
hestan, Mingrelia, Imeritia, and Abkhasia. On both sides the
treaty was regarded as a kind of armistice ; [2] this was understandable from the point of view of the humiliated party as well as from
that whose pride had been given such ample nourishment.
Unfaithful to his general principle that separate alliances were
harmful to the cause of Peace,[3] the Tsar, in 1817, sent General
Yermolov, Governor and Commander-in-Chief of the Caucasus,
to Teheran to propose an alliance against Turkey.[4] The offer
was refused, but it seems likely that the Persian invasion of the
Turkish dominions in 1821 was at least partly due to the influence
of Mazarovich, the Russian agent at Teheran.

On this south-eastern drive of Russia into Asia, Russian trade
naturally followed the flag. The comment to the Commercial
Statute of May 30th, 1817 emphasized that, since Russia's industry
was less highly developed than that of her Western neighbours,
she could export her industrial products only in an eastern
direction.[5] Two customs districts for Asia were created, there-

[1] Theodor von Bernhardi, *Geschichte Russlands*, III, p. 217.
[2] Sir Henry Rawlinson, *England and Russia in the East*, London, 1875, p. 35.
[3] Cf. the first Memorandum on the approaching Conferences at Aix-la-Chapelle
(Public Record Office).
[4] Sir Percy Sykes, *A History of Persia*, 3rd ed., London, 1930, II, p. 315.
[5] Valentin Wittschewsky, *Russlands Handels-, Zoll- und Industriepolitik*, Berlin,
1905, p. 57.

fore, at Orenburg and Astrakhan. Asiatic raw material was exempt from customs duties. By the ukase of October 8th, 1821, Transcaucasia was granted various privileges with regard to customs and taxes. The intention was that Transcaucasia should become a big transit centre for the trade from the Levant and Odessa to Persia and Central Asia. This idea went back as far as 1804. In 1811, at any rate, in a memorandum of the Trade Department, it was expressly stated that by transit trade through Russia India could most cheaply and speedily be supplied with foreign commodities.[1]

Anglo-Russian friction over India manifested itself in various ways. According to the *India Gazette* of May 13th, 1822, Russian officers in disguise were working on the northern frontiers of the British Indian territories in considerable number.[2] Lieut.-Col. de Lacy Evans, in his pamphlet of 1828 already mentioned, expressed a feeling widespread among British politicians when he wondered " whether Russia, if suffered to proceed in her career, and to arrange without obstruction her materials of operation, may not shortly acquire a degree of intercourse with India . . . whereby India must become untenable or unworthy of further retention ".[3] At about the same time, there appeared in *Blackwood's Edinburgh Magazine* this outspoken statement :

Much has been said, and a good deal written, on the possibility of our being called upon to defend our Indian possessions against the invasion of a European power, and there is still much question of the practicability of such an expedition. . . . It is almost unnecessary to say that Russia is the only European nation at all likely to undertake this enterprise.[4]

No doubt such apprehensions were strengthened by the fact that British rule in North-Western India had not yet reached the natural mountain barrier of the Karakorum.

However, the huge plateau of Iran still lay between the territories conquered by Britain and Russia respectively. It first occurred to Lord Minto, Governor-General of the East India Company, to establish a solid block of linked kingdoms between British India and Europe.[5] At that time—it was after Tilsit— Europe, of course, meant France as well as Russia. This *cordon sanitaire* was to consist of the Punjab, Afghanistan, and Persia.

---

[1] Wittschewsky, op. cit., p. 36.
[2] Cf. also the " Bengal Hurkara " of September 12th, 1822. (*Asiatic Journal*, XV, pp. 105, 403–4.)
[3] Pp. 18–19.   [4] Vol. XXII, September 1827.
[5] E. Thompson, op. cit., pp. 160–1.

The main concern was the protection of the route to India. For this purpose, Britain concluded a preliminary treaty with Persia in 1809, according to which Persia was to prevent any European force from passing through her territories towards India. In return, Britain pledged herself to protect Persia against foreign invasion, to supply her with arms and military forces for defensive purposes, and to subsidize her financially. Indeed some native horse artillery was sent from Madras to the Araxes to help the Persians against Russia.[1] This was not sufficient, for if Persia was to survive against one, or, as it might be, two European Powers, she too would need to be taught the " science of Europe ". French military instructors—for France had played the same game from another angle—were now superseded by British officers and gunners, who also took an active part in Persia's war with Russia. Not even Napoleon's invasion of Russia altered the situation essentially. The British officers and gunners were officially recalled, but they were probably encouraged unofficially to carry on.[2] It was obvious that, although Britain and Russia were for the time being allies in Europe, they were still rivals in Asia. After 1814 the subsidies came to an end, but the 6th article of the definitive Treaty of Teheran (November 25th, 1814) meant that Great Britain claimed a right to consider any spontaneous act of Russian aggression on Persia as a demonstration against India.[3]

On the Russian side this attitude found a highly critical response. Capodistria, anticipating the idea of spheres of influence, pointed out to Gagern in 1815 that the other nations did not interfere in what was going on in India.[4] The conclusion to be drawn was that Russia should be given a free hand in Persia. Similarly Nesselrode, in a letter to Lieven, the Ambassador in London, emphasized that there existed " dans notre politique asiatique le principe de ne jamais admettre dans de pareilles discussions l'intervention et même les bons offices d'une Cour étrangère et de les considérer plutôt comme des affaires domestiques ". In the same despatch, Nesselrode tried to justify this principle in typically imperialist fashion :

[1] Bernhardi, op. cit., p. 233.
[2] Ibid., p. 241 ; and more recently H. L. Hoskins, *British Routes to India*, New York, 1928, p. 78.
[3] The article provided that although Britain might be at peace with Russia, if Persia were attacked by Russia, and British good offices failed, the subsidies to support the Persian army were to continue, or alternatively a force from British India was to be sent.
[4] Gagern, *Mein Antheil an der Politik*, V, 1. Teil, Leipzig, 1845, p. 349.

Les relations de la Russie avec les États et les peuples de l'Asie placés sur nos frontières dans cette partie du monde sont d'une nature si distincte que l'on s'exposerait aux plus grands inconvénients en y appliquant les principes sur lesquels sont basés les rapports politiques de l'Europe.   Ici tout se fonde sur la réciprocité et la bonne foi ; chez les peuples de l'Asie, au contraire, la crainte offre le seul garant et la sainteté des traités est inconnue parmi eux.   Il est facile à prévoir combien un pareil mobile s'affaiblirait si dans leur esprit l'idée s'établissait qu'ils peuvent obtenir par l'influence d'une troisième Puissance, ce que leur refuse celle avec laquelle ils sont en contestation.[1]

No Power, Nesselrode thought, was in a better position to appreciate this reason than " l'Angleterre, dont les rapports avec les peuples de l'Inde offrent tant de rapprochement et d'analogie avec nos relations asiatiques ".

The Tsar himself fully subscribed to this view.   In a postscript to Nesselrode's despatch, Alexander described any such inter-ference on the part of England or any other Power as " illégitime et inadmissible ".   In later despatches to Lieven, he declared Russia's relations with Turkey and the other Asiatic states to be " interêts exclusifs de la Russie ".[2]   If the Tsar was more internationally minded than ever inside Europe, the same could no longer be said of his attitude to Asia.   The time when he had felt conscience-stricken over the annexation of Georgia was long past.

As for the second Russian expansionist drive, namely that towards the Levant, something has already been said about it in the present study in connection with the background of the Greek revolt.   A few facts remain to be added.   Only then it will be possible fully to appreciate the intricate character of the Greek Question.

Already during the reign of Catherine II, Russia had annexed the territory of the Crim Tatars on the northern shore of the Black Sea.   By the Treaty of Kutchuk Kainardji (1774), confirmed in 1779 and 1793, Russia was granted the right of sending her commercial vessels through the Bosphorus and the Dardanelles. A great step forward was made in 1799 when the Straits were opened to Russian warships.   Russia was thus enabled, among other things, to exercise, together with Turkey, a protectorate

---

[1] The despatch was dated April 14th (26th) 1816.   (F. de Martens, *Recueil des Traités et Conventions conclus par la Russie avec les Puissances Étrangères*, XI, St. Petersburg, 1895, p. 265.)
[2] The despatches were dated 11th (23rd) February 1817, and 2nd (14th) February 1818.   " Les autres états asiatiques " meant Russia's neighbours.

over the Ionian Islands.   After Tilsit, as we have seen, Alexander
coveted Constantinople ; but in addition he desired to gain complete control over the Dardanelles.   This Napoleon refused to
sanction.   Moreover, when Russia, threatened by Napoleon's
invasion, had to come to terms with Turkey, the Porte cancelled
the right of Russian warships to pass through the Dardanelles.

This stiffening of Turkish resistance was not only due, however, to Napoleon's deadly designs against her most dangerous
enemy.   To some extent it was due also to Great Britain.   Ever
since 1799 grave apprehension had been felt in this country over
Russia's privilege ; the overland route to India through Meso-
potamia seemed to be menaced.[1]   The resulting jealousy was,
according to Sir James Headlam-Morley, one of the principal
causes of the sudden change of policy by which Paul I came to
join Napoleon.[2]   Anglo-Russian friction in the Levant reached
a peak in 1804–5, during the Anglo-Russian negotiations concerning the formation of the Third Coalition.   The main point at
issue was Malta, for Russia demanded that island, or at any rate
the right to install a garrison there.   A few years later, after
Admiral Duckworth's voyage through the Dardanelles (1807)
had revealed the weakness of the Porte, Britain hastened to
conclude a Treaty with Turkey in 1809.   Clause XI of this
treaty ran :

As ships of war have at all times been prohibited from entering
the Canal of Constantinople, namely in the Straits of the Dardanelles
and the Black Sea ; and as this ancient regulation of the Ottoman
Empire is in future to be observed towards any Power in time of peace,
the Court of Great Britain promises on its part to conform to this
principle.

Great Britain had thus achieved her aim : the closing of the
Straits against Russian men-of-war.[3]

All the more important was the right of passage still granted
to Russian commercial vessels.   As trade relations between
Western Europe and the Baltic were greatly hampered by the
Continental blockade, the Black Sea ports gained in relative

[1] Colonel de Lacy Evans was still haunted by the same fear.   Among other things
he wished to ascertain " whether if the Russians establish themselves on the Hellespont,
it may not imminently endanger, if not lead on to the loss of, British India, British
maritime ascendancy—and even, not impossibly, British connection with Ireland ".
(On the Designs of Russia, p. 12.)
[2] Studies in Diplomatic History, London, 1930, pp. 220–1.
[3] Headlam-Morley, op. cit., p. 225.   In this connection it is well to remember
that the Russian fleet which took part in the Battle of Navarino, still had to make the
long voyage from the Baltic.

importance.[1]   Odessa became an important centre for the export of Russian wheat to European markets.   Between 1815 and 1824, an annual average of about 700,000 chetverts of wheat (100 chetverts = 72 British imperial quarters) were exported from Odessa, out of a total average of about 2,100,000 chetverts.[2] In May 1821 Turkey, desirous to diminish the Greek profits from this commerce, issued an order for the pre-emption of foreign produce found within the Straits.[3]   The effect of this order was that the market prices fixed by Turkey depressed the wheat prices at Odessa.   A year later, the Porte placed new restrictions on Russian commerce in the Straits, so that the very continuance of the grain trade in this direction seemed uncertain. One of the main claims of Russia was, therefore, the cancellation of these tiresome restrictions.

The Levantine trade of Great Britain, too, was increasing during and after the Napoleonic Wars.   Obviously her hold on the " strategic rock of Malta " and the Ionian Islands—as well as her temporary hold on Sicily—facilitated economic penetration.   In contradistinction to the Spanish-American revolt, the sympathies of the British merchants trading in these regions under the direction of the Levant Company were decidedly on the side of the decaying Empire.[4]   For, unlike Spain, the Porte as we have seen, had for some time, put few obstacles in the way of British trade.   On the other hand, there was from the merchants' point of view an obvious analogy between the two revolts, namely that their commerce was endangered by the piracy carried on by the armed privateers of the revolting party.

Whereas British commercial interest inclined towards the *status quo* in the Levant, British financial interest pointed rather to the cause of the insurgents ; for Turkey did not want any loans. Soon Greek loans found in England subscribers as eager and as credulous as did the previously mentioned loans which were supposed to serve South America.   In many cases speculation accounted for people's Philhellenism, as Thomas Moore not unfairly described it with his Irish wit :

> And still, as the premium higher went,
> His ecstasy rose—so much per cent,

[1] Vernon J. Puryear, " Odessa : Its Rise and International Importance, 1815–50 ", *Pacific Historical Review*, June 1934, p. 196.
[2] Ibid., pp. 196–7.
[3] Puryear, *France and the Levant from the Bourbon Restoration to the Peace of Kutiah*, Berkeley, 1941, p. 17.
[4] Crawley, *The Question of Greek Independence*, p. 29.

(As we see in a glass, that tells the weather,
The heat and the silver rise together)
And Liberty sung from the patriot's lip,
While a voice from his pocket whisper'd " Scrip ".[1]

As to the procedure of these loans, we possess a revealing series of articles under the title " The Greek Pie ", written by Cobbett with painstaking accuracy as well as his usual vigour. Particularly devastating is Cobbett's indictment of Joseph Hume, who with regard to one of these loans was at the same time " one of the lenders of the money, one of the owners of the bonds, and also one of the Commissioners for guarding the interest of the bond-holders ".[2] Small wonder that Hume did not live up to the superhuman task of serving all these interests impartially. In fact, he speculated for high stakes ; but when he lost he forced the Greek deputies in London to take back his fallen bonds for account of the Greek Government at par ; [3] even the interest of the loss had to be replaced.[4] According to the *Annual Register* of 1826 similar tactics were used by John Bowring.[5] Commissioners like these were naturally enough not very keen that large sums should be sent to Greece, and in fact little of the money subscribed ever arrived there. Far greater were the services rendered to the cause of Greek independence by such adventurers as Lord Cochrane and Sir Richard Church, whom we meet again in this theatre of war, and, on a higher plane, by Lord Byron who, weary of life, sought a death worthy of the Romantic fervour which he had enkindled all over Europe.

The attitude of the British Government towards the Greek revolt was not so straightforward as in the case of South America. Castlereagh, trying to hold the Tsar back, wrote to him about the Greeks on July 16th, 1821, that they formed " a branch of that organized spirit of insurrection ". Canning, on the other hand, recognized the Greeks as belligerents in March 1823. It is generally accepted that this was done for purely economic reasons [6] to protect British commerce which, as we have seen, suffered from the corsairs. Indeed, some British merchants now switched over to supplying the Greeks with arms and munitions,[7]

---

[1] From the poem " The Ghost of Miltiades ".
[2] *Cobbett's Weekly Register*, Vol. 60, 1826, p. 394.
[3] Ibid., pp. 398–9.   [4] Ibid., p. 443.
[5] P. 376.
[6] For example, *Cambridge History of British Foreign Policy*, II, p. 87 ; and R. W. Seton-Watson, *Britain in Europe, 1789–1914*, Cambridge, 1937, p. 99.
[7] The British Government did not interpose objections to this export. (Cf. Planta to G. D. Clark, 20th February, 1823, F.O. 78 T 119, quoted by Puryear, *France and the Levant*, p. 38.)

whereas the Levant Company was still more active in selling war supplies to Turkey.[1] In 1825 this Company was dissolved, and its diplomatic functions taken over by the Government. This measure has been interpreted as an indication that, from the Government's point of view, wider political considerations outweighed narrower economic ones.[2] It seems to the present writer that that might perhaps apply even to Canning's earlier recognition of the Greeks as belligerents ; for, if nothing else had to be done than to protect British Levantine trade, it would have been safer to side with the Turks.

In April 1823, the Abbé de Pradt wrote : " À defaut de la Turquie l'Europe à besoin de la Grèce pour barrer la route à la Russie." [3] We only have to read " England " for " Europe ", to arrive at Canning's fundamental conception of the Greek question. It was, however, extremely difficult to achieve this goal. On January 16th, 1824, with regard to the plan to create in Greece a strong and popular government which might be an effectual barrier against Russia, Canning said to Bowring : " Yes, that would be a proper argument for English policy, but what language could we hold to Russia to obtain her consent, knowing as we do that she can conquer Turkey and Greece when she pleases ? " [4] In the autumn of 1825, if not before, Canning thought that he had found the solution. In order to control Russian aggression, he offered to join her as an ally.[5] The intention of the Foreign Secretary, according to the later testimony of the King of the Belgians (who also referred to Lord Melbourne) was this : " He said we must remain with Russia, and by this means prevent mischief." [6]

In conclusion we shall have to examine how great was the danger of " Russian mischief ", and also whether Canning's ingenious move really helped matters. But before doing so, we must first cast a glance at the policy of the other two protagonists, France and Austria,[7] to set the whole stage for the dénouement.

To France, especially to Marseilles and other places in the south, the Levantine trade had previously been of great importance. By 1816, however, there remained only 23 French

---

[1] Puryear, op. cit., p. 38.   [2] Ibid., p. 37.
[3] Cf. also his Vrai systéme de l'Europe relativement à l'Amerique et à la Grèce, Paris, 1825, p. 283.
[4] Sir John Bowring, Autobiographical Recollections, London, 1877, p. 284.
[5] Crawley, op. cit., p. 48.
[6] Letter to Queen Victoria, 22nd September 1840. (A. C. Benson and Viscount Esher, The Letters of Queen Victoria, I, London, 1907, p. 289.)
[7] Prussia played a very inferior rôle. So did the U.S.

commercial houses in the Levant and Barbary out of about 80 at the turn of the century.[1] Some recovery was made before 1821, so that in that year the relative total trade value of Levant commerce from France was about three-fifths of its average for the immediate pre-revolutionary era.[2] Fully to regain the old position seemed impossible owing to the outbreak of the revolt. Soon, however, commercial and financial circles in France turned their attention to Egypt. In February 1825 the Government asked for information on the Egyptian methods of cotton culture and the possibility of extending its type to the French colony of Senegal. In July of the same year, Drovetti, French consul at Alexandria, learned officially that a new French company was forming for the exploitation of Egypt ; and that the Government had approved of this enterprise.[3] French economic penetration of Egypt was, no doubt, facilitated by the fact that Great Britain was at that time not much interested in that country ; this was to be the case until after 1835, when the overland route to India was established and the mails were sent by it. Nevertheless, French agents in Egypt knew how to create, or to exploit, Egyptian apprehensions of potential British designs.[4] Control of Egypt would have meant for France an easy access to the East ; also she would have been able to maintain her traditional interests in Syria.[5] But Egypt's main attraction for France lay in the hope that with her help it might be possible to recover " l'équilibre maritime " in the Mediterranean, an aim which had been earlier stressed by Richelieu in 1816.[6] This idea was now revived, for the new King Charles X took a great interest in sea-power. In 1824, Drovetti held out the prospect that the Egyptian navy might be used by France in future to balance more nearly her naval inferiority to Great Britain in the Near East.[7] Consequently, Mehemet Ali's request for the purchase of war vessels, which had been declined by Great Britain, was favourably received by the French Government. Owing to Philhellene pressure in oppositional papers such as the *Constitutionnel* and *Courier Français*, the Government had to act with some secrecy.[8] For the same reason little publicity was being given to the French

[1] Puryear, op. cit., pp. 2–3.
[2] Ibid., p. 9.   [3] Ibid., pp. 46–7.
[4] Cf. General Belliard's letter to General Boyer, of March 1st, 1825. (Georges Douin, *La mission militaire française auprès de Mohamed Aly*, Cairo, 1923, p. 32.)
[5] Hoskins, op. cit., p. 130.
[6] Instructions au Marquis d'Osmond. (Christian Schefer, op. cit., p. 144.)
[7] Puryear, op. cit., p. 42.
[8] Cf. Douin, *Les premières frégates de Mohamed Aly*, Cairo, 1926, p. 28.

military mission to Mehemet Ali which had arrived in Alexandria on November 24th, 1824. It had been recruited by the Napoleonic general Belliard, and was headed by Boyer, another Napoleonic general ; second in command was Marshal Livron, previously a merchant in Egypt. When, in the following year, Ibrahim Pasha, called by the Sultan, landed in Greece in order to smash the revolt, numerous French officers and men were under his command. On the other hand, a few adventurers like Fabvier offered their services to the Greek cause.

Austria, whose ships, since 1784, had been allowed to sail through the Dardanelles up to Constantinople, also held a strong trade position in the Levant. According to statistics for the year 1824, Austria sent 530 vessels to Constantinople, as compared with 438 Russian and 358 British vessels.[1] As to the Greek revolt, Metternich was hostile to it from the beginning and remained so throughout, even if at times for outward purposes his policy seemed to favour the insurgent cause.[2] Whereas Kaunitz had still regarded the Porte as a dangerous foe of the Austrian monarchy, views had changed round about the turn of the century when the new Russian bugbear made Turkey seem harmless in comparison. Thereafter, it became a dogma of Austrian diplomacy that the Porte should not be weakened.[3] In 1822, Ottenfels, Austrian Internuncio at Constantinople, thus described Metternich's Oriental policy : " Turkey is to be conserved, for on the one hand the dissolution of this Empire would result in incalculable complications ; and, on the other, its division among the European Powers would give Austria hardly enough to compensate her for the shares taken by other States." Obviously, Metternich was thinking mainly of Russia. As to Philhellenism, Gentz declared that it was based quite as much on people's gross ignorance as on their deep-rooted love of revolutions.[4] Metternich shrewdly noticed how strange it was that Liberalism, of all movements, should have become the spokesman of Christendom in its struggle against Islam.[5] His personal attitude to the whole problem was revealed in his letter to Gentz from Ischl on July 13th, 1825 : " I can assure you," he wrote,

---

[1] Puryear, op. cit., p. 30.
[2] For such a " ballon d'essai ", thought out by Gentz, cf. his despatch to Ottenfels of July 17th, 1825. (Josef Krauter, *Franz Freiherr von Ottenfels. Beiträge zur Politik Metternichs im griechischen Freiheitskampfe, 1822–1832*, Salzburg, 1914, p. 148.)
[3] Richard Charmatz, *Geschichte der auswärtigen Politik Österreichs im 19. Jahrhundert*, Leipzig, 1918, Vol. I, p. 104.
[4] Gentz to Ottenfels, December 17th, 1824. (Krauter, op. cit., p. 137.)
[5] Srbik, *Metternich*, Vol. I, p. 625.

" that the affair does not concern me any more than if I had to write an intricate melodrama. Thus it will not exercise an unfavourable influence upon my watering cure." [1]

This cynical detachment leads us, by way of antithesis, back to the Tsar. We have seen that Alexander, by armed intervention, could have decided the issue of the Greek revolt. It was clear that here more than anywhere else Russia was in a position to strike. This would have been in line with the policy of Catherine II, and also with that of Alexander's earlier rule, especially in the year 1808. Alexander refrained from it for various reasons. Unlike the Liberals, he was under no illusion as to how Christian the Greeks really were.[2] In his opinion they were as yet too barbarian to deserve full independence.[3]

Alexander's main objection to armed intervention he expressed in conversation with La Ferronays, the French Ambassador, in February 1825, in these words : " Ce n'est point par la guerre . . . que je veux mettre un terme à la guerre." [4] Rightly or wrongly, he anticipated that the first armed move on the part of Russia would be the signal for a general European war. Russia had many traditional grievances, economic and political, against Turkey, and the intransigent attitude of the Porte seemed to call for measures of coercion. But the ideal of European unity was still so strong in Alexander's mind that he refused to make war on Turkey, except by general consent of the Powers.[5] " Tout avec mes Alliés et rien sans eux ", he told La Ferronays. With this conception he grew more and more isolated in Russia.[6] This fact was testified to by a no less critical observer than Metternich,[7] who based his judgment on Lebzeltern's reports.[8] Similarly, Gentz informed the Hospodar Ghika on December 6th, 1822, that Alexander had no desire of aggrandisement.[9] In the following year, after the Emperor Francis had met Alexander at Czernowitz, Gentz wrote to Ottenfels : " The Emperor Alexander wants peace, and does

[1] Metternich, *Nachgelassene Papiere*, IV, p. 181.
[2] W. P. Cresson, *The Holy Alliance. The European background of the Monroe doctrine*, New York, 1922, p. 106.
[3] Alexander to La Ferronays in February 1825. (*Lettres et Papiers du Chancelier Comte de Nesselrode*, VI, p. 220.)
[4] Nesselrode, op. cit., p. 218.
[5] Cf. Alexander's remark to the Prussian diplomat Schöler, on November 30th, 1821. (Karl Ringhoffer, *Ein Dezennium preussischer Orientpolitik*, Berlin, 1897, p. 241.)
[6] Cf. Alexander to La Ferronays : " L'opinion de toute la Russie est contraire à la mienne." (Nesselrode, op. cit., p. 219.)
[7] Metternich to Ottenfels, April 18th, 1824. (Krauter, op. cit., p. 129.)
[8] Cf. Lebzeltern to Metternich, December 30th, 1823, and March 16th, 1825.
[9] *Dépêches inédites aux Hospodars de Valachie*, II, p. 147.

not wish to hear of any complications." [1]   Even as late as
August 15th, 1825, Gentz reported to Ghika : " En dépit de
toutes les instigations du parti nombreux parmi les Russes qui
la [guerre] regarde comme une nécessité et comme un point
d'honneur, il ne s'y décidera certainement pas, à moins de se
croire poussé à l'extremité." [2]   Not even Canning withheld his
praise altogether when he wrote in a private despatch to Bagot
on July 14th, 1823 : " In truth the Emperor's forbearance is very
great, and if it is really the offspring of moderation, and a
deference for the Alliance, it is singularly laudable." [3]

There was less unanimity with regard to the deeper reasons
of Alexander's moderation.   Few statesmen were as appreciative
as Richelieu, who had written to Louis XVIII from Aix-la-
Chapelle : " Il faut remercier la Providence d'avoir donné à
ce puissant souverain un caractère de modération qui ne changera
jamais, parce qu'il est fondé sur les sentiments religieux—c'est le
plus sûr garant de la conservation de la paix en Europe." [4]
Most of the worldly-wise, Görres reports, registered the fact as
an extraordinary paradox. [5]   To these critics who failed to understand an idealist approach to politics, the Tsar's attitude seemed
rather foolish. [6]   This is why, for example, Metternich remarked
sarcastically on the occasion of Capodistria's dismissal : " Russia
is playing rather a sad rôle."   Similarly, during his visit to Paris,
in March 1825, the Austrian statesman boasted publicly to the
effect that he had duped the Tsar.   In Canning's eyes the position
must have been very much the same, if we are to judge from his
instructions to Stratford Canning in the late autumn of 1824,
where he envisaged the possibility of " declaring frankly our real
motives ", which would have meant that it was necessary to
" betray the secret . . . and therewith destroy the illusion by
which the Emperor of Russia has to be fortified against the warlike
impulsion of his people ". [7]

Alexander, bitterly disillusioned, began once more in his life
to readjust his political system.   All that remains to be related
happened during the year 1825.

[1] Krauter, op. cit., p. 119.
[2] Dépêches inédites, III, p. 23.
[3] J. Bagot, George Canning and his Friends, II, p. 181.
[4] Raoul de Cisternes, Le Duc de Richelieu, Paris, 1878, p. 94.
[5] " Die heilige Allianz und die Völker ", Gesammelte Schriften, XIII, pp. 461-2.
[6] Cf. Alexander to La Ferronays : " Ma modération, qu'on attribue peut-être
à des causes peu flatteuses pour moi." (Nesselrode, pp. 219-20.)
[7] Strat. MSS., F.O. 352/9.   (Quoted by Temperley, The Foreign Policy of Canning,
p. 334.)

In the spring, Stratford Canning reported that the Tsar's mind was divided. In the summer, Nesselrode wrote to the Russian chargé d'affaires in Constantinople that the Porte's intransigence had provoked the Tsar's righteous anger and had opened his eyes to the rôle played by the ambassadors of Austria, France and Prussia at Constantinople.[1] Consequently, a circular despatch instructed the Russian diplomats in Vienna, Paris, and Berlin not to enter into any more negotiations about the Eastern Question with the governments to which they were accredited.[2] The Concert of Europe had definitely come to an end. Alexander now, in the autumn, authorized the Russian Cabinet to enter into separate negotiations with Great Britain—the other World Power which could not be neglected—with the limited object of finding a solution to the Greek question. As long as he lived he was still determined not to provoke a war in Europe. But he had warned La Ferronays : " Je suis un homme, je suis mortel, et peut-être entre-t-il dans les vues de la Providence de ne pas m'accorder une longue existence." And he had added : " Comment fait-il que cette réflexion semble échapper à tant de monde et surtout à M. Canning ? Rien ne me donne une plus pauvre idée de sa prévoyance politique." [3]

Indeed, before winter set in, Alexander left the stage of this world. He is supposed to have died at Taganrog on December 1st, 1825. According to another version, for which his latest biographer, N. Sementovsky-Kurilo,[4] offers the gist of the available evidence,[5] his death was only staged, and he withdrew into the Siberian wilderness where he could live up to the standards of Christianity without appearing unduly paradoxical.

---

[1] Prokesch-Osten, *Geschichte des Abfalls der Griechen*, I, p. 388.
[2] Schiemann, *Geschichte Russlands unter Kaiser Nikolaus I*, Vol. I, p. 346.
[3] Nesselrode, op. cit., p. 219.
[4] *Alexander I. Rausch und Einkehr einer Seele*, Zürich, 1939, Ch. XIII. The earlier standard work on the problem is Nicolas Mikhaïlovitch, *Légende sur la mort de l'Empereur Alexandre en Sibérie sous les traits du pèlerin Fedor Kousmitch*, St. Petersburg, 1907.
[5] For more detailed evidence, cf. the very interesting study by Prince Vladimir Bariatinsky, *Le Mystère d'Alexandre Ier. Le Tsar-a-t-il survécu sous le nom de Fédor Kousmitch ?*, Paris, 1929.

EPILOGUE

War is mischief upon the largest scale.

Bentham (1789).

Le roman est fini, nous entrons dans l'histoire.[1] Such was Metternich's comment when he heard the news of Alexander's death. To confront *roman* once more with *histoire*—in the sense which Metternich's words implied—will be the object of this epilogue.

It may be convenient to start with a few words about three chapters of that *roman* which have so far not been dealt with in the present study. They are, in the first place, Alexander's proposal for reduction of armaments ; in the second, his plan for a European army, and finally his scheme for a maritime league against the Barbary Powers.

The idea that large standing armies are dangerous to the cause of Peace had been put forward convincingly by Kant [2] as well as by Bentham.[3] The latter had therefore proposed a " reduction and fixation of the force of the several nations that compose the European system ". Shortly after announcing the Pact of the Holy Alliance to the world, Alexander, adopting this idea, opened negotiations with the other Powers.[4] Castlereagh politely rejected the proposal. The gist of his reply was that, since the Empire had expanded, its forces too had to expand.[5] Not only were the forces not reduced, but Castlereagh's successor had to ask for an increase in the expenditure upon Army and Navy. In 1824 six regiments of infantry were required to quell a serious unrest among the West Indian negroes who were somewhat prematurely expecting their immediate emancipation. In the following year Palmerston had to ask for another 8,000 men for the service of the Empire ; for the above-mentioned campaign in Burma was devouring a large number of soldiers.[6] Bentham's

---

[1] *Lettres du Prince de Metternich à la Comtesse de Lieven*, p. 333.
[2] *Zum ewigen Frieden. Ein philosophischer Entwurf*, Königsberg, 1795, p. 8.
[3] A Plan for an Universal and Perpetual Peace (MS. 1789), *Works*, ed. John Bowring, Vol. II, Edinburgh, 1843, pp. 550–51. Cf. O. Kraus, *Der Machtgedanke und die Friedensidee in der Philosophie der Engländer. Bacon und Bentham*, Leipzig, 1926, pp. 59–60.
[4] Martens, op. cit., p. 259.
[5] Headlam-Morley, op. cit., p. 256. This was at the time when the Whigs in Parliament belaboured the Government with the argument that the expense of the colonial garrisons was too high, and that the existence of any troops anywhere was a menace to civil liberties.
[6] Fortescue, op. cit., pp. 86–7.

other warning to the effect that distant dependencies increase the chances of war [1] was only too justified.

Metternich, too, had raised objections against Alexander's proposal. In a despatch to Castlereagh, in 1816, he wrote : " The disadvantage of affording in the outset information of this nature, and the difficulty always of obtaining any true data from Russia, no one could better appreciate than your Lordship. To take the initiative here, uncertain of a reciprocity of confidence, would be impossible." [2]

How far was Alexander himself prepared to go ? In conversations that took place, in 1816, between the Tsar and Barclay de Tolly on the one hand, and Lebzeltern on the other, he is reported to have said : " On ignore que j'ai dissous 150,000 hommes, le corps de Bennigsen, le corps de Langron . . . et 5 à 6 corps de milices licenciées." [3] For the rest—still a big force —the Tsar and his military expert offered numerous explanations as to the reasons why it was at that time impossible for Russia to reduce her army. The gist of these explanations was again the wide extent of the Empire. It is well to remember that Nesselrode, no doubt with the Tsar's approval, wrote in the same year : " Chez les peuples de l'Asie la crainte offre le seul garant." [4] Bentham's warning as to the danger of far-distant dependencies was applicable no less to the Russian elephant than to the British amphibian. Nevertheless, the fact remains that Alexander at least showed some intention of finding a way out of the dilemma.

When Alexander saw that, for various reasons, an appreciable reduction of armaments would not come off, he proposed at Aix-la-Chapelle what had already been anticipated in the Holy Alliance Pact, namely that the European Alliance should be supplemented by a European army to be directed by a permanent Allied General Staff. This measure, he felt, would at the same time allay the apprehensions of the weak and deter the malevolent from aggression. The proposal was warmly supported by the Prussians, but it met with Wellington's disapproval.[5] It was in the same vein that Alexander offered 100,000 Russian soldiers to support the intervention against the revolt in Naples ; for in his view this should have been an intervention on behalf of Europe. Canning, not without sarcasm, wrote to Granville on

[1] Op. cit., pp. 546–8.
[2] Headlam-Morley, op. cit., p. 258.
[3] Lebzeltern to Metternich, on 7th (19th) August, 1816.
[4] Cf. Chapter VIII of this book.
[5] Cresson, op. cit., p. 74.

January 10th, 1825 : "The Emperor would have no objection to help us in Ireland, so general and purely philanthropic are his principles of occasional intervention with unruly subjects of his friends or neighbours." [1]

The plan of a European army, too, was politely rejected. The main reason is mentioned in Castlereagh's despatch to Liverpool from Aix-la-Chapelle on October 19th, 1818, where he said that the Russian forces would constitute the most powerful element of that international police, and added : "They would have an irresistible claim to march through the territories of all Confederate States to the most distant points of Europe to fulfil her [Russia's] guarantee." [2] As to Alexander's later offers of Russian military contributions to European interventions, the higher motives which, I suggest, must have been present in his mind, were again entirely overlooked. In a private and secret despatch on August 20th, 1823, Canning wrote to Bagot : "In the prurient and tantalized state of the Russian army some vent must be found . . . Spain and France thus failing, is there any other theatre for a Russian force in the West of Europe ? None ; and therefore is Metternich apprehensive that the Turkish war must come at last." And Canning added : "Perhaps so." [3]

Another of Alexander's suggestions made at Aix-la-Chapelle had a similar fate. It had already been decided at the Congress of Vienna to stop the piracy and the enslavement of Christians which was carried on by the Regencies. In August 1814, the British admiral, Sir Sidney Smith, had suggested, in a memorandum to the European Powers, the employment of an international maritime force for this purpose. In the following month, this plan had been recommended to the French Government by Polignac, who hoped that France would derive great advantages from it. In the first place, it would give satisfaction to her desire for military activity and glory. But this would not only apply to France : "Une expédition contre les Barbaresques offre à quelques puissances de l'Europe la faculté de se débarrasser des mécontents que la carrière des armes peut seule satisfaire." [4] Anticipating his own policy of diversion which he was to carry out in 1830, and, to some extent, anticipating the whole trend

---

[1] *Some Official Correspondence of George Canning*, I, p. 232.
[2] Quoted in *Cambridge History of British Foreign Policy*, II, p. 28.
[3] Bagot, op. cit., II, p. 198. Cf. Wynn to the Duke of Buckingham, November 22nd, 1822. (Buckingham, *Memoirs of the Court of George IV*, Vol. I, p. 396.)
[4] Note sur l'expédition projetée contre les Barbaresques, 19/9/1814. (Archives des Affairs Étrangères, Mém. et doc. Afrique VI, quoted in F. Charles-Roux, *France et Afrique du Nord avant 1830*, Paris, 1932, pp. 500–1.)

of European nineteenth-century history, Polignac wrote in the same memorandum : " Des guerres intestines peuvent prochaine- ment déchirer l'Europe, si on ne s'occupe point de donner une direction à cette disposition guerrière." Algeria, moreover, seemed an auspicious place because there, to quote Polignac again, " France pouvait trouver l'occasion d'établissements avantageux et celle d'un acheminement vers l'Égypte."

What actually happened was that, in 1816, Great Britain sent an expedition under Lord Exmouth against the Dey of Algiers. An occasional coercive measure of this kind, supported from time to time by a pecuniary concession, seemed to Castlereagh the best method of dealing with this problem.[1] Similarly, the second memorandum on the approaching Conferences at Aix-la-Chapelle read : " The protection of British Commerce could not be better provided for than it had been under the Treaties with these Powers, and the respect in which the British flag was universally held." [2] As to a Defensive Maritime League, " the more the subject had been examined, the more the Cabinet were impressed with the inevitable complexity of any such system of League applicable to this object, and which, to be made equitable in its arrangements, and effectual to its object, must combine the naval contingents of so many different States ". Therefore : " So far as the separate interests of Great Britain were concerned, they continued to hold the opinion, on which they had first proceeded, namely that no League of this description was desir- able." Indeed, of all the diplomats at Aix-la-Chapelle Castle- reagh and Wellington showed the strongest disinclination to study the Russian proposal.[3]

That British aversion to the scheme was not based on its complexity alone is shown by Castlereagh's despatch to Bernstorff. There he explained that the destruction of the Regencies would lead to the establishment on the African coast of States which, united with France, might be harmful to British influence and commerce.[4] Obviously Russia was meant. In 1816–17 there were rumours that the Tsar intended to acquire Minorca as a base against the Algerine pirates. When Lebzeltern made inquiries on this point, Capodistria was reported to have replied : " I don't know why England should have the privilege of occupy- ing islands in the Mediterranean." One more piece of evidence

---

[1] Castlereagh to Bernstorff, quoted in Charles-Roux, op. cit., p. 505.
[2] F.O. 92/34. (Public Record Office.)
[3] Martens, *Recueil des Traités et Conventions par la Russie avec les Puissances Étrangères*, VII, p. 301.　　　　[4] Charles-Roux, op. cit., p. 505.

may be mentioned to show the degree which British apprehension of Russian sea power had reached. It is taken from the Austrian Archduke Ludwig's report on his journey in England in 1816 :

A Power which is not in friendly esteem [wrote the Archduke] is Russia. The Englishman, calculating and jealous of his trade, knows that that Empire, which is so vast, provided with all resources, and touching all seas, might one day come forward as a Sea Power. England has been made attentive of late by repeated Russian sea voyages, which had for their purpose more than discovery ; by the establishment of settlements on islands between Asia and America, and even on the North-West coast of this continent ; by the connection with Kamchatka, the Continent of Russia ; by the mission to China, and by the conquests over Persia.[1]

We thus arrive at the conclusion that an effective Concert of Europe implied, from the British point of view, the danger of Russian preponderance. Nevertheless, so long as there was a real or, for that matter, a widely imagined danger of social revolution in England, the British Government did, to some extent, participate in the Concert system.[2] When the apprehensions of the ruling classes were decreasing, owing to the return of prosperity which, as we have seen, was caused partly by the expansion of the South American trade, the Concert system was completely abandoned as a hindrance, and Canning fell back upon the old Balance of Power game. In a speech in the House of Commons on April 29th, 1823, he advertised it as " the only safeguard of nations ; the protection of the weak against the strong, the principle by which small states flourished in the vicinity of great ones ".[3]

As we have seen, British sea power greatly enlarged the board on which the game could be played. In fact, much of Britain's attention was now focused upon that new side of the board from which the Atlantic disjoined the other European players. This is why Canning, using a metaphor of Bolívar's which had come to his knowledge on December 11th, 1826,[4] was in a position to announce in his famous speech in the House on the

---

[1] Erzherzog Rainersches Privatarchiv. (Eduard Wertheimer, " Aufenthalt der Erzherzöge Johann und Ludwig in England 1815–1816 ", Archiv für österreichische Geschichte, LXXVIII, 1892, pp. 425–6.) Cf. also Sir Robert Wilson, A Sketch of the Military and Political Power of Russia, in the Year 1817, p. xi : " England devoted all her resources to remove the danger of one domineering rival, France ; but Russia, profiting by the occasion, mounted to a higher pinnacle than that rival ever reached." Cf. also D. Gerhard, England und der Aufstieg Russlands, München, 1933, and N. Nozikov, Russian Voyages Round the World, transl. E. and M. Lesser, London [1945].
[2] Cf. Chapter VI of this book.   [3] Hansard, N.S., VIII, p. 1407.
[4] Adolf Rein, " Über die Bedeutung der überseeischen Ausdehnung für das europäische Staatensystem ", Historische Zeitschrift, Vol. 137, 1928, pp. 76–8.

following day : " I have called the New World into existence
to redress the balance of the Old."

As to the Old World, Canning wrote to Frere on August 7th,
1823 : " For Alliance read England, and you have the clue to
my policy." [1] His policy with regard to South America helped
to promote Free Trade, which has often been identified with a
certain cosmopolitanism. C. R. Fay, however, points out that
the fall of mercantilism between 1820 and 1853 did not mean
that England fell away from nationalism, but that the tendency
was the other way about. [2] The misconception about the implications of free trade was not the only one. As shrewd an observer
as Heine saw in Canning the " Spartacus of Downing Street ".
Yet Canning had written to Monsieur on February 1st, 1823,
that " Mr. Burke's last works and words [are] still the manual
of my politics ". [3]

England's interest, as he understood it, was the only principle
to which Canning really adhered. On March 20th, 1821, he
had pointed out in the House that " Queen Elizabeth had assisted
the Protestants throughout Europe only when the interests of
England demanded that she should do so ". [4] On much the
same lines was Castlereagh's explanation of the varying attitude
of Great Britain towards the revolts in Naples and in Greece.
The Turkish question, he said, was a practical matter, unlike the
Neapolitan, which was theoretical. This brings us back to Canning, whom Disraeli, in the dedication of his second pamphlet previously mentioned, praised for his " sublimity of conception which
distinguishes the practical statesman from the political theorist ".

Hazlitt, describing " The Character of Mr. Canning ", saw
it in a somewhat different light : " At one time the honour of the
country sways him, at another its interest. At one moment he
is all for liberty, and the next for slavery. First we are to hold
the balance of Europe, and to dictate and domineer over the
whole world ; and then we are to creep into our shells and draw
in our horns ; one moment resembling Don Quixote, and the
next playing the part of Sancho Panza ! And why not ? All
these are topics, are cues used in the game of politics, are colours
in the changeable coat of party, are dilemmas in casuistry, are
pretexts in diplomacy ; and Mr. Canning has them all at his
fingers' ends." [5]

---

[1] Cf. also Canning to Bagot, 3/11/1822.   [2] *C.H.B.E.*, II, p. 388.
[3] *Canning Correspondence*, I, p. 74.   [4] Hansard, N.S., IV, p. 1372.
[5] *The Examiner*, 11/7/1824.

Pretexts in diplomacy, if successful, are called practical politics. Of course, they are not always successful. For example, as Halévy has rightly pointed out, the " untoward event " of the Battle of Navarino, the logical outcome of Canning's policy, facilitated instead of averting the Russian War against Turkey.[1] As early as 1822, Goethe in his wisdom had seen what was coming : " If the aim is to establish a less powerful State or a republic in Greece, the greater Powers will continuously strive to raise their influence there, and the result will be a fatal disruption of power (Gewaltenzersplitterung)." [2]

Taking a wider view, we might say that when the excitement of the Napoleonic Wars and their immediate aftermath was over, Europe relapsed into that trend of secularization which has characterized her history at least since 1660. Jean Paul's apprehension turned out to be justified : " Unfavourable and bright-cold is our time for religion," he wrote in 1809. " Some people hope that the tempest of the War is driving us again to religion, just as a thunderclap drove Luther to theology, but it is still undecided whether the conflagration of the War is a purgatory leading to bliss, or rather a hell leading to greater evil." [3]   Indeed, before long, religion was again pushed into the background until that stage of indifference was reached which La Mennais, full of eloquent horror, had anticipated as early as 1817.[4] In the same year, Goethe in his essay *Geistes-Epochen* (which hitherto has not found the attention it deserves) was obviously referring to the contemporary intellectual situation when he described in a few forceful words " the Prosaic Epoch ". On repeated occasions during the 1820s, Hegel, lecturing on the Philosophy of Religion, reminded his students : " Es hat eine Zeit gegeben, wo alles Wissen Wissenschaft von Gott gewesen ist."   And he continued : " Unsere Zeit hat dagegen das Ausgezeichnete, von Allem und Jedem, von einer unendlischen Menge von Gegenständen zu wissen, nur nichts von Gott." [5] Nor was this only the opinion of an " abstract " philosopher. The great realist Balzac, one of the most reliable witnesses for our period, makes one of his characters, a country doctor, say in 1829 : " Au lieu d'avoir des croyances, nous avons des intérêts." [6]

[1] Histoire du Peuple Anglais au XIXe siècle, II, Paris, 1923, p. 238.
[2] Conversation with F. von Müller, May 22nd, 1822. (*Goethes Gespräche*, ed. Biedermann, II, p. 572.)
[3] *Über die jetzige Sonnenwende in der Religion*. (In : Dämmerungen für Deutschland.)
[4] *Essai sur l'Indifférence en matière de Religion*, tome I.
[5] *Werke*, XI, Berlin, 1840, p. 36.   [6] *Le Médecin de Campagne*, Ch. I.

Similarly, Friedrich von Schlegel described his epoch as being based—not on creed but—on credit.[1]

What then of the new creed, nationalism or patriotism ? The curate in Balzac's novel gravely dismisses it : " Le patriotisme n'inspire que des sentiments passagers, la religion les rend durables. Le patriotisme est un oubli momentané de l'intérêt personnel, tandis que le christianisme est un système complet d'opposition aux tendances dépravées de l'homme." [2]

George Canning claimed for himself, to some extent rightly, the rôle of awakener of nationalism. Referring to the development in South America, he proudly paraphrased Vergil's famous lines in a letter to Granville on December 17th, 1824 :

Novus saeclorum nascitur ordo.

New ? Yes, that must be conceded. *Order ?* No, definitely not ; rather the opposite. *For centuries ?* Here the historian must be more cautious than the politician. All he can say is this : after little more than one century, towards the end of the Second World War, an increasing number of people, it seems, are realizing, firstly, what Saint-Simon had already felt,[3] namely that our European Society is disintegrating ; and secondly, that if every nation is for itself, God is against us all.

It was towards the end of the Napoleonic Wars that Jean Paul prophesied : " Probably Europe will be raised and sublimated into the paradise of religion only by a still more violent purgatory ; only from dust and ashes does Phœnix arise." [4] At that time, however, no one could have visualized the extreme violence of the purgatory through which Europe is now passing.

---

[1] *Signatur des Zeitalters*, Concordia, VI, pp. 394-5.

[2] Ibid., Ch. III.

[3] Saint Simon, Thierry, *De la Réorganisation de la Société Européenne*, Paris, Oct., 1814, pp. VIII, 111.

[4] *Über die jetzige Sonnenwende in der Religion* (1809). Cf. also E. M. Arndt, *Geist der Zeit*, 2. ed., 1807, p. 90.

INDEX